*In honor of the One who is
holy, harmless and undefiled*

Contents

Chapter 3
The Cross Was Hell..................49

Chapter 4
Hell Fire and The Cross..................83

Chapter 5
Our Suffering Father...........105

Chapter 6
The Cross and Beauty..........117

Chapter 7
God's Law of Love................133

Chapter 8
The Bride and The Groom..............161

Chapter 9
Job and Fire, Pigs and Lies..............177

Chapter 10

Faith..................................213

Chapter 11

Sin..................................231

Chapter 12
The Old Versus The New..................255

Acknowledgments

My friend and mentor, Kazuo Yoshitake, your humble and wise example has taught me as much as your words, which have been full of wonder. Your Christ-centered insights into Genesis have been extraordinary. The same goes for Revelation. The stuff in between was pretty good too. Thank you.

Ozzie Grant, your consistent depth of understanding and clarity of presentation on the character of Jesus are without parallel. Only eternity will fully reveal the results of teaching such a beautiful view of God and the plan of salvation. Thank you.

Thank you, Isaac Heckman. I will always fondly remember discussing Jesus, vengeance, self-defence, and related issues with a small group of friends in the warmth of the sun. Thank you for the invitation to the church and the study group. No seminary could have presented Jesus more clearly and powerfully.

Having you as my loving father, Rudy James, has given me strength. Your mercy toward your enemies reminds me of King David. I have enjoyed the hours we have spent discussing the Bible. Thank you.

Ever willing, Dianna James, thank you for helping me with grammar, punctuation, form and style. Your encouragement, good suggestions, and quick mind have been a blessing to me on many levels. Thank you.

Reading, correcting, and checking the manuscript for clarity, Cindy Robinson, your help has been vital, thank you. Ken, from installing solar panels and inverters to proofreading, I thank you for being a great neighbor.

Calling on you, my brother, Scott James, has meant a lot to me. The hours spent wrestling with spiritual principles have strengthened me and helped me to gauge the effectiveness of my presentation of the concepts in this book. Thank you.

Jesus, You started it all. You are the Author and finisher of this book, and my life. To know you is to love you.

Introduction

As humans we take it for granted that fear of punishment is the only foundation which can maintain social order. But fear, greed, and force cannot heal the human heart.

Many forms of government have been established in order to usher in a Utopia. All have failed in this endeavor. That is because the human heart is self-centered by nature.

Only love has the power to change our hearts. Love awakens love. That is why it is so important to understand God's love as displayed by Jesus on the cross of Calvary.

The powers of darkness have tried to obscure God's love from our sight, with great success. Hundreds of religions attempt to explain the spiritual dimension. All seem to stumble in explaining the immensity of human suffering.

In a world where might makes right, human suffering steadily increases. War, genocide, ethnic cleansing, famine, and disease, charge throughout the Earth, propelled by the spiritual darkness that results from a misconception of our heavenly Father.

Indeed, if God is good and all-powerful, why does he allow such vast and intense suffering? This issue has led many to reject God altogether.

Only Christianity can satisfactorily answer this question. And then only if it properly explains the sovereignty of God in the light of his all-powerful love and the crucially important concept of human freedom.

As you might expect, the cross of Calvary points the way to unifying the thousands of various Christian denominations. I also believe that Jesus's love can draw followers of all religions into his fold.

Surprisingly, a better understanding of God's goodness and wisdom as revealed through the life, infinite suffering, and death of Jesus will explain the awful problem of human suffering.

Holy Spirit, help us as we examine these issues in the light of the deeper beauty, the glory of Jesus's life and death.

And there was war in heaven:
Michael and his angels
fought against the dragon;
and the dragon fought and his angels,
(Revelation 12:7, KJV)

1

War in Heaven

"And there was war in heaven: Michael and his angels fought against the dragon; and the dragon fought and his angels" (Revelation 12:7 KJV). Imagine that! War in Heaven.

Now, imagine that you hold the scepter of power; you are the ruler of the universe. Your character and personality, though, remain the same. With one word you can speak a world, a solar system, or even an entire galaxy into existence. With one word you can cause a world to vanish into nonexistence.

All the mighty angels, your friends, are at your command. With one word you could create more beautiful angels, or any other kind of intelligent being that you desired. With a mere word you also could cause anyone to cease to exist. Over eons of time, you have successfully established a society that is based on kindness, friendship, and love.

How would you handle it if one of your closest friends, the head angel, Lucifer, had taken advantage of his lofty position, your kindness, and friendship and had started a rebellion by insinuating unkind, untrue things about you, behind your back? I don't know about you, but I'd be inclined to nip it in the bud.

Wouldn't it be nice if sin and rebellion had been erased before it ever got started? You could threaten Lucifer with demotion or even destruction to bring him into line. With one word you could confine him to fiery torment. Or you could destroy him.

But then the questions would come. Your angel friends would wonder what happened to your close friend and their leader, Lucifer. Would it bother you if even your closest friends were afraid of you? Can anyone really love a ruthless dictator?

It is nice to have friends who enjoy your company, who love and trust you. Would your integrity be so great that you would allow the rebellion to run its course, knowing that one third of your dear friends would join Lucifer's side? These are only some of the delicate, though vitally important issues that God faced when war broke out in Heaven.

In all wars there are rules of engagement. There are principles and territory that are disputed. Take the Civil War for example. National territory and unity, as well as national and state sovereignty were disputed. Another important issue was slavery. The South favored slavery. The North condemned the South's slavery.

The war in Heaven followed a similar pattern. The unity of Heaven, the sovereignty of God over the entire universe and Earth were disputed. The law of God, and slavery were also disputed. Lucifer desired to rule in Heaven and on Earth. Lucifer tried to change or even do away with God's law of love.

The war that started in Heaven continues, and as in every war, there are rules of engagement. And each side has chosen to use certain weapons. Satan (Lucifer) uses deceit, lies, coercion, and any other malignant principle that he can think of. God, however, has chosen the powerful weapons of truth and love. Paul encourages us, telling us that we can live, "in hope of eternal life which God, who never lies, promised ages ago" (Titus 1:2, KJV). The beloved disciple tells us, "He who does not love does not know God; for God is love" (1John 4:8, KJV).

God in his wisdom has chosen to remain faithful to certain principles, "If we are not faithful, he remains faithful, because he cannot be false to himself" (2Timothy 2:13, TEV). In other words, God never steps out of character.

Satan favors and uses the principle of slavery. Jesus brought this out, "I am telling you the truth: everyone who sins is a slave of sin. A slave does not belong to a family permanently, but a son belongs there for ever. If the Son sets you free, then you will be really free" (John 8:34-36, TEV).

Jesus's brother tells us, "But he who looks into the perfect law, the law of liberty, and perseveres, being no hearer that forgets but a doer that acts, he shall be blessed in his doing" (James 1:25, RSV).

There is also the principle of equal access. Both God and Lucifer must have an equal opportunity to present their case to the inhabitants of Heaven and Earth. Satan cannot force anyone to join his side. Adam and Eve were free to choose whom they would follow. They were free moral agents. In other words, neither God nor Satan would be able to force Adam or Eve to join his side.

God placed the tree of the knowledge of good and evil and the tree of life in the Garden of Eden to provide Adam and Eve with freedom of choice. Adam and Eve chose, on the basis of incomplete information and Satan's lies, to rebel against God. Satan deceived them. The war in Heaven had spread to Earth.

In order to learn more about the war in Heaven, we will examine the story of Absalom's rebellion against his father, King David. The story of David and his rebellious son Absalom has many parallels to the war between Christ and Satan. We will also weave in other Bible texts.

At first, Lucifer and Absalom had each responded to his father's love. Over time, however, each allowed vanity, pride, and ambition to block the blessings of love.

In order to understand Absalom's rebellion, we will first need to look at the story of David and Bathsheba, and the story of Amnon and Tamar. These stories give us important background information that will help us understand why David did not punish his sons for their serious crimes, and why Absalom grew to hate his father, David:

3

Bathsheba

It was now spring, the time when kings go to war. David sent out the whole Israelite army under the command of Joab and his officers. They destroyed the Ammonite army and surrounded the capital city of Rabbah, but David stayed in Jerusalem.

Late one afternoon, David got up from a nap and was walking around on the flat roof of his palace. A beautiful young woman was down below in her courtyard, bathing as her religion required. David happened to see her, and he sent one of his servants to find out who she was.

The servant came back and told David, "Her name is Bathsheba. She is the daughter of Eliam, and she is the wife of Uriah the Hittite."

David sent some messengers to bring her to his palace. She came to him, and he slept with her. Then she returned home. But later, when she found out that she was going to have a baby, she sent someone to David with this message: "I'm pregnant!"

David sent a message to Joab: "Send Uriah the Hittite to me." Joab sent Uriah to David's palace, and David asked him, "Is Joab well? How is the army doing? And how about the war?" Then David told Uriah, "Go home and clean up." Uriah left the king's palace, and David had dinner sent to Uriah's house. But Uriah didn't go home. Instead, he slept outside the entrance to the royal palace, where the king's guards slept.

Someone told David that Uriah had not gone home. So the next morning David asked him, "Why didn't you go home? Haven't you been away for a long time?"

Uriah answered, "The sacred chest and the armies of Israel and Judah are camping out somewhere in the fields with our commander Joab and his officers and troops. Do you really think I would go home to eat and drink and sleep with my wife? I swear by your life that I would not!"

Then David said, "Stay here in Jerusalem today, and I will send you back tomorrow."

Uriah stayed in Jerusalem that day. Then the next day, David invited him for dinner. Uriah ate with David and drank so much that he got drunk, but he still did not go home. He went out and slept on his mat near the palace guards. Early the next morning, David wrote a letter and told Uriah to deliver it to Joab. The letter said: "Put Uriah on the front line where the fighting is the worst. Then pull the troops back from him, so that he will be wounded and die." Joab had been carefully watching the city of Rabbah, and he put Uriah in a place where he knew there were some of the enemy's best soldiers. When the men of the city came out, they fought and killed some of David's soldiers—Uriah the Hittite was one of them. (2Samuel 11:1-17, CEV)

God sent Nathan the prophet to relate a parable to King David, about a rich man stealing a poor man's only lamb. It illustrated the evil that David had done. Without noticing the similarity to his actions, David condemned the rich man to repay fourfold and to be killed. After King David had sentenced the imaginary man, Nathan drew the parallel to David's actions. He revealed how David had condemned himself:

Why, then, have you despised the word of the Lord and done this horrible deed? For you have murdered Uriah and stolen his wife. From this time on, the sword will be a constant threat to your family, because you have despised me by taking Uriah's wife to be your own. (2Samuel 12:9, 10, NLT)

When David understood how the parable applied to him, a strong sense of guilt engulfed him. In spite of the darkness of guilt, David's faith in God's mercy remained strong. David repented and asked for forgiveness of his sin. Though God forgave him, David still suffered some of the consequences of his sin. David and Bathsheba's son died shortly after birth. But God, being full of mercy and forgiveness, spared David's life. David wrote a poem about this experience:

Nathan's Parable

To the chief Musician, A Psalm of David, when Nathan the prophet came unto him, after he had gone in to Bathsheba. Have mercy upon me, O God, according to thy lovingkindness: according unto the multitude of thy tender mercies blot out my transgressions. Wash me throughly from mine iniquity, and cleanse me from my sin. For I acknowledge my transgressions: and my sin is ever before me... Purge me with hyssop, and I shall be clean: wash me, and I shall be whiter than snow. Hide thy face from my sins, and blot out all mine iniquities. Create in me a clean heart, O God; and renew a right spirit within me. Cast me not away from thy presence; and take not thy holy spirit from me. Deliver me from bloodguiltiness, O God, thou God of my salvation: and my tongue shall sing aloud of thy righteousness. (Psalm 51:1-3, 7, 9-11, 14, KJV)

David knew that his example would lead others to regard sin lightly. He felt the responsibility deeply. David knew the cleansing power of God's mercy, forgiveness, and reconciliation. He also knew the destructive power of guilt, hatred, and vengeance. Having received such abundant mercy from God, David became quite probably the most merciful king to ever rule on this Earth. Some would contend that King David was too merciful. Absalom certainly did:

The Rape of Tamar

David's son Absalom had a beautiful sister named Tamar. And Amnon, her half brother, fell desperately in love with her. Amnon became so obsessed with Tamar that he became ill. She was a virgin, and it seemed impossible that he could ever fulfill his love for her...

So Amnon pretended to be sick. And when the king came to see him, Amnon asked him, "Please let Tamar come to take care of me and cook something for me to eat."

So David agreed and sent Tamar to Amnon's house to prepare some food for him.

When Tamar arrived at Amnon's house, she went to the room where he was lying down so he could watch her mix some dough. Then she baked some special bread for him. But when she set the serving tray before him, he refused to eat. "Everyone get out of here," Amnon told his servants. So they all left. Then he said to Tamar, "Now bring the food into my bedroom and feed it to me here." So Tamar took it to him. But as she was feeding him, he grabbed her and demanded, "Come to bed with me, my darling sister." "No, my brother!" she cried. "Don't be foolish! Don't do this to me! You know what a serious crime it is to do such a thing in Israel. Where could I go in my shame? And you would be called one of the greatest fools in Israel. Please, just speak to the king about it, and he will let you marry me."

But Amnon wouldn't listen to her, and since he was stronger than she was, he raped her. Then suddenly Amnon's love turned to hate, and he hated her even more than he had loved her. "Get out of here!" he snarled at her.

"No, no!" Tamar cried. "To reject me now is a greater wrong than what you have already done to me."

But Amnon wouldn't listen to her. He shouted for his servant and demanded, "Throw this woman out, and lock the door behind her!"

So the servant put her out. She was wearing a long, beautiful robe, as was the custom in those days for the king's virgin daughters. But now Tamar tore her robe and put ashes on her head. And then, with her face in her hands, she went away crying.

Her brother Absalom saw her and asked, "Is it true that Amnon has been with you? Well, don't be so upset. Since he's your brother anyway, don't worry about it." So Tamar lived as a desolate woman in Absalom's house. When King David heard what had happened, he was very angry. And though Absalom never spoke to Amnon about it, he hated Amnon deeply because of what he had done to his sister. (2Samuel 13:1, 2, 6-22, NLT)

Notice that while David was angry, and had the authority and the power to put Amnon to death for the rape of Tamar, he did not do it. David had committed adultery. He then had committed murder to try to cover up the adultery. Having felt the restoring power of God's incredible mercy, David condemned his son's sin, but still extended mercy, reconciliation, and rehabilitation rather than resorting to a punishment that would result in death. David also felt that his adultery with Bathsheba and murder of her husband Uriah made him partially responsible for his son's crime. Even though his motives were not perfect, David's mercy made him a man after God's own heart.

Absalom, on the other hand, did not share in his father's tendency toward mercy. While Absalom had no authority to put Amnon to death, he nevertheless allowed a desire for vengeance to burn in his heart.

The Old Testament story of Absalom's rebellion against his father, David, highlights the differences between the principles of God and Satan. Many Christians will be familiar with the story of David and Absalom. Many will also understand that in the Bible, David often represents Christ, the Son of God. Perhaps some have seen that Absalom represents Lucifer, now known as the Devil or Satan. The story of David and Absalom has much in common with the history of the war between Christ, the Son of God, and Satan. Absalom's heart overflowed with venomous hatred, but he hid it behind a smiling face.

Absalom's Revenge on Amnon

Two years later, when Absalom's sheep were being sheared at Baal-hazor near Ephraim, Absalom invited all the king's sons to come to a feast. He went to the king and said, "My sheep-shearers are now at work. Would the king and his servants please come to celebrate the occasion with me?"

The king replied, "No, my son. If we all came, we would be too much of a burden on you." Absalom pressed him, but the king wouldn't come, though he sent his thanks.

"Well, then," Absalom said, "if you can't come, how about

sending my brother Amnon instead?" "Why Amnon?" the king asked. But Absalom kept on pressing the king until he finally agreed to let all his sons attend, including Amnon. Absalom told his men, "Wait until Amnon gets drunk; then at my signal, kill him! Don't be afraid. I'm the one who has given the command. Take courage and do it!" So at Absalom's signal they murdered Amnon. Then the other sons of the king jumped on their mules and fled... Meanwhile Absalom escaped... Absalom fled to his grandfather, Talmai son of Ammihud, the king of Geshur. He stayed there in Geshur for three years. And David, now reconciled to Amnon's death, longed to be reunited with his son Absalom. (2Samuel 13:23-29, 34, 37-39, NLT)

This story reveals the stark contrast between the characters of David and his son Absalom. David's heart and character represent God. Because he had deserved to die and yet had received so abundantly of God's mercy, King David had mercy on Absalom.

In a similar manner, though based on different, holier principles, God's wisdom constrained him to have mercy on Lucifer and the rebellious angels.

Lucifer despised and yet exploited God's mercy. Absalom's heart and character reflect Satan's heart and character. Absalom also despised and yet exploited David's mercy and forgiveness. He felt that these were weaknesses that prevented the proper application of justice. Rebellion and resentment filled Absalom's heart:

Reconciliation

Joab knew that David couldn't stop thinking about Absalom, and he sent someone to bring in the wise woman who lived in Tekoa. Joab told her, "Put on funeral clothes and don't use any makeup. Go to the king and pretend you have spent a long time mourning the death of a loved one." Then he told her what to say.

The woman from Tekoa went to David. She bowed very

low and said, "Your Majesty, please help me!" David asked, "What's the matter?" She replied: "My husband is dead, and I'm a widow. I had two sons, but they got into a fight out in a field where there was no one to pull them apart, and one of them killed the other. Now all of my relatives have come to me and said, 'Hand over your son! We're going to put him to death for killing his brother.' But what they really want is to get rid of him, so they can take over our land.

Please don't let them put out my only flame of hope! There won't be anyone left on this earth to carry on my husband's name." "Go on home," David told her. "I'll take care of this matter for you." The woman said, "I hope your decision doesn't cause any problems for you. But if it does, you can blame me." He said, "If anyone gives you any trouble, bring them to me, and it won't happen again!" "Please," she replied, "swear by the Lord your God that no one will be allowed to kill my son!" He said, "I swear by the living Lord that no one will touch even a hair on his head!" Then she asked, "Your Majesty, may I say something?" "Yes," he answered. The woman said: "Haven't you been hurting God's people? Your own son had to leave the country. And when you judged in my favor, it was the same as admitting that you should have let him come back. We each must die and disappear like water poured out on the ground. But God doesn't take our lives. Instead, he figures out ways of bringing us back when we run away." (2Samuel 14:1-14, CEV)

Joab knew how to reach the heart of King David. Joab knew that David was merciful, forgiving, and always looked for ways to reconcile those who had been separated by sin and guilt. In this way, David truly was a man after God's own heart. Truly, Absalom was a man after Satan's heart.

The story of merciful King David and his vengeful, rebellious son, Absalom, accurately portrays the contrasting methods and principles of the war in Heaven. Lucifer began his rebellion against the Almighty God slowly, craftily, and deceitfully. Absalom also began his rebellion against his powerful and popular father using similar methods. It is no coincidence that the rebellion of Absalom is patterned after Lucifer's rebellion. Satan molded Absalom's willing heart and mind after his own motives, methods, and madness:

Absalom Returns to the Court

Absalom lived in Jerusalem for two years without seeing his father. He wanted Joab to talk to David for him. So one day he sent a message asking Joab to come over, but Joab refused. Absalom sent another message, but Joab still refused. Finally, Absalom told his servants, "Joab's barley field is right next to mine. Go set it on fire!" And they did. Joab went to Absalom's house and demanded, "Why did your servants set my field on fire?" Absalom answered, "You didn't pay any attention when I sent for you. I want you to ask my father why he told me to come back from Geshur. I was better off there. I want to see my father now! If I'm guilty, let him kill me." Joab went to David and told him what Absalom had said. David sent for Absalom, and Absalom came. He bowed very low, and David leaned over and kissed him. (2Samuel 14:28-33, CEV)

As we have seen, David was merciful, kind, forgiving, and valued reconciliation over punishment. Before David became king, when King Saul was trying to kill him, David did not take revenge, even though he had easy opportunities to do so. Even though Samuel had anointed him to be the next king, David did not try to seize the kingdom from Saul. These are the qualities that distinguished David as a man of God, "The Lord has sought out a man after his own heart. The Lord has already chosen him to be king over his people" (1Samuel 13:14, NLT).

While David shared many of the attributes of God, Absalom shared many of the attributes of Lucifer. For example, both were renowned for their beauty. Absalom was the most handsome man in Israel:

Now no one in Israel was as handsome as Absalom. From head to foot, he was the perfect specimen of a man. He cut his hair only once a year, and then only because it was too heavy to carry around. When he weighed it out, it came to five pounds! (2Samuel 14:25, 26, NLT)

In like manner the Bible describes Lucifer's beauty as perfect. Compare Absalom's description with the following description of Lucifer:

Thus says the Lord God: "You were the seal of perfection, full of wisdom and perfect in beauty. You were in Eden, the garden of God; Every precious stone was your covering: The sardius, topaz, and diamond, beryl, onyx, and jasper, sapphire, turquoise, and emerald with gold. The workmanship of your timbrels and pipes was prepared for you on the day you were created. You were the anointed cherub who covers; I established you; You were on the holy mountain of God; You walked back and forth in the midst of fiery stones. You were perfect in your ways from the day you were created, till iniquity was found in you." Your heart was lifted up because of your beauty; you corrupted your wisdom for the sake of your splendor. (Ezekiel 28:12-15, 17, NKJ)

Lucifer in Heaven walked among the stones of fire. He was a covering cherub, which is the highest position among the angels. It was his job to shield the glory of God, as symbolized by the two golden, covering cherubs above the Ark of the Covenant in the Hebrew sanctuary. It was Lucifer's privilege and blessed responsibility to share and teach the other angels about the glory of God. God freely shared his light, wisdom, knowledge, and love through an organized chain of command. Lucifer was the highest created being. Lucifer shared his ever-deepening understanding and appreciation of the light of God's love with all the angels. As the covering cherub, Lucifer was God's ordained leader of all the heavenly hosts. Lucifer means

Light-Bearer, Day Star, or *Primeval Dawn.* The Hebrew gives the sense that Lucifer was the prototype, or template—the first angel. All the angels in Heaven respected Lucifer. All the angels looked to Lucifer as God's ordained source for the knowledge of God's love.

Just like Lucifer, Absalom allowed vanity, pride, and a burning desire for harsh punishment of sinners to fill his heart. Both Lucifer and Absalom felt that patience, mercy, kindness to enemies, and the desire for reconciliation were fatal weaknesses that could be exploited for their own gain.

We know that Satan and his angels lost the war in Heaven. Let's take a look at what Scripture reveals and see if we can determine some of the main principles of that war. We'll look at Scripture passages that describe Lucifer, and how he became Satan, the great rebel, destroyer, liar, and murderer. We'll also look at some other passages to see if we can fill in some of the details in order to get a clearer picture of what the war in Heaven was like:

> How art thou fallen from heaven, O Lucifer, son of the morning! how art thou cut down to the ground, which didst weaken the nations! For thou hast said in thine heart, I will ascend into heaven, I will exalt my throne above the stars of God: I will sit also upon the mount of the congregation, in the sides of the north: I will ascend above the heights of the clouds; I will be like the most High. (Isaiah 14:12-14, KJV)

Lucifer's Jealousy

Lucifer allowed pride and self-seeking to fill his heart. Instead of worshiping his Creator, Lucifer began to worship himself. The greater the blessings received and the more exalted the position, the greater the capacity for evil. Among the angels, Lucifer had the greatest potential for good. He also had the greatest potential for evil. Lucifer's pride began to alter the way he thought. He was the leader of the angels. He was second only to the Son of God. He began to resent being second.

He knew that the Son of God cooperated with the Father in the creation of the universe:

> Christ is the visible likeness of the invisible God. He is the firstborn Son, superior to all created things. For through him God created everything in heaven and on earth, the seen and the unseen things, including spiritual powers, lords, rulers, and authorities. God created the whole universe through him and for him. Christ existed before all things, and in union with him all things have their proper place. (Colossians 1:15-17, TEV)

Lucifer felt that he too could participate in the creation of new worlds and new beings. He was jealous of the Son of God, and even of the Father himself. Lucifer's true goal was to ascend to the throne of God. As Lucifer cherished the desire for self-exaltation, he lost sight of the true nature of God's throne.

The throne of God, the foundation of his government, is based on the unselfish principles of love, mercy, and reconciliation. That is why his created children praise and worship him. That is what makes the society of Heaven secure.

"So we have known and believe the love that God has for us. God is love, and those who abide in love abide in God, and God abides in them" (1John 4:16, NRSV). God's law of unselfish love is very simple. "'You shall love the Lord your God with all your heart, and with all your soul, and with all your mind, and with all your strength.' The second is this, 'You shall love your neighbor as yourself.' There is no other commandment greater than these" (Mark 12:30, NRSV).

"We each must die and disappear like water poured out on the ground. But God doesn't take our lives. Instead, he figures out ways of bringing us back when we run away" (2Samuel 14:14, CEV). Our loving Heavenly Father is merciful and always seeks to bring back his wandering ones:

> God did not keep an account of their sins, and he has given us the message which tells how he makes them his friends.

Here we are, then, speaking for Christ, as though God himself were making his appeal through us. We plead on Christ's behalf: let God change you from enemies into his friends! (1Corinthians 5:19, 20, TEV)

Love is patient and kind; it is not jealous or conceited or proud; love is not ill-mannered or selfish or irritable; love does not keep a record of wrongs; love is not happy with evil, but is happy with the truth. Love never gives up; and its faith, hope, and patience never fail. Love is eternal. (1Corinthians 13:4-8, TEV)

"But You are holy, Enthroned in the praises of Israel" (Psalm 22:3, NKJ). Love is the foundation of God's throne or government. He never forces or coerces anyone to belong to his kingdom. It is composed only of those beings that freely love, worship, and praise him. God's law of unselfish love guided the society of Heaven before sin entered. The same law governs God's kingdom now, and will continue to do so after sin comes to an end. All the angels lived in happy, holy, harmony. That is, until Lucifer allowed the mystery of iniquity to enter his heart.

As the anointed, covering Cherub, the leader of the angels, Lucifer allowed pride and jealousy to blind him, making the step to the throne of God seem within his grasp. He felt that with enough of the angels on his side, and some careful scheming, he could force God to acknowledge and exalt him. He had to plan carefully, subtly, and slowly.

Lucifer Schemes

Keep in mind that Lucifer was well aware of God's infinite power. Lucifer well knew that as a finite, created being, physical force would be useless against the omnipotence of God. Lucifer also knew that God's love and mercy were infinite. In Heaven, there was a perfect sense of freedom.

Consider carefully that if Lucifer had thought that God would immediately, or even eventually, punish disobedience with death, he would never have rebelled. God had taught

Lucifer that unselfish love is the only foundation for a secure and harmonious government. Lucifer knew that God would not threaten him or punish him. Otherwise, fear, not love would have motivated him to obey. But, obedience based on fear is not really obedience at all.

God loves all his creatures and wants only obedience and worship that spring from a heart of love. He created angels and humans with freedom of choice. If God had created robots, then there would be no sin, suffering, or death. The continued existence of sin with its high cost of suffering and death is strong evidence that God values freedom of choice.

As covering cherub, Lucifer knew God better than any other created being. He knew that God loved him and valued his freedom. He knew that rebellion would cause God deep sorrow. He also knew that God would not directly punish his rebellion.

He was right. Lucifer and his fallen angels are still alive. They are free to come and go upon this Earth and tempt all six billion of us humans. I am quite sure that you know this by experience, as I do. Lucifer and his fallen angels exist only by the mercy and sustaining power of God.

Lucifer and his angels have long since passed the point of no return, but God has not killed them. Nor has God confined them to hellfire. The first two chapters of the book of Job show that Satan was free to present himself in the heavenly courts, before the throne of God. Other evil angels also spoke in the heavenly courts:

> And the LORD said, Who shall persuade Ahab, that he may go up and fall at Ramothgilead? And one said on this manner, and another said on that manner. And there came forth a spirit, and stood before the LORD, and said, I will persuade him. And the LORD said unto him, Wherewith? And he said, I will go forth, and I will be a lying spirit in the mouth of all his prophets. And he said, Thou shalt persuade him, and prevail also: go forth, and do so. (2Chronicles 18:20-22, KJV)

God's holy angels never tempt anyone, nor do they put lying spirits into prophets' mouths! Jesus is divine and he is the truth. Clearly, then these were evil angels seeking to bring destruction to king Ahab. Notice, though, that they needed God's permission before they could act. "No temptation has taken you but what is common to man; but God is faithful, who will not allow you to be tempted above what you are able, but with the temptation also will make a way to escape, so that you may be able to bear it" (1Corinthians 10:13, MKJ).

What Lucifer did not understand was that, in the end, sin itself destroys all those who allow its evil seeds to be planted and grow in their hearts and minds. Lucifer knew that God would be a formidable Opponent. He had witnessed God's creative power. But depending on God's love and mercy, Lucifer decided to go ahead with his rebellion!

If Lucifer had merely declared open rebellion, none of the angels would have followed him. The deception must have been very hard to detect. He had to have moved carefully and slowly. Based on the texts in Isaiah 14, Ezekiel 28, and the story of David and Absalom, I believe that Lucifer used a two-pronged plan of attack. He decided to subtly attack the very throne of God, his law of mercy, unselfish love, and reconciliation.

First, Lucifer used his exalted position to gain support among the angels. He made it look like he was trying to improve upon the government of Heaven. He claimed that he was trying to expand the freedom of the angels and at the same time strengthen Heaven's security. Hadn't God created angels to be noble, holy, wise, and loving? Hadn't he created the angels to be perfect? He hinted to some of his closest angel friends that they did not need the restraints imposed by God's law of unselfish love.

Lucifer used the same deception on the angels that he would later use on Eve, "And the serpent said unto the woman, Ye shall not surely die: For God doth know that in the day ye eat thereof, then your eyes shall be opened, and ye shall be as gods, knowing good and evil" (Genesis 3:4, 5, KJV).

Lucifer insinuated that God's law was holding the angels back from reaching their full potential as gods. Many of the angels listened to his subtle insinuations. His words were so subtle that they thought that they had come up with the ideas themselves. These angels then talked with other angels. A minor note of discord rippled through the angel ranks.

Rebellion Spreads

Lucifer, as the "covering cherub," (the highest position among the angels) then pointed to this discord in the harmony of Heaven as evidence that there was room for improvement in the underlying structure of Heaven. He proposed that God's law of love unnecessarily limited the angels. God had made them perfect—they did not need any law to govern them. Lucifer told them that they could become like God, knowing good and evil. In other words, the angels could be a law unto themselves. Satan was saying "ignore God's law of love and just follow your heart."

Second, Lucifer took advantage of the discord in Heaven's harmony that he himself had so artfully caused, to attack another of God's principles, the principle of mercy and reconciliation. Under the cover of seeking to remedy the unrest among the angels in Heaven, Lucifer promoted his "superior" idea for insuring security and harmony in Heaven.

On Earth, Lucifer instilled his self-centered, unmerciful, and hate-filled sense of justice to Absalom. In Heaven, Lucifer had insinuated that, in order to be just and to maintain Heaven's security, God must punish any angel or other created being who did wrong. The ultimate punishment of course, would be death. The threat of death would be a great deterrence to rebellion. This alternate "justice" was abhorrent to God. Our Father is a God of love, mercy, and reconciliation. "For I have no pleasure in the death of him that dieth, saith the Lord GOD: wherefore turn yourselves, and live ye" (Ezekiel 18:32, KJV). "For he doth not afflict willingly nor grieve the children of men" (Lamentations 3:33, KJV).

"The wages of sin is death; but the gift of God is eternal

life through Jesus Christ our Lord" (Romans 6:23, KJV). Our Father longs to give us the gift of eternal life. The inevitable consequence or wages of sin is death. Force cannot produce love.

God does not condone or cause anyone to sin. Although, when we do sin, God can still turn some aspects of it around to his glory. Some would say that David's sin and restoration caused him to be perhaps too merciful. When his son Absalom rebelled and was trying to kill him, David still requested that his officers spare his son's life.

God faced a similar situation when Lucifer, the highest angel in Heaven, rebelled. When, after repeated warnings, Lucifer and one third of the Heavenly angels willfully continued in rebellion against God's government of love, they hardened their hearts and passed the point of no return. Their probation closed. They had slammed the door to God's love so many times that God could no longer find an opening into their hearts. If God had not stepped in and shielded them from the burning, crushing weight of their sin and guilt they would have perished.

However, all of Heaven would have been afraid of God. Many would have been led to believe Satan's false charges that God was an unfair, self-centered tyrant. True obedience and worship can only be based on love and freedom.

God in his infinite wisdom shielded the rebellious angels from reaping the natural consequences of their sin in order to allow the time necessary to reveal to all of Heaven the horrible, inevitable results of rebellion against God's perfect law. "But of the tree of the knowledge of good and evil, thou shalt not eat of it: for in the day that thou eatest thereof thou shalt surely die" (Genesis 2:17, KJV).

God's promises, principles, and warnings about sin would apply to all created beings. But the Lamb slain from the foundation of the world has taken all sin upon himself. Yet in his mercy, Jesus shields men and angels from the full destructive results of sin and guilt.

Lucifer took advantage of God's mercy. He claimed that

it proved that God knew that the rebellion was justified or else they would have been killed.

Lucifer had charged God with selfishly, arbitrarily holding back the angels from their true potential, and at the same time being too compassionate to provide Heaven with the necessary security. One third of the angels sided with Lucifer. Two thirds of the angels sided with God. In order to permanently bring an end to rebellion, God had to allow sin to develop fully. God's newest creation, Earth, became a battleground.

Freedom and Equal Access

God created Adam and Eve, endowed with perfect love. Nevertheless, God had to allow Adam and Eve freedom to choose. Their natural tendency was to love God and each other. However, they had to develop their characters. That would take time.

Both Lucifer and God would have opportunity to talk with Adam and Eve. God visited with Adam and Eve in the cool of the day. "And they heard the voice of the LORD God walking in the garden in the cool of the day" (Genesis 3:8, KJV). Lucifer was limited to the tree of the knowledge of good and evil to present his case.

Satan tempted Adam and Eve and they fell. Satan thought he had won the war, but it was only the first battle. Satan had shown that he could deceive sinless beings. Now God would have to show that he could woo sinful beings back to a love relationship. Both God and Lucifer would need a lot of time to present their case to the human race.

In order to be fair, both God and Satan would have to have equal access to the hearts and minds of each human being. Each person would be free to choose between Christ and Satan. The war between Christ and Satan has been going on for about six thousand years. Earth's history, as a battleground between good and evil, will soon draw to a close. Each of us has a part to play in this battle.

Each day we must choose between good and evil, Christ and Satan, selfishness and love. We can choose to behold and partake of the grace of Christ, or we can choose to behold and partake of Satan's lies, sin, and selfishness. By beholding we become changed. Behold your God. Behold his infinite sacrifice, his mercy, grace, and love, his righteousness.

Our heavenly Father, in his great wisdom, has chosen to deal with Lucifer's rebellion patiently, carefully, and at very high cost to himself. King David also chose to deal with Absalom's rebellion patiently, carefully, and at very high cost to himself.

Abuse of Freedom

Absalom abused his lofty position as a prince. In the same way, Lucifer's high position gave him tremendous influence in the courts of Heaven. When the mystery of iniquity, the seeds of rebellion, began to grow in Lucifer's heart, he turned his exalted position to his perverted purposes.

The more richly that God blesses his creatures, the greater the potential curse when used in rebellion. God had more richly blessed Lucifer than any other created being. Let's examine the Scripture story of Absalom's rebellion against his Father David and see if we can find the parallels with Lucifer's rebellion against his "Father," his Creator, Jesus Christ:

Absalom Undermines His Father

Absalom then bought a magnificent chariot and chariot horses, and hired fifty footmen to run ahead of him. He got up early every morning and went out to the gate of the city; and when anyone came to bring a case to the king for trial, Absalom called him over and expressed interest in his problem. He would say, "I can see that you are right in this matter; it's unfortunate that the king doesn't have anyone to assist him in hearing these cases. I surely wish I were the judge; then anyone with a lawsuit could come to me, and I would give him justice!" And when anyone came to bow to him, Absalom wouldn't let him, but shook his hand instead! So in this way Absalom stole the hearts of all the people of Israel. After four years, Absalom

21

said to the king, "Let me go to Hebron to sacrifice to the Lord in fulfillment of a vow I made to him while I was at Geshur—that if he would bring me back to Jerusalem, I would sacrifice to him." "All right," the king told him, "go and fulfill your vow." So Absalom went to Hebron. But while he was there, he sent spies to every part of Israel to incite rebellion against the king. "As soon as you hear the trumpets," his message read, "you will know that Absalom has been crowned in Hebron." He took two hundred men from Jerusalem with him as guests, but they knew nothing of his intentions. While he was offering the sacrifice, he sent for Ahithophel, one of David's counselors who lived in Giloh. Ahithophel declared for Absalom, as did more and more others. So the conspiracy became very strong. (2Samuel 15:1-12, Living Bible)

Absalom hated David's ways of mercy and forgiveness. Yet Absalom depended on it. In fact, Absalom laid the groundwork for his rebellion counting on his father's mercy. Absalom surely reasoned in his heart that he had to take justice into his own hands because his father the king was too weak and softhearted to do justice.

Lucifer had said the same thing about our heavenly Father—that God was too softhearted to keep the kingdom of Heaven secure. Just as Lucifer had done, Absalom equated mercy and forgiveness with weakness. This feeling was inspired from Satan. Pride, selfishness, hatred, vengeance, a desire for power, and a desire to be worshiped warped Absalom's heart just as these flaws had warped Lucifer's heart. Absalom was molded after Lucifer's pattern.

Lucifer gathered one third of the angels in Heaven and with subtle sophistry and lying words, attacked the loyal angels and God's throne. Just like Lucifer, Absalom gathered a large army and came to attack David and his loyal followers. David stepped off his throne and left the holy city of Jerusalem, the city of peace. David only accepted willing followers. At first David and his loyal followers didn't engage Absalom's large army. At first, things looked bad for King David and his loyal band of followers. Absalom and his army quickly conquered everywhere he led them. Rather than fight in the holy city, David decided to conduct the battle in the wilderness. David's men finally made their stand in a large wooded area. Even then, David asked his men to spare Absalom's life. God was with David and his men. David's experienced men loved him and fought fiercely and wisely.

Lucifer and his army of angels attacked the heavenly kingdom. At first Jesus didn't seem to respond. He didn't seem to openly engage Lucifer and his followers. Lucifer seemed to conquer everywhere he went. Things didn't look so good for Jesus and his loyal followers. For example, consider the wickedness of the people before the flood. Jesus also stepped off his throne, set aside his golden crown, laid aside his royal robes, and left Heaven. Rather than fight in the holy city, Jesus decided to engage Lucifer and his army in the "wilderness" that is our planet Earth. Jesus also only accepts willing followers.

When David's loyal followers turned to fight, Absalom's inexperienced, halfhearted men became confused and fled. Absalom, too, fled. Absalom ran into a tree. Absalom's long, beautiful hair, a symbol of his pride and vanity, got caught in the low branches of an oak tree. Absalom's pride cost him his life.

Lucifer's pride caused him to battle his Father. Lucifer also ran into a tree—Calvary's tree. At the end of the age, all will see that Lucifer's pride has cost him his life too. Jesus became a man, taking human flesh. "He did this so that through his death he might destroy the devil, who has the power over death" (Hebrews 2:14, TEV).

When King David heard of Absalom's death, he grieved for his son. "And the king was much moved, and went up to the chamber over the gate, and wept: and as he went, thus he said, O my son Absalom, my son, my son Absalom! would God I had died for thee, O Absalom, my son, my son!" (2Samuel 18:33, KJV). David loved Absalom more than his own life. Jesus loved Lucifer even more than David loved Absalom.

23

David's grief is a type of God's grief over Lucifer. But just like Absalom, Lucifer has sealed his own fate.

Lucifer Looks for Weakness in God's Government

As the mystery of iniquity silently grew in Lucifer's heart, his mind began to separate that which God had joined together.

Intellect, knowledge, reason, and facts blend with love, truth, beauty, and emotions. Reason separate from love, knowledge separate from truth, facts separate from beauty, and intellect without emotion become curses instead of blessings. For example, the Grand Canyon could factually be described as just a huge ditch in the ground. Fact combined with beauty would describe the multitude of colors, the interplay of light and shadow, and the feeling of awe and wonder at the immense proportions of the canyon. Fact plus beauty equals truth.

Lucifer's Catch-22*

Lucifer began to analyze God's government of unconditional love. God had given Lucifer an incredible mind, endowed with exalted powers of reason. Lucifer knew that God granted his creatures freedom. He knew that God would not destroy him for proposing a "more secure" form of government than Heaven's law of unconditional love.

Lucifer selfishly thought he saw a way that he might achieve equality with God. He reasoned that God's unconditional, reconciling law of love had a fatal flaw. Lucifer reasoned that if he could manipulate a large number of angels to rebel, God would have to respect him. Lucifer knew that if God destroyed him and his fellow rebellious angels, fear and doubt would become permanently entrenched in the hearts and minds of the rest of the angels.

God's government, founded on obedience to the principle of unconditional love, would be compromised. Lucifer knew that if God destroyed him and his angels, Heaven would be

*Catch-22: [from the novel *Catch-22* (1961) by J. Heller] a paradox in a law, regulation, or practice that makes one a victim of its provisions no matter what one does.

turned into hell. The very essence of love requires freedom. Love cannot be forced, coerced, or bought, "There is no fear in love; but perfect love casteth out fear: because fear hath torment. He that feareth is not made perfect in love" (1 John 4:18, KJV). As love casts out fear, so does fear cast out love.

Lucifer explained to the angels that God had only two options. God could allow the mutinous angels to live in open rebellion. Or he must destroy them. Either way the rebels' claims would be proven right. Lucifer thought he had found the perfect Catch-22. God must acknowledge Lucifer's wisdom by setting aside his law of unconditional love and mercy, the very foundation of his throne, in favor of Lucifer's idea of conditional love, justice, and punishment. Or God must destroy his law of love by destroying Lucifer and his angels.

Lucifer was sure that he had our freedom-loving God backed into a corner with no way out. Having formulated the new law of Heaven, Lucifer would be exalted to the very throne of God. Lucifer would have the prerogatives of God. He would be able to help design and create new worlds.

And all Lucifer's loyal followers, who had risked their lives to stand up for the rights and progress of all the angels would be exalted as heroes. All the angels would advance to a higher level of existence that God had selfishly and arbitrarily withheld from them. They would be as gods.

When it became clear that God was not going to destroy Lucifer and his fallen angels, the rebellious angels declared that was proof God's government was flawed and that God knew their rebellion was just.

Love is God's Power

But God is Master of the third option. After patiently waiting four thousand years, God countered Satan's rebellion. The plan to sacrifice his Son on the cross of Calvary stunned Satan. Satan's selfish heart couldn't conceive of that level of unselfishness. Satan understood the prophecies, but he couldn't imagine the effect that Jesus's sacrifice would have on sinful men and the heavenly beings.

25

Yet our merciful heavenly Father was patient with Satan. He did not kill or punish Satan and his angels for their rebellion. God did not even force them out of Heaven. "And the angels which kept not their first estate, but left their own habitation, he hath reserved in everlasting chains under darkness unto the judgment of the great day" (Jude 6, KJV).

Jude asserts that Satan and his angels voluntarily left Heaven, their first estate, their own habitation. They have forged their own chains by hanging onto selfishness, pride, hatred, and sin with its attendant shame, guilt, stress, and fear. The horror of sin and guilt has changed their perception of the light, love, and truth of God into dark lies from the pit of hell.

The Testimony of Demons

Dear reader, have you come to believe some of Satan's lies? Do you accept as truth the testimony of demons? Please do not answer too hastily:

> And when he was come to the other side into the country of the Gergesenes, there met him two possessed with devils, coming out of the tombs, exceeding fierce, so that no man might pass by that way. And, behold, they cried out, saying, What have we to do with thee, Jesus, thou Son of God? art thou come hither to torment us before the time? (Matthew 8:28, 29, KJV)

The devils that possessed these two men falsely accused Jesus of coming to torment them before the time. Sin and guilt have so darkened and distorted their debased minds that they believe that God desires to torment them.

Nevertheless, their own sin and guilt torment them now. Furthermore, at the judgment, their sense of sin and guilt will be excruciatingly accentuated in the presence of the perfect purity of God's holiness, his perfect character of unselfish love, his glory.

At the judgment all will see that from the beginning Satan has lied to men and angels in order to exalt himself. Lucifer thought he could win the war for the hearts and minds of Heaven's angels:

A War of Words

And war broke out in heaven: Michael and his angels fought with the dragon; and the dragon and his angels fought, but they did not prevail, nor was a place found for them in heaven any longer. So the great dragon was cast out, that serpent of old, called the Devil and Satan, who deceives the whole world; he was cast to the earth, and his angels were cast out with him. (Revelation 12:7-9, NKJ)

This war was fought with words, ideas, thoughts, and feelings. The hearts and minds of each citizen of Heaven had to be brought to a point of decision. Was God's law of unselfish love a firm, secure foundation for the government of Heaven? Did God the Father himself live by the same principle of unselfish love? Or did Lucifer, the covering cherub, the highest created being in Heaven, really have a better idea? Was God holding the angels back, limiting their potential to become gods? The great Dragon, Lucifer, deceived one-third of God's holy angels.

"Nor was a place found for them in heaven any longer." The disharmony, dissension, and differences eventually reached a crescendo. John, in Revelation 12:9, informs us that Satan and his angels were "cast out." Jude 6, asserts that they left voluntarily. Both Scriptures are true.

The key lies in understanding how they were cast out. The next verse will give us that key. "Then I heard a loud voice saying in heaven, "Now salvation, and strength, and the kingdom of our God, and the power of his Christ have come, for the accuser of our brethren, who accused them before our God day and night, has been cast down" (Revelation 12:10, NKJ).

Jesus's Death Wins the War in Heaven

"Now salvation" clearly refers to the crucifixion of the Son of God. This passage gives us the time and the method by which Satan and his angels were cast out of Heaven. When the loyal angels saw how Satan and his angels treated the beloved Son of God, their hearts and minds overflowed with outrage. Paul explains it, "Forasmuch then as the children are partakers of flesh and blood, he also himself likewise took part of the same; that through death he might destroy him that had the power of death, that is, the devil" (Hebrews 2:14, KJV).

The suffering and death of the Son of God on Calvary's cruel tree, in contrast with Satan's self-centered, malignant hatred, decided the outcome of the war in Heaven. They cast out what little sympathy they might have retained for Satan's cause.

The loyal angels no longer had any desire to listen to Satan's accusations. Truly, God had cast Satan and his angels out of Heaven. God did this by contrasting his unconditional love, mercy, and forgiveness with Satan's brutal concept of justice, his selfishness, and hatred. God accomplished all this through his Son's suffering on Calvary's tree. At the same time, Jesus demonstrated the infinite beauty of his Father's character of love and the hideous destructiveness of sin.

Victorious in the battle for Heaven, God won the hearts and minds of all the loyal angels. He vanquished Satan and his evil mob of angels, and banished their evil lies and accusations from the heavenly realms. However, in his great mercy and wisdom, God sustains Satan's life. Nevertheless, God did not lie. Sin does result in death. Satan will come to an end. And it won't be pretty. But remember, how the end comes is equally important as the end itself. We will examine that concept in a later chapter.

God's Sovereignty and Human Freedom

God has the power to do anything that he wants, but God's character governs his actions. Our God is a God of principles. God's character, his principles are eternal, unchanging. "Every good gift and every perfect gift is from above, and cometh down from the Father of lights, with whom is no variableness, neither shadow of turning" (James 1:17, KJV). God created mankind free to choose. Sin could not make our Creator change his mind. In fact sin is proof that we are free moral agents. If Adam and Eve hadn't been free, sin would never have raised its ugly head.

Listen to what God reveals to Israel about himself, "For I am the LORD, I change not; therefore ye sons of Jacob are not consumed" (Malachi 3:6, KJV).

Paul also affirms the same thing about Jesus, "Jesus Christ the same yesterday, and to day, and for ever" (Hebrews 13:8, KJV). The presence of sin cannot change God's principles, which are the very foundation of his heavenly government.

Our Creator-God has the physical power to destroy Satan and all his sympathizers. But that would not solve the sin problem. Our heavenly Father, in his wisdom, knows that if he were to kill Satan and his followers, many would seek to obey motivated by fear. Fear-based obedience is not really obedience at all. Force cannot make Heaven secure. Selfishness and sin can only be overcome by love's warm embrace. God, in his wisdom, chose not to use force because he knew that it could not change human or angel hearts. The battle for the universe rages from heart to heart.

There is another reason that God has not destroyed Satan and his sympathizers. The exercise of force is contrary to the principles of God's government. Or in other words, compelling power and the exercise of force are contrary to, and in fact the opposite of, his glorious character of love.

God has written with his own finger, on stone tablets, the foundation principles of his government and his glorious character of love. The life and death of Christ exemplified, honored, and expanded our understanding of the Ten Commandments. His authority rests upon his character of mercy, and love; the presentation of these principles is how God does battle.

This principle can be found in Psalm 22:3, "But You are holy, enthroned in the praises of Israel" (NKJ). I used to struggle with this verse. It seemed out of place and even a little silly. How could the foundation of God's throne, his government have its foundation on something as weak and changeable as the praises of Israel? Human praise seemed like a strange place for the foundation of God's government. I prayed about it and asked the Holy Spirit to give me deeper understanding.

Praise God, he did! He brought to mind Solomon's words "In a multitude of people is a king's honor, But in the lack of people is the downfall of a prince" (Proverbs 14:28, NKJ). God is not a dictator. He is a benevolent king. He desires only willing subjects in his kingdom. "Enthroned in the praises of Israel," means that our Father's kingdom is only as strong as the enlightened loyalty of each of his children. A king without followers is no king at all. Our Father also knows that his eternal principles are the only path to happiness and eternal life.

Severity, harshness, force, military weapons of mass destruction, revenge, and punishment may have the illusion of expediency and power to our warped human minds. These may seem necessary to deal with bold, sin-hardened minds. But these have no place in our Father's kingdom, which is founded on love. His kingdom is ruled and guided by love.

Our Father has only one weapon, namely the presentation of the principle of unselfish, unconditional, self-sacrificing love. If you don't think that love alone can win, you don't understand the power of the cross. If you don't think God knows how to let sin burn itself out, you underestimate the self-destructiveness of sin, and the wisdom of God.

Christ's sacrifice on the cross shows us that the Almighty Creator-God wields the mightiest weapon in the universe: his infinite, self-denying love. If anyone's mind were ever forced or coerced our Father's kingdom would suffer. Heaven's foundation would not be secure. People would doubt the goodness of the King. Sooner or later Heaven's harmony would disintegrate.

Fear and force can never bring true loyalty! Money or material rewards cannot win our hearts. Our Father's government, founded on the principle of love, is holy and pure. It is untainted by unwise human ideas. Only love can win the heart. Only God's perfect love can win our complete loyalty.

Therefore I will divide Him
a portion with the great,
And He shall divide
the spoil with the strong,
Because He poured out His soul unto
death. (Isaiah 53:12, NKJ)

2

Gethsemane

Innocent Or Guilty

Over the past several years a number of men have been freed from prison. Some of these men had been on death row. Though convicted in a court of law, DNA evidence has now shown them to be innocent of the crimes they had been convicted of. Imagine serving hard time for a crime you did not do! Have you ever been accused of something you did not do? It does not feel very good.

It is human nature to quickly deny an accusation, insisting, "I didn't do it! I wouldn't do that!" When we are guilty, we still start pointing fingers at others in order to share the blame. Isaiah discloses to us that Jesus, on the other hand, even though innocent, chose to take the responsibility, the blame, shame, and guilt for all our misdeeds.

All of Heaven thinks Jesus is great because he was willing to be identified with sinners, that is, to take the fall for our sins, even though that meant risking everlasting death. Jesus had to be willing to cease to exist in order to rescue us from hell:

> Therefore I will divide Him a portion with the great, And He shall divide the spoil with the strong, Because He poured out His soul unto death, And He was numbered with the transgressors, And He bore the sin of many, And

33

made intercession for the transgressors. (Isaiah 53:12, NKJ)

How did Jesus "pour out his soul unto death"? Let's look at how Jesus tried to prepare his disciples to understand his imminent suffering. He gave them a view of Heaven's understanding of service and self-sacrificing love.

The Last Supper

A brief overview of Jesus's last few hours will provide us important background information that will give us some insights into Jesus's suffering. We'll start with the Last Supper.

Jesus's closest friends, his twelve disciples, were arguing over which of them would have the highest place of honor in the kingdom of Heaven. The desire for glory, honor, and self-exaltation filled their hearts. Selfishness crowded out love.

Jesus saw that they did not understand the spiritual nature of his kingdom. He feared for their souls; the disciple's selfishness grieved Jesus.

To demonstrate to them the nature, the very foundation of God's kingdom, Jesus showed them that he was their Servant. Jesus laid aside his outer garment. This action symbolized how he laid aside his kingly robes, left Heaven, and came to Earth as a man.

It also symbolized how he was about to lay aside his robes of innocence by carrying the sin and guilt of the whole world. Jesus tied a towel around his waist and took the role of a servant. Even though Jesus was their Master and their God, he then washed each of the 12 disciples' feet. Jesus did not do this to shame them, but to reveal to them the true order of God's kingdom.

All Heaven worships almighty God because he is humble, kind, and serves all of his created beings by upholding them with his mighty power. Though he is our Creator, King, and Savior, Jesus is humble and kind:

Come unto me, all ye that labour and are heavy laden, and

I will give you rest. Take my yoke upon you, and learn of me; for I am meek and lowly in heart: and ye shall find rest unto your souls. For my yoke is easy, and my burden is light. (Matthew 11:28-30, KJV)

"Tell the city of Zion, Look, your king is coming to you! He is humble and rides on a donkey and on a colt, the foal of a donkey" (Matthew 12:5, TEV). Jesus is the rightful King of Israel, the Saviour of the world, God in human flesh. However, he is meek and lowly in heart. Jesus came to show us what the Father is like:

Jesus and the Father are One

Philip said to Him, "Lord, show us the Father, and it is sufficient for us." Jesus said to him, "Have I been with you so long, and yet you have not known Me, Philip? He who has seen Me has seen the Father; so how can you say, 'Show us the Father?'" (John 14:8, 9, NKJ)

If the Father had come to the Earth as a man instead of Jesus, no one could have told the difference. We have seen that Jesus is meek and lowly in heart. Then the Father is also meek and lowly in heart. Heavenly society has different values than what is normally found here on Earth.

In earthly society the talented, the young and the beautiful, the rich and the powerful are exalted and idolized. But in Heaven it is not so. Heaven places high value on character. He, who through unselfish love, stoops the lowest to serve others is considered great and is exalted, "So the last shall be first, and the first last" (Matthew 20:16, MKJ).

God's love is the strongest and the most unselfish in the universe. No one can ever stoop lower than God did in the person of Jesus Christ. Jesus outlined Heaven's view of greatness:

But Jesus called them and said, You know that the rulers of the nations exercise dominion over them, and they who are great exercise authority over them.

35

However, it shall not be so among you. But whoever desires to be great among you, let him be your servant. And whoever desires to be chief among you, let him be your servant; even as the Son of man did not come to be served, but to serve, and to give His life a ransom for many. (Matthew 20:25-28, MKJV)

Grief in the Garden

Now we will look at what began to crush Jesus's heart in the garden of Gethsemane. The garden of Gethsemane is located on the Mount of Olives. Gethsemane means an oil press, the device used to crush the oil out of the olives. Olive oil is a symbol of the Holy Spirit (see 1Samuel 16:13). The garden of Gethsemane was the place where the dark weight of the sins of the world began to crush out Jesus's sense of closeness to his Father. Through the Holy Spirit he had enjoyed oneness with God from his mother's womb. The meaning of the name, "Gethsemane" accurately symbolizes the experience of our Savior on the night before the crucifixion.

"Then Jesus went with them to a place called Gethsemane; and he said to his disciples, 'Sit here while I go over there and pray'" (Matthew 26:36, NRSV). As Jesus entered the garden of Gethsemane, he knew the terrible struggle that he was about to endure. Although suffering terrific stress, he carefully weighed the spiritual condition of his disciples. Always kind and considerate, Jesus had eight of his disciples wait for him at a distance. He knew that they were not ready to comprehend the suffering he was about to undergo:

He took Peter with him and Zebedee's two sons James and John, and began to be filled with anguish and despair. Then he told them, "My soul is crushed with horror and sadness to the point of death . . . stay here . . . stay awake with me." He went forward a little, and fell face downward on the ground, and prayed, "My Father! If it is possible, let this cup be taken away from me. But I want your will, not mine." (Matthew 26:37-39, The Living Bible)

The Cup of Sin and Guilt

Even with the inner circle of Peter, James, and John, Jesus felt that it was necessary to put some distance between them in order to shield them from witnessing the fullness of his agony. Jesus was beginning to drink from "the cup of God's wrath."

This caused Jesus to cry out, "My soul is crushed with horror and sadness to the point of death." What was this cup that caused Jesus, the Son of God such intense grief? "The Lord holds a cup in his hand, filled with the strong wine of his anger. He pours it out, and all the wicked drink it; they drink it down to the last drop" (Psalm 78:8, TEV).

In order to save mankind, Jesus had to drink the full cup of the sufferings of sin. To drink from this "cup" then, is to suffer the consequences of sin. This is an extremely bitter cup. Contained within this cup are all the rage, murder, rape, fighting, torture, divorce, abuse, anguish, suffering, shame, and guilt of our fallen world. "But we see Jesus, who was made a little lower than the angels, for the suffering of death crowned with glory and honor, that He, by the grace of God, might taste death for everyone" (Hebrews 2:9, NKJ).

Christ was headed toward the cross where he would experience the full consequences of sin and taste death for everyone, so that we would not have to. Christ's experience in the garden of Gethsemane shows the horrifying consequences of sin. Jesus dreaded to drink from this cup. But it was the only way to save you and me.

His great love for us was stronger than his dread of the fearful consequences of sin. The results of sin are not pretty. The terrible experiences of Israel and other nations are often described as a cup. The descriptions of this cup provide us with hints of the depths of suffering that Jesus went through on our behalf:

Thus says your Sovereign, the Lord, your God who pleads the cause of his people: See, I have taken from your hand the cup of staggering; you shall drink no more from the bowl of my wrath. And I will put it into the hand of your

37

tormentors, who have said to you, "Bow down, that we may walk on you"; and you have made your back like the ground and like the street for them to walk on. (Isaiah 51:22, 23, NRSV)

In this world, the good and bad alike suffer from the consequences of sin. However, those who continue in sin will experience a fiery bitterness that is the natural consequence of selfish, sinful rebellion against God's government of unselfish love. The Bible uses a variety of words to describe the contents of this "cup:" terror, horror, bitterness, intoxicating wine, and wrath, etc. Ezekiel describes the experience of a nation that turns its back on God:

Yes, this is what the Sovereign Lord says: You will drink from the same cup of terror as your sister—a cup that is large and deep. And all the world will mock and scorn you in your desolation. You will reel like a drunkard beneath the awful blows of sorrow and distress, just as your sister Samaria did. In deep anguish you will drain that cup of terror to the very bottom. Then you will smash it to pieces and beat your breast in anguish. For I, the Sovereign Lord, have spoken! (Ezekiel 23:32-34, NLT)

Obadiah also warns us about the consequences of rejecting the principles of God's love:

For the day of the LORD is near upon all the heathen: as thou hast done, it shall be done unto thee: thy reward shall return upon thine own head. For as ye have drunk upon my holy mountain, so shall all the heathen drink continually, yea, they shall drink, and they shall swallow down, and they shall be as though they had not been. (Obadiah 15, 16, KJV)

This cup of sin that all the wicked must drink will horrify them beyond what our easy-chair understanding of hell can grasp. Nevertheless, we do know that "they shall be as though they had never been." Jesus, to be our Savior, had to be willing to step through eternal death's dark door.

John the Revelator talks about this awful cup and describes the degradation, distress, the fiery guilt and torment that flow from that cup. Those who worship the beast and its image, instead of our loving God, destroy their own souls:

> And the third angel followed them, saying with a loud voice, If any man worship the beast and his image, and receive *his* mark in his forehead, or in his hand, The same shall drink of the wine of the wrath of God, which is poured out without mixture into the cup of his indignation; and he shall be tormented with fire and brimstone in the presence of the holy angels, and in the presence of the Lamb. (Revelation 14:9, 10, KJV)

Jesus Decides to Drink Our Cup of Woe

Christ was the only man that could ever be tempted to use his divinity to escape his captors. But, Christ was a willing victim in the garden of Gethsemane. He had to choose of his own free will to drink down to its bitter dregs the awful cup of our sin. This cup contained all the burning guilt, shame, horror, separation, fiery indignation, and wrath that are the natural, inevitable results of the sins of the whole world. What an awful cup! Only his great love for us could impel him to do this. It is no wonder then that Jesus prayed three times to his Father, asking if there were any other way to save us:

> Then he returned to the three disciples and found them asleep. "Peter," he called, "couldn't you even stay awake with me one hour? Keep alert and pray. Otherwise temptation will overpower you. For the spirit indeed is willing, but how weak the body is!" Again he left them and prayed, "My Father! If this cup cannot go away until I drink it all, your will be done." He returned to them again and found them sleeping, for their eyes were heavy, so he went back

to prayer the third time, saying the same things again. Then he came to the disciples and said, "Sleep on now and take your rest . . . but no! The time has come! I am betrayed into the hands of evil men! Up! Let's be going! Look! Here comes the man who is betraying me!" At that very moment while he was still speaking, Judas, one of the Twelve, arrived with a great crowd armed with swords and clubs, sent by the Jewish leaders. Judas had told them to arrest the man he greeted, for that would be the one they were after. So now Judas came straight to Jesus and said, "Hello, Master!" and embraced him in friendly fashion. Jesus said, "My friend, go ahead and do what you have come for." Then the others grabbed him. (Matthew 26:40-50, The Living Bible)

The Cup and the Second Death

Our Heavenly Father, up to this point, had always shielded Jesus from the full weight of the dark knowledge of the guilt, grief, woe, and sin of humanity. Powerful angels had also protected Jesus from physical harm. Now Jesus would face physical and spiritual torture and death. Now Jesus would open his heart and mind to experience the full weight, agony, and darkness of sinful humanity's grief and woe. Even now Jesus was entering into the second death. He began to experience the fullness of the wrath of God. In Psalm 89, Ethan the Ezrahite, through the power of the Holy Spirit, foretells the hellish sufferings of Jesus:

The days of his youth You have shortened; You have covered him with shame. Selah. How long, Lord? Will You hide Yourself forever? Will Your wrath burn like fire? Remember how short my time is; For what futility have You created all the children of men? What man can live and not see death? Can he deliver his life from the power of the grave? Selah. Lord, where are Your former lovingkindnesses, Which You swore to David in Your truth? Remember, Lord, the reproach of Your servants—How I bear in my bosom the reproach of all the many peoples, With which Your enemies have reproached, O Lord, With which they have reproached the footsteps of Your anointed. (Psalm 89:45-51, NKJ)

Note, "Will Your wrath burn like fire?" The psalmist, Asaph, describes the cup of suffering that the wicked will endure as a result of their stubborn rebellion against the Lord:

For in the hand of the LORD *there is* a cup, and the wine is red; it is full of mixture; and he poureth out of the same: but the dregs thereof, all the wicked of the earth shall wring *them* out, *and* drink *them*. (Psalm 75:8, KJV)

Again and again the psalmists prophesied regarding the second death experience that our Savior would endure to rescue us from the power of sin (Psalms 22, 30, 31, 40, 42, 43, 55, 57, 69, 75, 86, 88, 89, 102, 116, 129, 130, and others). These prophecies describe Christ's torturous, hellish time of suffering, which began in the garden of Gethsemane and ended with his death on the cross. These Psalms of innocent suffering prefigure the innocent suffering of the Lamb of God:

I will praise thee, O Lord my God, with all my heart: and I will glorify thy name for evermore. For great is thy mercy toward me: and thou hast delivered my soul from the lowest hell. O God, the proud are risen against me, and the assemblies of violent men have sought after my soul; and have not set thee before them. But thou, O Lord, art a God full of compassion, and gracious, longsuffering, and plenteous in mercy and truth. (Psalm 86:12-15, KJV)

One of David's weapons against despair, against the temptation to feel forsaken of God, is to praise God's name. God's name is synonymous with his character. Jesus also rested on the name, the character of Almighty God:

41

I love the LORD, because he hath heard my voice and my supplications. Because he hath inclined his ear unto me, therefore will I call upon him as long as I live. The sorrows of death compassed me, and the pains of hell gat hold upon me: I found trouble and sorrow. Then called I upon the name of the LORD; O LORD, I beseech thee, deliver my soul. Gracious is the LORD, and righteous; yea, our God is merciful. (Psalm 116:1-5, KJV)

The Sons of Korah Foretell Gethsemane
While in the Garden of Gethsemane, Jesus knew full well what our salvation would cost him. Putting the cup of our sin and guilt to his lips meant drinking down all the horrors of hell. Centuries before Christ, the Holy Spirit gave the sons of Korah insights into Jesus's agonizing decision:

Psalm 88
1 O Lord, God of my salvation, when, at night, I cry out in your presence,
2 let my prayer come before you; incline your ear to my cry.

This refers to Jesus's three seasons of earnest, pleading prayer that night in Gethsemane.

3 For my soul is full of troubles, and my life draws near to Sheol.
4 I am counted among those who go down to the Pit; I am like those who have no help,

In the garden of Gethsemane Christ said, "My soul is sorrowful, even unto death." Sheol is a Hebrew word that is often translated as hell or the grave. After three agonizing seasons of prayer, Jesus saw that the only path by which he could save humanity would lead him right through the pit of hell.

5 like those forsaken among the dead, like the slain that lie

in the grave, like those whom you remember no more, for
they are cut off from your hand.
6 You have put me in the depths of the Pit, in the regions
dark and deep.

Remember we are talking about Jesus, the Creator-God.
He voluntarily left the warmth of Heaven, the praise and adoration of myriads of angels, and the intimate friendship with his
Father, for the cold slap of human rejection and the hellish,
soul-burning guilt of sin. Christ faced the cruel result of sin,
which is the second death. We will continue to explore the second death in the next two chapters. Jesus felt forsaken of God,
cut off from his life-giving hand. Jesus felt that he would cease
to exist, and enter into the dark abyss of eternal death.

7 Your wrath lies heavy upon me, and you overwhelm me
with all your waves. Selah

Though perfectly innocent, Jesus chose to face the wrath
of God against sin. The hot anger, the seething indignation,
the ocean of grief that a father would feel upon learning of the
brutal torture and murder of his precious, innocent child gives
us a window into the heart of God. Now multiply that by the
billions of God's children that have suffered under the tyranny
of sin. That is one part of God's wrath against sin. *Selah* is a
word that is similar to "amen." It means, hesitate, meditate,
slow down; don't miss the importance of these words.

8 You have caused my companions to shun me;
you have made me a thing of horror to them.
I am shut in so that I cannot escape;
9 my eye grows dim through sorrow. Every day I call on
you, O Lord; I spread out my hands to you.

All Jesus's disciples deserted him. Peter denied his God
and friend three times. Jesus felt that the death that he faced
would hold him forever and ever. Jesus did know the prophe-

cies that foretold his resurrection in three days. However, it was by faith alone that he could grasp these prophecies.

It is a very different thing to read about something than it is to experience it! Theory versus the real world never seemed further apart. Jesus's five senses told him that if he accepted the sin and guilt of the world that he would die, forever separated from his Father, forever trapped in the grave.

10 Do you work wonders for the dead?
Do the shades rise up to praise you? Selah
11 Is your steadfast love declared in the grave,
or your faithfulness in Abaddon?
12 Are your wonders known in the darkness,
or your saving help in the land of forgetfulness?

Meditate on these words. Clearly, Jesus confronted the emotions, the physical sensation of reality that screamed out in his heart, mind, and soul that if he took on our sins, his Father would reject him, he would cease to exist, and he would never experience the joys of Heaven again!

Also, Jesus was overwhelmed with a strong sense of the futility of his death. He was tempted to fear that it would do no good. Every fiber of Christ's being longed to bless others. He was tempted to fear that his death would not bring salvation to fallen humanity. His heart and mind abhorred the thought that death would prevent him from praising his Father, leading the angels, and serving humanity.

13 But I, O Lord, cry out to you; in the morning my prayer comes before you.
14 O Lord, why do you cast me off? Why do you hide your face from me?

While still in the Garden, before anyone had laid a hand on him, Jesus began to feel the darkness of separation from his Father.

15 Wretched and close to death from my youth up, I suffer your terrors; I am desperate.

Jesus's identification with sinful humanity had been placing the foul, bitter cup of sin to his lips from his youth up. Jesus embodied holiness, purity, and absolute perfection. Even while growing up, the presence of sin in his family, friends, and neighbors caused him pain in proportion to his holiness, purity, and affection for others.

16 Your wrath has swept over me;
your dread assaults destroy me.
17 They surround me like a flood all day long;
from all sides they close in on me.
18 You have caused friend and neighbor to shun me;
my companions are in darkness. (NRSV)

Jesus's sacrifice brings to light important lessons about the wrath of God and the second death. Jesus Christ is the only man to have ever experienced the fullness of the wrath of God, which is the second death.

The wrath of God flooded over Jesus and engulfed him. Jesus drowned in our sins. Christ endured the burning anguish and guilt of the world's sins, the horrific lake of fire. There is only one thing in the entire universe that could motivate the Son of God to open his heart, mind, and body to this infinite torture—infinite love!

How few understood his sacrifice. How dark appeared the condition of human guilt and the dense ingratitude of men! Satan presented to Jesus the worst possible view of sinful humanity. Satan forcefully brought to Christ's attention the fact that his special people whom he had blessed above all others were rejecting him. Not only were they rejecting him, they were seeking to take his life.

Judas, one of his own disciples was about to betray him. Peter, one of the inner three, was about to deny him three times. All his disciples and other followers would desert him.

This pierced Jesus's heart and soul. The leaders of the nation that he had come to save, even his own closest followers that he loved so dearly, were about to become pawns that Satan would use for his evil purposes.

Sweating Blood

Grief upon grief, woe upon woe, Satan was arranging for everything to fall upon Christ Jesus. All this sadness and grief was piled on top of the sense of separation from his heavenly Father, caused by the infinite weight of the world's sin and guilt. Luke adds an important detail to the picture of grief and woe that Christ experienced in the garden of Gethsemane:

> And he was withdrawn from them about a stone's cast, and kneeled down, and prayed, Saying, Father, if thou be willing, remove this cup from me: nevertheless not my will, but thine, be done. And there appeared an angel unto him from heaven, strengthening him. And being in an agony he prayed more earnestly: and his sweat was as it were great drops of blood falling down to the ground. (Luke 22:41-44, KJV)

And "His sweat was as it were great drops of blood falling down to the ground." Many people have faced imminent torture and death without sweating blood. Very few people ever sweat blood. It was not fear of the coming physical torture that caused Jesus such intense agony. Only intense mental anguish, an abyss of horror and dread can cause this phenomenon. Extreme mental stress and strain can cause the outer capillaries to burst, mixing blood with sweat.

Jesus had greater spiritual and emotional strength than any man that had ever lived. Jesus was also physically strong, for he had worked as a carpenter until he was thirty years old and had taken perfect care of his body. Picture then, if you can, the kind of mental and spiritual stress and anguish it would take to cause Jesus to sweat blood!

Mortal humans can endure a finite amount of suffering.

Beyond that point, the human body fails. But Christ was fully human, and fully divine. His capacity for suffering was immense, far greater than ours. His capacity for suffering was and is proportionate to his capacity to love! The intense agony that Christ began to suffer in the garden of Gethsemane broadens and deepens our understanding of God's infinite love and the heinous, hideous nature of sin. His sufferings also give us insights into how God views sin, and what will come upon those who hang on to sin. Behold your God! Behold Jesus sweating blood before suffering any physical torture or abuse! Behold the Lamb of God!

*He who overcomes
shall not be hurt by the second death.
(Revelation 2:11, NKJ)*

*And about the ninth hour Jesus cried
with a loud voice, saying,
Eli, Eli, lama sabachthani?
that is to say,
My God, my God,
why hast thou forsaken me?
(Matthew 27:46, KJV)*

3

The Cross Was Hell

Sleep, the First and Second Death

Providence and an "Empty" Prayer Meeting

It was Tuesday and I was driving north of the small town of Ketchikan, Alaska. I saw a young man hitchhiking. It is my custom and privilege to pick up hitchhikers. I asked him if he ever read the Bible. He told me that he did. We eagerly entered into the pleasure of a lively spiritual conversation. We each shared our testimony of how we came to know Jesus. As in all such cases time passes much too rapidly and we still had much to share with one another when we came to Lighthouse Grocery, which was his destination. As we pulled in front of the store, he invited me to a seven o'clock Wednesday evening prayer meeting at his pastor's house. I said that I would be delighted to come. He gave me directions.

I continued on my way toward one of the many lovely parks north of town. With the joy of sharing the love of God in my heart, the warmth of the summer sun seemed more pleasant, the bird songs seemed happier, and the lush greens of the Alaska rainforest seemed more vibrant.

The next evening I headed toward the pastor's house for prayer meeting. I normally like to arrive at meetings early, but because this would be my first time to meet these people, I felt more comfortable in timing my arrival for exactly seven o'clock. I did not want to be the first person there. Much to my surprise there were no other cars parked around the house. I double-checked the address. It was correct. I checked my watch. Yes, it was seven o'clock, Wednesday evening. I hesitated, unsure of what to do. But because I'd spent the time and effort to find the place, I decided to go and ask.

I rang the doorbell and presently a man opened the door. I told him that I was looking for a prayer meeting and asked him if I had the right place. He smiled and explained that I had the right place, but that prayer meeting was on every other Wednesday evening. I laughed and said that it seemed that I was in the right place at the wrong time. I then said that I was sorry to have troubled him and that I would come back the next Wednesday. But he introduced himself as the pastor and graciously invited me into his home. He said that he would find it a pleasure to fellowship for a while. I introduced myself, mentioning the young man that I had enjoyed talking with the day before.

There is a special joy in fellowshipping with someone who loves Jesus that transcends denominational issues. Noting that we did come from different denominations, the pastor asked me what I believed in regard to hell. I stated that I believed in hell, but perhaps differently than he did. I then requested permission to ask him a couple of questions, in order to establish some common ground. He nodded his assent. I asked him if it was his understanding that Jesus died the second death as punishment for our sins. He said that was his belief. I then asked him if it was his understanding that the second death was eternal torment in fire and brimstone forever and ever. He said that was his understanding of the second death. I then asked him, "Well then, if Jesus died the second death for our sins, and the second death is eternal torment in fire and brimstone forever and ever, why isn't Jesus still burning?" Head in hands, the pastor thoughtfully stared at the floor for a few moments, which, as I waited for his answer, seemed like an eternity to me. At length he straightened up and looked me square in the eyes, conceding that it was a good question and he did not know the answer. He would have to study it further.

I pray that we all will be motivated to study this question further, to examine our beliefs, our doctrines in the perfect light that shines from the cross of Calvary. Hell is much more than physical torment. Jesus's suffering on the cross involved much more than physical torment as well.

The movie "The Passion of the Christ" focused on the physical aspect of Jesus's sufferings. In the graphic movie, Roman soldiers tortured Jesus horribly. His face became so swollen and bloody that it was hard to see any expression of feeling. Jesus did suffer intense physical pain.

Was a few hours of physical suffering by a perfect man all that was necessary for our salvation? No. Did Jesus suffer emotionally, mentally, and spiritually as well as physically? Yes. Jesus's sacrifice entails much more than physical suffering. Jesus suffered the full wages of sin for all humanity, which is the second death.

A Multitude of Denominations

Let us look to the cross for our answers. It is because we as Christians have not done this that there are hundreds of different Christian denominations.

Most denominations claim the Bible as their authority. Each denomination claims to be led by the Holy Spirit and yet interprets the Bible differently. Many denominations feel that they are the only ones that have the truth.

Negotiations resulting in compromise will not fulfill Jesus's desire for Christian unity. However, God has graciously provided us with an infallible guide with which to check our interpretations. This is the foundation of the only safe path to the unity that Christ desires for his church. Listen to what Paul proclaims on the subject, "For other foundation can no man lay than that is laid, which is Jesus Christ" (1 Corinthians 3:11, KJV).

This is true for the reading of the New Testament and is

also true for the reading of the Old Testament. Jesus's sacrifice on Calvary is the foundation on which all truth must be built. I invite you to reexamine all your beliefs and doctrines in the light of Jesus's sacrifice. One of the most unpleasant and awkward doctrines is that of everlasting torment in hell. But before we take a deeper look at hell in the light of the cross, we need to distinguish between the first and the second death. "And death and hell were cast into the lake of fire. This is the second death" (Revelation 20:14, KJV).

There is no more death because God has cast death into the lake of fire and destroyed it. There is no more hell because God has cast hell into the lake of fire and destroyed it as well. The second death is the lake of fire. Death is the end of life, a state of nonexistence. What kind of fire can consume death and hell? Physical fire cannot ignite, burn, or consume death. Neither can physical fire destroy hell. But the fire of God's love can bring an end to sin, death, and hell.

Jesus died the second death on the cross of Calvary in order to pay the price for our sins. The second death is hell. The cross was hell. Christ died to pay the penalty of sin—the whole world's sin. The penalty of sin is death—the second death. The good and the bad alike face death—the first death. The first death (physical death) is a result of sin; nevertheless, it is not punishment for sin.

The First Death and Sleep

The Bible refers to the first death as rest or sleep, "Consider and hear me, O LORD my God: lighten mine eyes, lest I sleep the sleep of death" (Psalm 13:3, KJV). Sleep is used to describe David's death, "So David slept with his fathers, and was buried in the city of David" (1 Kings 2:10, KJV).

Jesus's first choice to refer to those who were no longer living was the word *sleep*:

While He spoke these things to them, behold, a ruler came and worshiped Him, saying, "My daughter has just died, but come and lay Your hand on her and she will live." So

52

Jesus arose and followed him, and so did his disciples...
When Jesus came into the ruler's house, and saw the flute
players and the noisy crowd wailing, He said to them,
"Make room, for the girl is not dead, but sleeping." And
they ridiculed Him. But when the crowd was put outside,
He went in and took her by the hand, and the girl arose.
And the report of this went out into all that land. (Mark
9:18, 19, 23-26, NKJ)

Jesus raised this girl from the dead. He did not just wake
her up from a nap. Jesus used the word sleep to show the temporary nature of the first death. Jesus preferred to reserve the
word death to refer to the spiritually lost. These word choices
serve to highlight the difference between the physical life and
the spiritual life. Jesus considered the end of the physical life
to be of relatively small importance in comparison with the
eternal consequences of spiritual death. "Then another of His
disciples said to Him, 'Lord, let me first go and bury my father.' But Jesus said to him, 'Follow Me, and let the dead bury
their own dead'" (Matthew 8:21, 22, NKJ).

In other words, let the spiritually dead bury the physically
dead. The apostle Paul also teaches that although we may be
alive physically, when we are living in our sins we are dead.
Those who are not saved are referred to as dead, spiritually
dead:

You were dead through the trespasses and sins in which
you once lived, following the course of this world, following the ruler of the power of the air, the spirit that is now
at work among those who are disobedient. All of us once
lived among them in the passions of our flesh, following the desires of flesh and senses, and we were by nature
children of wrath, like everyone else. But God, who is
rich in mercy, out of the great love with which he loved us
even when we were dead through our trespasses, made us
alive together with Christ—by grace you have been saved.
(Ephesians 2:1-5, NRSV)

As Christians we want to see things as God does. The first death is just like sleeping; it is temporary. We don't need to be afraid to sleep the sleep of death. The only thing that we as Christians need to fear is that which can separate us from Jesus. When the dead in Christ hear the trumpet of God, they will rise to everlasting life:

> Lo! I tell you a mystery. We shall not all sleep, but we shall all be changed, in a moment, in the twinkling of an eye, at the last trumpet. For the trumpet will sound, and the dead will be raised imperishable, and we shall be changed. (1Corinthians 15:51, 52, RSV)

> For this we say to you by the word of the Lord, that we who are alive and remain until the coming of the Lord will by no means precede those who are asleep. For the Lord himself will descend from heaven with a shout, with the voice of an archangel, and with the trumpet of God. And the dead in Christ will rise first. Then we who are alive and remain shall be caught up together with them in the clouds to meet the Lord in the air. And thus we shall always be with the Lord. Therefore comfort one another with these words. (1Thessalonians 4:15-17, NKJ)

"The dead in Christ will rise first." The word *rise* is the same Greek word Christ often used to describe *resurrection* (see Matthew 17:9; 20:19; Mark 8:31; 9:9, 9:31; 10:34; Luke 11:32; 16:31; 18:33; 24:7; 24:46; and John 6:39, 40, 44). We can see from the words of Scripture that God considers the first death much like we would consider going to sleep at night.

From God's point of view our spiritual condition is what counts. If we have accepted Christ as our Savior, we will live eternally, although we may sleep in the grave until the blessed resurrection at the second coming. Therefore, Christians have nothing to fear from the first death. Stephen, for example, was more concerned for the spiritual well being of his murderers than he was about being stoned to death:

And they stoned Stephen as he was calling on God and saying, "Lord Jesus, receive my spirit." Then he knelt down and cried out with a loud voice, "Lord, do not charge them with this sin." And when he had said this, he fell asleep. (Acts 7:59, 60, CEV)

When Jesus's friend Lazarus died, he described him as sleeping:

These things He said, and after that He said to them, "Our friend Lazarus sleeps, but I go that I may wake him up." Then His disciples said, "Lord, if he sleeps he will get well." However, Jesus spoke of his death, but they thought that He was speaking about taking rest in sleep. Then Jesus said to them plainly, "Lazarus is dead." (John 11:11-14, NKJ)

Jesus here tried to teach the disciples Heaven's perspective regarding physical death. His disciples then, and even many now, two thousand years later, misunderstand the concepts of death as sleep, the second death, and the resurrection.

Jesus cried at Lazarus's tomb in sympathy with his friends' feelings of sorrow and loss, "When Jesus saw that Mary and the people with her were crying, he was terribly upset and asked, "Where have you put his body?" They replied, "Lord, come and you will see." Jesus started crying" (John 11:33-35, CEV).

The first death causes separation and sorrow, but it is nothing to be afraid of. The second death, however, is different and a much more serious thing:

Do not fear any of those things which you are about to suffer. Indeed, the devil is about to throw some of you into prison, that you may be tested, and you will have tribulation ten days. Be faithful until death, and I will give you the crown of life. "He who has an ear, let him hear what the Spirit says to the churches. He who overcomes shall not be hurt by the second death. (Revelation 2:10, 11, NKJ)

Jesus encourages us not to be afraid of physical suffering, torture, or even death. Even in the face of torture we can choose to abide in Christ. The attractions of sin separate more people from Jesus than threats of torture do. Through faith in Christ we will overcome sin and so escape its punishment—the second death.

The Second Death

He who does not overcome sin and selfishness will be hurt by the second death. The second death will have power over those who do not have part in the first resurrection:

Blessed and holy is he who has part in the first resurrection. Over such the second death has no power, but they shall be priests of God and of Christ, and shall reign with him a thousand years. The sea gave up the dead who were in it, and Death and Hades delivered up the dead who were in them. And they were judged, each one according to his works. Then Death and Hades were cast into the lake of fire. This is the second death. And anyone not found written in the Book of Life was cast into the lake of fire. (Revelation 20:6, 13-15, NKJ)

"But the cowardly, unbelieving, abominable, murderers, sexually immoral, sorcerers, idolaters, and all liars shall have their part in the lake which burns with fire and brimstone, which is the second death" (Revelation 21:8, NKJ). Even if we die the physical, first death, we can look forward to the resurrection and eternal life.

The Contrast between the First and Second Death

Now we'll look to the cross to see what God has revealed to us there in regard to sin and its punishment, which is the second death. Christ has paid the penalty for sin by experiencing the second death, so we don't have to, "But we see Jesus, who was made a little lower than the angels for the suffering of death, crowned with glory and honour; that he by the grace of God should taste death for every man" (Hebrews 2:9, KJV).

The first death is not punishment for sin. Therefore, no matter how brutal, the first death cannot atone for sin. As the Son of Man, Jesus did experience physical torture and the first death, but that wasn't atonement for sin. Jesus had to die the second death to make atonement.

Jesus died to rescue us from the second death. Therefore the death that he tasted for every man was the second death. This is the same thing as the cup of suffering that Jesus prayed about in the garden of Gethsemane. Christ tasted the second death for every man on the cross of Calvary. Different events that caused Jesus sorrow hint at the anguish and suffering that would later engulf him on the cross:

Triumph and Sorrow

And when he came near the foot of the Mountain of Olives, all the disciples with loud voices gave praise to God with joy, because of all the great works which they had seen; Saying, A blessing on the King who comes in the name of the Lord; peace in heaven and glory in the highest. And some of the Pharisees among the people said to him, Master, make your disciples be quiet. And he said in answer, I say to you, if these men keep quiet, the very stones will be crying out. And when he got near and saw the town, he was overcome with weeping for it, Saying, If you, even you, had knowledge today, of the things which give peace! but you are not able to see them. For the time will come when your attackers will put a wall round you, and come all round you and keep you in on every side, And will make you level with the earth, and your children with you; and there will not be one stone resting on another in you, because you did not see that it was your day of mercy. (Luke 19:37-44, BBE)

Jesus wept over Jerusalem. Huge crowds gave Christ honors fit for a king during his triumphal entry into Jerusalem. All the poor of Israel were looking for a Saviour to rescue them from poverty and hunger as well as a Messiah to heal their physical diseases.

Rich and poor alike waited impatiently for a King to lead Israel to victory over their Roman enemies. All of Israel would have welcomed Jesus as King on a physical, worldly level.

How few were ready to receive Jesus into their hearts as the Messiah-King on a spiritual level to rescue them from sin and selfishness. That wounded the heart of Jesus to the point of tears.

Jesus's heart-rending sorrow fit in like funeral music at a wedding. The multitudes of Israel were eager to crown Jesus king. Can you imagine the amazement of the vast crowds of Israelites when Jesus, the One they were eager to crown king, burst into tears of inexpressible sorrow?

To the crowds, the future of Israel looked bright. Jesus could heal the sick and wounded, raise the dead, and feed vast multitudes. Jesus would be their great and powerful King. He would lead Israel's army against the hated Romans. With Jesus as Israel's King, Israel would crush all her enemies.

On the other hand Jesus saw things on a spiritual level. And Israel's future did not look so good. Jesus's sudden sorrow sounded a discordant note of wailing in the sweet chorus of praises and hallelujahs. While everyone was rejoicing, honoring Jesus, the Messiah, the son of David, the King of Israel, he interrupted the joyous praises to weep tears of bitter anguish. His sobbing, mournful tones cast a pall over the triumphal entry. Christ's outburst of grief and tears showed the depths of God's love for unrepentant, sinful Israel as she, by rejecting him, separated herself from the only Source of life and hope.

Jesus also knew that Jerusalem was a type of the world at the end of time. Looking down the ages to our time, just before his glorious second coming, he saw that the majority of nominal Christians, unnumbered millions, would by rejecting him, seal their own doom (see Matthew 24:5, 10, 24; Luke 21:8, 12,

58

16, 17, 35; John 16:2; and Revelation 13:4, 7, 8, 12, 14, 15).

Jesus's Unselfish Sorrow

From the descent into Jerusalem Jesus could see the garden of Gethsemane. He knew that was where the sin and guilt of our rebellious world would begin to fall on him. Jesus knew that he was headed for the cross of Calvary.

But Jesus did not weep because of the infinite suffering that he soon faced. No. Jerusalem's approaching doom broke Jesus's heart. Jerusalem was rejecting him, their only hope. He had come to save them from the ruin and degradation of sin and guilt.

Nevertheless, the very concept of love demands freedom. Israel must be free to accept or reject their Saviour. Love cannot exist without freedom. It is also true that freedom cannot exist without love.

Jesus's reaction to Jerusalem gives us an insight into one aspect of the sorrow and anguish that filled his heart to the point of breaking as he hung on the cross of Calvary. Jesus's love for sinners has ever been infinite. Infinite love brings the possibility of infinite sorrow. Jesus loves each of us sinners more than he loves his own life.

Have you ever had someone that you cared for reject your love? It hurts doesn't it? Jesus's heart is much more sensitive than ours, so the pain of rejection would be much more intense for him. All the more so because Jesus knows that all those who reject his saving love are headed for destruction and eternal death.

Now try to imagine that intense pain of rejection, multiplied by the hundreds of thousands of precious souls in the nation of Israel that were rejecting the saving love of Jesus. Can you imagine how much it must have hurt our Savior to see the whole chosen nation of Israel choose Satan's path of death and destruction instead of Jesus's path of salvation and life? No wonder Jesus broke down and wept! The wonder is that anguish of soul did not kill him right there! It was only because his Father was in him, strengthening him that Jesus was able to endure that magnitude of grief.

It is my hope and prayer as we study God's love, as displayed by Jesus on the cross, that the Holy Spirit will win our hearts and minds to Jesus's noble cause.

Sin and selfishness cause guilt and separation. These lead to stress, sickness, disease, and death. That is why our sin was torture to Christ's spirit. Sin destroys his creation, his children that he loves. Sin and guilt warp the spiritual eyesight of those who hang onto their self-centered ways. Unrepentant sinners feel condemned by God, the very One who gave his life to save them. This separation causes God intense anguish of soul.

A Mother's Love

Would you like to get a mother's perspective into the suffering of God? Ask any loving mother that has gone through the agony of watching cancer or some other illness steal the life of her dear child. The deeper the mother's love, the deeper her sympathy, and the more intense her grief will be as she endures the suffering of her dear child.

God's love is infinitely deeper and more sensitive than any father or mother's love. The sacrifice of Jesus on the cross proves that God loves each individual human being more than his own life. Imagine the agony Christ and the Father felt, and feel now, when one of their precious children refuses Jesus's free, and totally effective cure for the cancer of sin. Now multiply that infinite agony by the staggering number of lost angels and of lost human beings!

I plead with you, dear reader, on behalf of God, please allow God's message of love and mercy to enter and fill your heart. By beholding we become changed:

> But we all, with open face beholding as in a glass the glory of the Lord, are changed into the same image from glory to glory, even as by the Spirit of the Lord. (2Corinthians 3:18, KJV)

Behold the infinite love of God with the eye of your heart

60

until sin and selfishness become hateful in your eyes, and are fully replaced by love for God and man.

Victory Behind Enemy Lines

Preach the love of Jesus by living a life that is in harmony with God's law of unselfish, unconditional love. Love your enemies. Pray for those that hate you. As you do this you will be establishing a stronghold behind enemy lines. The enemy will attack your stronghold. But remember the King of the Universe is on our side. He has already won the victory. Selfishness is the enemy, an enemy that sneaks up on us when we take our eyes off of Jesus.

Strong willpower may change our actions temporarily, but it cannot change our heart. We must give the Holy Spirit the time and the opportunity to change our hearts by investing the time every day to meditate on Christ's unselfish, infinite heart of love that overflowed in the self-sacrifice of the cross. God's love can rule only where it is invited.

Jesus voluntarily became our Sin-Bearer. He carried the sins of the whole world. Paul asserts: "For I handed on to you as of first importance what I in turn had received: that Christ died for our sins in accordance with the scriptures" (1 Corinthians 15:3, NRSV). Again in Hebrews 10:12, Paul writes: "But when Christ had offered for all time a single sacrifice for sins, he sat down at the right hand of God" (NRSV).

The prophet Isaiah, centuries before Christ, foretold that Christ would be our Sin-Bearer. "All we like sheep have gone astray; we have turned every one to his own way; and the LORD hath laid on him the iniquity of us all" (Isaiah 53:6, KJV).

Interestingly, Isaiah, in verse nine of the same chapter, used the Hebrew plural form for the word death. "And he made his grave with the wicked, and with the rich in his death[s]; because he had done no violence, neither was any deceit in his mouth" (Isaiah 53:9, KJV, Brackets mine, to express the literal Hebrew).

The Old Testament as well as the New Testament reveals

that Jesus died the second death in order to rescue us from sin and its destruction and eternal death. The scribes and Pharisees did not understand that the scriptures pointed to the suffering of the Messiah:

The Sign of Jonah

Then some of the scribes and Pharisees answered, saying, "Teacher, we want to see a sign from You." But He answered and said to them, "An evil and adulterous generation seeks after a sign, and no sign will be given to it except the sign of the prophet Jonah. For as Jonah was three days and three nights in the belly of the great fish, so will the Son of Man be three days and three nights in the heart of the earth." (Matthew 12:38-40, NKJ)

When these church leaders asked Jesus for a sign, he gave them the sign of Jonah. Had the church leaders' (the Scribes and Pharisees) hearts and minds been open to the Holy Spirit, the sign of Jonah would have been enough to convince them that Jesus was the divine Messiah, that he must suffer and die, and that he would be resurrected after three days. Jesus gave notice that Jonah's prayer was a messianic prophecy.

Jonah 2

1 Then Jonah prayed unto the LORD his God out of the fish's belly,
2 And said, I cried by reason of mine affliction unto the LORD, and he heard me; out of the belly of hell cried I, and thou heardest my voice.

On the cross, Jesus cried out from the depths of hell "My God, my God, why hast thou forsaken me?"

3 For thou hadst cast me into the deep, in the midst of the seas; and the floods compassed me about: all thy billows and thy waves passed over me.

The depth is another reference to the abyss of hell. The Old Testament people considered the seas to be inhabited by Leviathan, Rahab, the Dragon and other sea monsters representing demonic entities. The floods, billows, and waves refer to the realm of demons and evil men as well as separation from God (see Ezekiel 28:2, where the King of Tyre symbolizes Satan). For example, When Moses parted the seas for the Children of Israel it revealed that God was protecting them against Satan, Pharaoh and the heathen peoples (see also Psalm 74:13; Isaiah 27:1; Job 41; Isaiah 17:12; and Revelation 17:15).

> 4 Then I said, I am cast out of thy sight; yet I will look again toward thy holy temple.
> 5 The waters compassed me about, even to the soul: the depth closed me round about, the weeds were wrapped about my head.

Jonah's words "Cast out of thy sight" parallels Christ's feeling of rejection and separation from God. Soul means the mind. Jesus carried our sins in his mind and heart. He felt trapped, buried, forsaken, and lost. The weeds symbolize the crown of thorns thrust on Jesus's head (Matthew 27:29). The waters represent the wicked multitudes that called for Jesus's crucifixion.

> 6 I went down to the bottoms of the mountains; the earth with her bars was about me for ever: yet hast thou brought up my life from corruption, O LORD my God.

Jonah felt that because of his sin he would be stuck in the grave forever. "The earth with her bars was about me forever," foretells Jesus's second death experience. Every fiber of Jesus's being, all his senses thrust upon his heart and mind that he was going to die, to cease to exist, forever. Moreover, our sins buried Jesus under oceans of despair and darkness.

> 7 When my soul fainted within me I remembered the

63

LORD: and my prayer came in unto thee, into thine holy temple.

Jesus's soul fainted within him as well, to the point of breaking his heart. He too, remembered the Lord and cried out in prayer and supplication.

8 They that observe lying vanities forsake their own mercy.

Jonah and Jesus both knew that lying vanities, or false gods, separate people from their merciful Father. Lying vanities can also result from accepting Satan's cruel lies about our merciful Father.

9 But I will sacrifice unto thee with the voice of thanksgiving; I will pay *that* that I have vowed. Salvation *is* of the LORD.

Praise is an acceptable sacrifice to God. Jesus was born to die as a sacrifice for sin. "I will pay that that I have vowed." Jesus looked the darkness of everlasting death square in the face. He didn't blink. He reaffirmed his decision to save sinful humanity at all cost while in the garden of Gethsemane. He laid down his life, his soul.

The phrase, "Salvation is of the Lord," indicates that Jesus's faith rested entirely on his Father. Jesus placed his soul, his existence, in his Father's hands. Only by faith was Jesus able to grasp the hope of the resurrection, and only after plumbing the depths of the hell that was rightfully ours. As his breaking heart was ceasing to beat, Jesus spoke the words of triumph and faith, "It is finished."

10 And the LORD spake unto the fish, and it vomited out Jonah upon the dry *land*. (KJV)

By faith, Jesus won the victory over death, hell, and

64

Satan's lies. As Jonah spent three days of soul anguish in the belly of the whale, in the midst of the dark seas, Jesus spent three days in the heart of darkness. When the rude multitude seized Jesus, he entered into the grasp of the satanic powers of darkness.

In the garden, Jesus announced the beginning of his fulfillment of Jonah's three days, "But this is your hour, and the power of darkness" (Luke 22:53, KJV). Jesus had earlier said, "For as Jonah was three days and three nights in the belly of the great fish, so will the Son of Man be three days and three nights in the heart of the earth" (Matthew 12:40, NKJ).

We have listened to Jonah's anguished prayer, which foreshadows Jesus's last three days. It was Jonah's own sin that caused him to feel separated from God. When we sin, our guilt causes us to feel separated from our heavenly Father, "But your iniquities have separated between you and your God, and your sins have hid his face from you, that he will not hear" (Isaiah 59:2, KJV). Imagine, then, what Jesus must have felt, carrying the sin and guilt of the whole world!

Darkness and Separation

The apostle Matthew records Christ's words for us, "And about the ninth hour Jesus cried with a loud voice, saying, Eli, Eli, lama sabachthani? that is to say, My God, my God, why hast thou forsaken me?" (Matthew 27:46, KJV). Christ was quoting from Psalm 22:1, "My God, my God, why hast thou forsaken me? why art thou so far from helping me, and from the words of my roaring?" (KJV). Jesus was the perfect Son of God. Nevertheless, when he carried the sin and guilt of the whole world, an infinite darkness settled on his heart and mind, his soul.

The terrible darkness of sin blocked Jesus's sense of the Father's presence. As Jonah was separated from the light of the sun, Christ experienced the dark horror of separation from the light of his Father, the Source of life.

How terrible are the effects of sin on even the perfect Son of God! Christ's sense of separation from God crushed down heavily on his heart. This crushing weight of separation contributed to Jesus's death from a broken heart.

There are other dark factors to consider that took our gallant Savior down to the depths of the pit of hell. Only infinite love could bring Jesus to face the dire consequences of our sin. But God never deserted his Son.

Paul confirms the understanding that the Father was with his Son on Calvary, "To wit, that God was in Christ, reconciling the world unto himself, not imputing their trespasses unto them; and hath committed unto us the word of reconciliation" (2Corinthians 5:19, KJV). On the cross of Calvary, God was in Christ.

Because of the darkness of sin and guilt, Jesus was not able to sense his Father's presence. Nevertheless, the Father was in Christ, reconciling the world unto himself. Jesus willingly chose the cross because of his great love for fallen humanity. The Father loved Jesus even more because of his great sacrifice for fallen humanity:

> And I lay down my life for the sheep. I have other sheep that do not belong to this fold. I must bring them also, and they will listen to my voice. So there will be one flock, one shepherd. For this reason the Father loves me, because I lay down my life in order to take it up again. (John 10:15-17, NRSV)

Consider as well, "For he hath not despised nor abhorred the affliction of the afflicted; neither hath he hid his face from him; but when he cried unto him, he heard" (Psalm 22:24, KJV). Christ's view of the divine light of God's presence was fading because he began to carry the sins of the world, not because his Father hid his face from his Son. Our heavenly Father was not angry with his Son. No. God the Father's love is ever consistent no matter how large the mountain of guilt that any person might carry.

The Father was not frowning at his Son, but at sin. Jesus's infinite love for us led him to identify with our sin and guilt.

This, combined with the terrible enormity of his sense of separation from God, filled his soul with dismay and horror. He experienced the fullness of God's wrath against sin. All this caused his view of the Father's infinite love for sinners to be blocked.

Who could keep the Father from being with his Son at such a time? "For God so loved the world, that he gave his only begotten Son, that whosoever believeth in him should not perish, but have everlasting life" (John 3:16, KJV). Even though his children are sinners, God loves them with all his heart.

Infinite Suffering Reveals Infinite Love

Notice that God the Father chose to experience all that Jesus did. Who could stop Almighty God from going through this with his Son? Notice also the difference in consequences between the Father and the Son. Both suffered infinite pain, but God the Son had taken human form in order to be able to experience the second death as a man. He endured the natural consequences of carrying the world's sin and guilt.

On the cross of Calvary, Jesus showed all mankind the inevitable, horrifying death that all unrepentant sinners must face. Not because God has made an arbitrary decree declaring that those who break his law must be punished in this manner. No. The natural, inevitable result of sin is guilt. Guilt results in the sinner's inability to appreciate, believe, or receive God's love. Sin and guilt lead to death.

Guilt embodies a sense of condemnation, separation, and deep despair. Guilt and condemnation do not come from God, "For God sent the Son into the world, not to condemn the world, but that the world might be saved through him" (John 3:17, RSV). When a person hangs on to sin and guilt, he becomes unable to receive the cleansing, saving power of God. On the cross, Jesus felt forsaken and alone, but God the Father was in Christ, experiencing all that Jesus did. However, God alone is immortal. He cannot die:

I charge you to keep the commandment unstained and free

from reproach until the appearing of our Lord Jesus Christ; and this will be made manifest at the proper time by the blessed and only Sovereign, the King of kings and Lord of lords, who alone has immortality and dwells in unapproachable light, whom no man has ever seen or can see. To him be honor and eternal dominion. Amen. (1 Timothy 6:14-16, RSV)

It was love for their helpless children that led the Father and the Son to choose to experience the sufferings of sin. There was no other way to save humanity from the power of sin and guilt.

The Holy Spirit also has a personality, feelings that can be hurt, "And do not grieve the Holy Spirit of God, by whom you were sealed for the day of redemption" (Ephesians 4:30, NKJ). We don't often think of the Holy Spirit as a person. I think it is helpful to consider each member of the godhead as a person with thoughts and feelings. Jesus certainly had thoughts and feelings. If we have seen Jesus, we have seen the Father. And the Holy Spirit reveals Jesus to us. That means that the Holy Spirit has to be able to express to our hearts and minds the thoughts and feelings of Jesus.

The Consequences of Sin

Jesus's suffering for our sins goes to deep levels of anguish, agony, sorrow, and despair that our finite minds will never fully understand. Nonetheless, it is our privilege to bring glory to Jesus by studying and meditating on these holy, sacred topics. Let us prayerfully consider the anguish and despair of soul that Jesus endured as the dense darkness of sin and guilt blocked his view of his Father's love.

Though sinless, Jesus shared the consequences of our sin. Though the perfect Son of God, Jesus chose to identify himself with our sin, guilt, and shame. Through Jesus we begin to see God's great love for us. Faith begins to grow in our hearts. Our desires, thoughts, and habits begin to change. To be born again is to become a new person. The old person, self-centered, sin-loving, must go. The new person loves Jesus more than he loves sin. He is a new creation.

It takes more of God's creative power to redeem one sinner than it does to speak a world into existence. Undoing the destructive effects of sin, creating a new heart, a right spirit within us, forming a new life within us is a marvelous work that only God can do.

However, God cannot do this work without our permission and cooperation. That is why God poured out his great love through Jesus. Only by such an incredible demonstration of unselfish, unconditional love could God break through the dark fortress walls of sin and guilt that Satan had built around the whole world.

Wonderful, powerful love! When I, though a sinner and enemy of God, first began to understand, through Jesus, his great love for me, the Holy Spirit planted a seed of faith and love in my heart. Sin began to be less attractive to me. Jesus's sacrifice demonstrated to me the horrible, eternal consequences of hanging on to sin. I began to fear and hate sin and its consequences.

Jesus willingly chose to experience the punishment, the awful consequences of sin so that I wouldn't have to. As through the Scriptures I continue to meditate on the life and death of Jesus, my love for him and my faith in him continues to grow. Satan's lies lose their power.

Jesus willingly lifted the indescribably heavy and destructive burden of our shame, guilt, and despair, "Looking unto Jesus the author and finisher of our faith; who for the joy that was set before him endured the cross, despising the shame, and is set down at the right hand of the throne of God" (Hebrews 12:2, KJV).

Jesus weighed the guilt and shame of all humanity's sin against his great love for each of us and decided to save us even though the cost was beyond human comprehension. Jesus's hatred of sin was as strong as death. Jesus's love for sinners was stronger than death, stronger than his repugnance, his hatred for guilt, shame, and pain.

Love, Freedom, Risk, and Suffering

In this sinful world you have been the victim of injustice. Your thoughts, words, feelings, and even perhaps your attempts to help others have been angrily misunderstood. People have said hurtful words to you, perhaps even physically striking you.

The hurt, the anger, and the resentment may have simmered in the back of your mind for years. Relationships have been strained or even damaged beyond repair. You have been used; you have been abused. Even as a Christian, your forgiveness of others has often been more successful in your mind than in your heart.

Have you ever seen an injustice that grieved your heart? Of course you have. Perhaps you have seen an enraged parent screaming at or even beating their helpless toddler, for crying out in the only way she knew how for the love and attention that she craved. Perhaps you have been that child. Or perhaps you have seen an angry man taking out his rage and frustration on a defenseless, undeserving dog or other animal. I'm sure that you have wrestled with the world's injustice. Your staggering heart, mind, and soul have stumbled in different directions in the effort to understand the immensity of humanity's innocent suffering and pain, some of it your own.

If you could bring an end to all human suffering and pain by merely giving up all your money and material possessions, would you do it? Of course you would. What if the price were a little higher? What if you had to cease to exist, forever, would you do it then? I am certain that some Christians and even some non-Christians would agree to such a sacrifice. I also believe that even many "wicked" people would agree to such a sacrifice. Ah, but only because they do not understand the value that God places on each individual soul.

God allows the suffering to continue because in his wisdom he knows that there is no other way. He wants to save as many of his precious children as he can. He loves you and every other human being on the Earth more than his own life. Our suffering causes God deeper pain than we ourselves can experience. Yet our Father feels that our personal freedom to choose to accept or reject his love is more important than bringing an end to our suffering. Love and freedom cannot exist without one another. Certainly, we cannot truly love, worship, or obey God unless we are free not to. Love and worship require freedom. Freedom carries the risk of pain.

If God had wanted to, he could have created good-looking robots that he could order about to carry out his every whim. However, robots don't have freedom of choice and therefore do not have the ability to love.

If God had created us as beings that could not sin, there would have been no opportunity for selfish rebellion and death, but neither would we be able to love. Robots can have no meaningful interaction with God. If you were to program a robot to say "I love you," it would have no meaning; It would be like saying it to yourself.

Even the animals are not robots. Jeffrey Masson, in his book, *When Elephants Weep*, relates numerous stories that clearly portray that animals have emotions. When they are hurt, they cry out in pain. Yet some animals have risked or even sacrificed their lives for other animals and for people as well. They have feelings. Elephants shed tears. They mourn for their dead.

Feelings bring meaning. When we pray we shouldn't pretend that we are telling God something he doesn't already know. We cannot give God new information. He knows everything. But we can share our feelings with him. He cares about our hopes and desires, our disappointments and triumphs. God cares. He wants us to learn to care for each other and for him. Feelings combined with freedom bring the risk of pain. We can express our love for him.

If God had created us without freedom, there would have been no need for a Saviour, but neither would there be any appreciation of God's character, or any true worship. There would have been no suffering and death, but neither would there be any glory or victory.

God takes no pleasure in robotic service. God wanted intelligent, reasoning beings that could freely decide whether or not to love, which is the only foundation for true obedience and worship.

God inspired wise King Solomon to express a fundamental principle that holds true on Earth, and in Heaven, "A king's greatness depends on how many people he rules; without them he is nothing" (Proverbs 14:28, TEV). Jesus, our King, on the cross proved Solomon's point. Jesus would rather die forever, that is, cease to exist, than allow his precious children to be wiped out, annihilated by Satan.

God's Wisdom Beyond Selfish Reasoning

God in his wisdom, love, and prudence invites you to examine his record, his character, which is the principle that forms the foundation of his kingdom, "Come now, and let us reason together, saith the LORD" (Isaiah 1:18, KJV).

Friend, through the words on these pages, I invite you to examine, approve, and receive our wise Father's kingdom principle of unselfish love into your heart, mind, and soul, "In whom we have redemption through his blood, the forgiveness of sins, according to the riches of his grace; Wherein he hath abounded toward us in all wisdom and prudence" (Ephesians 1:7, 8, KJV).

Jesus, in his love, wisdom and prudence, freely chose to die for his enemies. That is the foundation principle, or law of Heaven. Through the power of the Holy Spirit, Jesus will implant that kind of love into your heart and mind.

To be willing to die for your enemies sounds risky, even foolish. Nevertheless, that is the mind of Christ, which is the only basis for peace, harmony, happiness, and security in Heaven as well as on Earth. "For the message of the cross is foolishness to those who are perishing, but to us who are being saved it is the power of God" (1Corinthians 1:18, NKJ). We should seek to be like Jesus:

Your attitude should be the same that Christ Jesus had. Though he was God, he did not demand and cling to his rights as God. He made himself nothing; he took the humble position of a slave and appeared in human form.

72

And in human form he obediently humbled himself even further by dying a criminal's death on a cross. (Philippians 2:5-8, NLT)

Benevolent, unselfish love is the power of God. If we want to be like Jesus, we must be willing to die the second death for those that hate us. That is the mind, or attitude of Christ. Obviously, self-denying love can only exist where intelligent beings can freely examine, freely judge, and freely choose to accept or reject it. The account of Jesus's death in the Scriptures provides the opportunity and the means for the examination of this principle of self-sacrificing love. The acceptance of it is justification. Choosing to live by it is sanctification. We are free to choose, but choose we must.

Freedom is risky. God has given every person tremendous potential. We are free to use our abilities to help others or to hurt others. The intense malignity and vast extent of human suffering serve to accentuate the importance that God places on our freedom.

Sowing and Reaping

God wants a love relationship with each person. He grants us freedom to say yes or no to his offer of love. When we say no to the power of God, which is his self-sacrificing love, which is the blood of Christ, he leaves us to make self-centered choices. Remember, though, we reap what we sow.

The prophet Hosea describes the positive side of this principle, "Sow to yourselves in righteousness, reap in mercy; break up your fallow ground: for it is time to seek the LORD, till he come and rain righteousness upon you" (Hosea 10:12, KJV). He also describes the negative side of sowing and reaping, "But instead you planted evil and reaped its harvest. You have eaten the fruit produced by your lies" (Hosea 10:13, TEV).

Self-centered choices always cause suffering for us and for others. Selfishness causes guilt, stress, separation, broken relationships, sickness, and sooner or later, death. Self-sacrificing love brings peace, rest, purpose, strong relationships, health, and life. Selfishness or self-sacrificing love, beloved reader, which will you choose? All must choose. To put off the choice is to say no for now.

God will never stop loving you, but your ability to receive his love diminishes each time you put him off. Say yes! Join in the battle against Satan's lies, and the resulting darkness, suffering, and death. Remember that Jesus, and all of Heaven suffer when we do.

All Heaven watches the suffering we endure. Each heavenly being longs to intervene and relieve our pain. However, our Father, in his wisdom has decided to give evil the time and space necessary to burn itself out. Even so, we can do much to turn Heaven's sympathetic sorrow and suffering to joy! We must try to understand more of our Father's suffering on account of our wretched self-centeredness. We must strive to be living channels of blessing and light to others through the power of the Holy Spirit.

Righteous Indignation and Guilt

How would you feel, if by circumstances, you were forced to watch as an angry, obscenity-screaming mob physically mistreated, tortured, and killed your innocent child? A strange mixture of anguish and burning anger would explode in your heart, straining it to its very limits. Is it right to feel grief and even anger at the blatant injustices in this world? Yes, it is called righteous indignation for good reason. Righteous indignation is the strong mix of emotions that we feel in regard to others for the cruel, unfair things that they have done to innocent people.

God's love and wisdom constrain him to allow us to inflict suffering on each other and ourselves. That is the only way that we can truly grasp the difference between Christ and Satan. We must see and experience it. Only then can we properly exercise our freedom to choose.

Satan has charged God with being an unfair, self-centered dictator. That is all the more reason that God goes to great lengths to make it evident that we have freedom to choose. We must be free to believe in Christ's love or in Satan's lies.

Declaring that we believe in and love Jesus is a good starting place. Our thoughts, feelings, words, actions, reactions, and interactions, will demonstrate whether we truly love Jesus or whether we actually follow Satan. Satan's lies have caused the world to reject God and his rescuing power. Jesus Christ died to heal and save us from the results, the presence, the disease of sin and guilt.

Jesus did not die as a clever legal maneuver that would allow us to continue in the sickness and suffering of sin and yet merely be declared to be well, to be righteous. Christ is the Great Physician. He did not die in order to lie! He died in order to reveal the truth about God and his incredible love, his saving, healing love. If we love and trust God, he will work in and through us to heal us, and others from the cancer of sin, with its suffering and guilt.

Innocent human suffering is one side of the coin, one half of the experience, the inevitable result of Satan's rebellion against God's law of unselfish love. Guilt is the other side of the same coin. Guilt is inward directed righteous indignation, the same explosive mixture of burning anger and anguish, but inwardly directed. The hurtful things that we have done to others violate our own sense of justice. Guilt is inward directed anger; it is self-hatred, and remorse.

Certainly you have also experienced the guilt-side of this coin. Have you ever done something really wrong? Perhaps you have betrayed the trust of a close friend or relative. Perhaps you have lost your temper and said hurtful, angry words that you did not mean.

How did you feel afterwards? Did you find it easy to look into the eyes of the person that you hurt, or did your eyes drop to the ground? When she looked into your eyes you likely felt tightness in your heart, and nausea in your stomach. The guilt that you felt caused you mental and emotional pain and even affected you physically. Guilt is inward directed anger and grief, a natural, and inevitable result of our sins. If you are like me, your mind has replayed these bitter scenes over and over.

75

Guilt causes us deep distress. Many people go to great lengths to try to escape the feelings that guilt brings. Many turn to alcohol, drugs, sexual promiscuity, or other self-destructive kinds of behavior. Sin and guilt are destructive.

Nevertheless, remember that no matter how bitter the guilt that you feel, God has shielded you from its full effects. God allows us to experience just enough guilt so that we can understand some of the bitterness of sin. If any of us were to experience, all at once, the fullness of our sin and guilt, we would perish in agony of soul.

But Jesus experienced the full sin and guilt of each person ever to exist on this Earth! Even as I try to find the words to convey this concept, my heart and mind reel at the magnitude, the enormity of the burden of guilt that Jesus agonizingly endured on our behalf, so that we wouldn't have to!

Jesus had no one to shield him! Try to wrap your mind around this aspect of the massive truth that Jesus was fully God and fully man. As the Son of God, his sensitivity and capacity to accept into his heart our burning guilt and shame were infinite.

As the Son of Man, his ability to physically endure our guilt resulted in the destruction of his life. Amazing love! Amazing love that soars beyond our comprehension, plunges to the depths of hell, yet beckons and urges our attention, our study, our meditation, our adoration, and our awe. Not, however, in order to merely call attention to himself, but to woo us away from sin and toward life eternal.

God Feels Our Pain

Furthermore, Jesus Christ experienced both sides of our bitter human experience, the guilt and shame of every perpetrator of wrong, as well as the injustice and pain of every victim. No wonder the angels worship him! Keep in mind that though Jesus was fully human he was also fully God. He was not forced, nor coerced into drinking this bitter cup of human sin and woe. No. He chose to leave the pleasures and glory of Heaven, the adoration and willing service of the angels, and the intimate fellowship with his Father, rather than to abandon us to experience our own sin and guilt.

Have you met anyone else likes this? Can your heart and mind grasp the fullness of Jesus's infinite love? God is love. God is fair, kind, sensitive, tenderhearted, patient, wise, and sovereign. In his wisdom, God has allowed the cancer of sin, with all its suffering, to continue for a time. He has done this in order that the whole universe may see the terrible malignancy of rebellion against the principle of unselfish, unconditional love.

God hates all human suffering. His tender heart ever suffers with all humanity, with each person, as he suffered long ago with Israel, "In all their affliction he was afflicted, and the angel of his presence saved them: in his love and in his pity he redeemed them; and he bare them, and carried them all the days of old" (Isaiah 63:9, KJV).

On the cross of Calvary, Jesus, through his infinite heart of mercy joined us in our afflictions. He carried us. His love and pity led him to suffer our guilt and shame. That is how our sins were laid upon him. God the Father (He is the law) did not force, or even demand that Jesus die for our sins.

Jesus freely, willingly laid down his life for our sins, "For this reason the Father loves me, because I lay down my life, that I may take it again. No one takes it from me, but I lay it down of my own accord. I have power to lay it down, and I have power to take it again; this charge I have received from my Father" (John 10:17, 18, RSV).

God the Father is not angrily looking for a way to destroy sinners. No, on the contrary, the reason that the Father loves Jesus is because Jesus is willing to lay his life down for sinners. Amazing love!

Will you join me as I pray, Father, fill my heart with your powerful, amazing love until sin and selfishness are crowded out. I claim Jesus as my assurance of Your love for me. Amen. God is our Creator, our Father. He will create a new heart in us, if we give him permission.

Jesus Earned the Right to Save

God the Father laid our sins on Jesus by withdrawing the layers of protection that had up to then surrounded Jesus and by allowing the infinitely sympathetic and loving Jesus to open his heart to the fullness of the human experience.

The heavenly angels had physically protected Jesus from the time he was a babe. God's mighty angels would never have allowed the Roman soldiers to tie Jesus's hands. They would have stopped the soldiers from flogging Jesus. Yet our heavenly Father ordered the angels to step back. The first layer of protection was withdrawn.

God is fair, more than fair. He allowed those under Satan's control to afflict Jesus physically, in order to demonstrate the difference between Satan's government and the government of Heaven. Jesus's physical suffering is a good starting point for studying God's love. It serves to get our attention. All the hosts of Heaven and all the people of Earth must see the contrast between the two governments.

The next layer of protection was the Holy Spirit. Jesus's close sense of connection with the Holy Spirit was lost. This happened at the same time, and as a consequence of, Jesus's taking into his heart the full experience of sinful humanity's guilt and woe. As God allowed Jesus to open his tender heart to the dark, hellish depths of our sin, guilt, and shame, Jesus began to sweat blood.

God had to intervene and send an angel to strengthen Jesus to endure this brutal experience, or he would have died right there. God did not arbitrarily withdraw his Holy Spirit. But in order to taste death for every man, Jesus had to experience the fullness of sin and the burning guilt of every person that has ever, or will ever walk this Earth. Our sins crushed out Jesus's close sense of communion with the Holy Spirit.

Jesus did not give us a gift that came solely from divine power. No, Jesus earned the right to be our Savior. Jesus, like David, presents his offering, his sacrifice before God from what he had earned. Araunah had offered his threshing floor to King David as a gift, "But the king said to Araunah, 'No, I will not have it as a gift. I will buy it, for I don't want to offer to the Lord my God burnt offerings that have cost me nothing.' So David paid him for the threshing floor and the oxen" (2Samuel 24:24, Living Bible).

Jesus is God. But he earned the right to save us through living a perfect, loving life and taking humanity's woe into the depths of his heart and mind.

We never suffer the fullness of our own sin and guilt. When God allows us to get a small taste of our own burning guilt, (in order to show us how dreadful sin is) we sometimes cry out, as did Cain that this is heavier than we can bear. God shields us from the full, crushing, and fatal weight of our guilt.

But, at the cross, our merciful heavenly Father did not shield his Son from this brutal experience. And Jesus experienced the totality of human guilt. It was only Jesus's infinite love that could give him the capacity to experience the enormity of human guilt and grief. Only Jesus's infinite heart of love could motivate anyone to choose such an experience in order to save rebellious mankind!

With God's mighty angels standing back, and Jesus's connection with the Holy Spirit broken up, Satan and his evil angels had full access to the heart and mind of Jesus to tempt and torment him. Satan is a liar. He mixes just enough truth with his lies in order to make them plausible. Knowing Jesus's tender, vulnerable heart of love and Satan's twisted, venomous, hatred, we can imagine Satan's attacks on Christ.

Satan pressed upon our Savior the futility of his sacrifice. Satan pointed out to Jesus the multitudes of Earth that had rejected the foundation of God's kingdom, the principle of unselfish love. Satan said, "Look at Cain, the people destroyed by the flood, the people of Sodom and Gomorrah, and even your own disciple, Judas. The whole Earth has rejected your law of unconditional love.

Your own chosen nation has rejected you. The leaders of Israel cannot distinguish between you and me. They are following my principles even while claiming your Father's name! No one understands or appreciates your sacrifice. You are wasting your time. You do not even know if your sacrifice will be accepted. Even if God did accept your sacrifice, it would not do you any good. The world is mine. They have chosen me. If you accept mankind's sin, guilt, and shame, you will be separated from your Father, forever. How do you even know that you are the Son of God? If you are the Son of God why don't you come down from the cross? Then Israel would follow you."

Satan subtly tempted and brutally tormented Jesus. Satan wanted Jesus to die, but not before he had turned back from his mission. Satan wanted Jesus to die as a failure. Satan pressed his torments and temptations harder and harder on the vulnerable Son of God. However, he did not want Jesus to die until he had given in to temptation. Satan continued to press the cup of humanity's sin, guilt, and woe to our Saviour's lips. Jesus willingly drank down the cup of suffering that was rightfully ours.

The Father covered Jesus's suffering and shame with dense darkness. The Father was there with his Son. But it was only through faith that Jesus could know that:

> When the waves of death encircled me, the floods of ungodly men made me afraid. The sorrows of hell hemmed me in. The snares of death went in front of me. In my distress I called upon the LORD and cried to my God. And He heard my voice out of His temple, and my cry entered into His ears. And the earth shook and trembled. The foundations of the heavens moved and shook because He was angry. Smoke went up out of His nostrils, and fire out of His mouth devoured. Coals were kindled by it. He bowed the heavens also, and came down. And darkness was under His feet. (2Samuel 22:5-10, MKJ)

Jesus drank down that cup to its bitter end. The experience broke Jesus's heart. As he hung on the cross, dying, Jesus cried out "It is finished." Jesus's death at once revealed and vanquished Satan. Love conquered. Hatred and selfishness failed.

Amazing love! Amazing hatred! Never has Heaven's light shined brighter. Never has Hell's deep darkness hung heavier.

Our Father's law of unselfish, unconditional love has never been demonstrated more clearly. The malignant viciousness of Satan's self-centered principle of perverted "justice" was revealed in its grandest fury. What a tremendous, infinite contrast! Never before and never again will the universe witness such an infinite contrast between light and darkness, and good and evil.

*The sinners in
Zion are afraid;
fearfulness hath
surprised the hypocrites.
Who among us shall dwell
with the devouring fire?
who among us shall dwell
with everlasting burnings?
(Isaiah 33:14, 15, KJV)*

4

Hell Fire and
The Cross

Digging for Truth

In the introduction to her book *HEART IN THE WILD*
Susan Chernak McElroy quotes L. Shefer: "Truth is fire, and to
speak the truth means to illuminate and burn." She also shares
her thoughts about:

> the fires of the year 2000—the ones that burned the West
> and the one that took my home in January of that year.
> My catastrophic house fire was not the first fire to have
> touched my life. If you imagine fire not in its flaming form
> but as a transitional force that sweeps in, consuming and
> transmuting all it touches, then the soul of fire had certain-
> ly entered me before. None of us is immune to the spirit of
> fire that rushes upon us, signaling profound and deep life
> changes with a terrifying rush of obliterating smoke that
> blackens out the meaning and oftentimes the very sense of
> reality of our former lives.
> Here in the West, the fires of 2000 were only fully ended
> when the winter snows came. The land went from black to
> white, and for six months it looked as if nothing were hap-

pening. But beneath the snow and deeper still, beneath the scorched ground, change was moving forward resolutely, undeniably. In accordance with a process as mysterious, enduring, and unstoppable as our own life changes, powerful, unnameable forces were remapping the vision of the forest to come. But the regrowth would not begin instantly or at the surface level.[1]

Just as life exists beneath the black ashes of a forest fire, hidden from sight, so the Bible also contains truths, deeper principles that elude the surface reader. The Bible does describe literal fire, but it also uses fire as a symbol. God is a consuming fire. Sin is also a blazing, consuming fire, but of a different sort. God's fire purifies, while sin's fire destroys. On one hand, because God is all-powerful and immortal, and we are weak and mortal, God's warnings about the severe, fiery consequences of sin may sound like threats to us.

Jesus's Death Reveals Sinners' Fate

On the other hand, we look at Jesus's love that led him to the cross to die in our place. We need to bring our fears to the cross of Calvary. Jesus did not threaten those who mistreated him. No, he prayed for those who nailed him to the cross! God is not two-faced. He does not smile at the righteous and snarl at the wicked. Remember, we are all sinners and fall short of the glory of God. Yet sin and unrepentant sinners do come to an end:

No, you would not learn, and you refused to respect the Lord. You rejected my advice and paid no attention when I warned you. "Now you will eat the fruit of what you have done, until you are stuffed full with your own schemes. Sin and self-satisfaction bring destruction and death to stupid fools. But if you listen to me, you will be safe and secure without fear of disaster." (Proverbs 1:29-33, CEV)

Sinners reap what they have sown. They eat the fruit of

84

what they have done. Sinners bring destruction on themselves:

> For the ways of man are before the eyes of the Lord, and He ponders all his paths. His own iniquities entrap the wicked man, and he is caught in the cords of his sin. He shall die for lack of instruction, and in the greatness of his folly he shall go astray. (Proverbs 5:21-23, NKJ)

The burning anguish that Christ endured upon the cross, the unfathomable weight of sin and guilt, and the sense of separation from God, caused Christ to experience the horrors of the second death. Christ endured the intense, yes infinite, spiritual, mental, emotional, and physical agony of the second death. Make no mistake, it was our sin, not the nails of the cross that killed the Son of God. Nor did God the Father kill his Son. The ancient Molech worshipers sacrificed their sons. But God does not operate by pagan principles. God did not kill his Son:

> "For this reason the Father loves me, because I lay down my life, that I may take it again. No one takes it from me, but I lay it down of my own accord. I have power to lay it down, and I have power to take it again; this charge I have received from my Father" (John 10:17, 18, RSV).

Jesus did experience God's "wrath and the power of Sheol:

> How long, O LORD? Will you hide yourself forever? How long will your wrath burn like fire? Remember how short my time is—for what vanity you have created all mortals! Who can live and never see death? Who can escape the power of Sheol? (Psalm 89:46-48, NRSV)

Psalm 89 foretells Jesus's experience on the cross. He suffered the "wrath of God." "How long will your wrath burn like fire?" Christ endured the fullness of the power of Sheol—hell. In the book of Revelation, John writes about the second death and hell. Jesus's deep love for fallen humanity brought him to the cross of Calvary, where he suffered the fullness of the second death and hell. Jesus suffered the fiery guilt and shame of sin, and the dark, destructive separation from God. Jesus's experience foreshadows the hell unrepentant sinners will experience, bound by their own unbreakable fetters of self-centered sin.

Our guide to interpreting the book of Revelation must be the cross of Christ. Our Father in Heaven did not torment his Son, Jesus. Cruel men crucified Jesus. Our sins killed him. Remember that Jesus died to pay the penalty for the sins of the whole world. That means that Jesus experienced the same fate that awaits unrepentant sinners at the end of the age. Jesus will not change from a gentle Lamb into a fire-breathing dragon that takes pleasure in the torture of his children. Neither will our heavenly Father.

Hell in the Light of the Cross

Our understanding of hell has been inconsistent with the character of God as revealed by the life and death of Jesus. Let's look at some texts that will help us understand the principles involved, "He will bring the people of the world to judgment. He will convict the ungodly of all the evil things they have done in rebellion and of all the insults that godless sinners have spoken against him" (Jude 15, NLT).

At the end of the age, the lost will stand before God's judgment throne. God will enable the lost to remember their evil thoughts, feelings, words, and actions. He will show them how they have stubbornly rejected his mercy, his free gift. The burning guilt of their sins will overwhelm them in the same way that the sin and guilt of the whole world overwhelmed the Son of God. Sinners will die the same death that Jesus did. The infinite weight of our sin and guilt and the sense of separation from God broke the heart of Jesus. The mental anguish Christ endured on the cross far exceeded the physical torment that he endured:

The sinners in Zion are afraid; Fearfulness has seized the

hypocrites: "Who among us shall dwell with the devouring fire? Who among us shall dwell with everlasting burnings?" He who walks righteously and speaks uprightly, He who despises the gain of oppressions, Who gestures with his hands, refusing bribes, Who stops his ears from hearing of bloodshed, And shuts his eyes from seeing evil. (Isaiah 33:14, 15, NKJ)

The nations fall into the pitfalls they have dug for others; the trap they set has snapped on them. The Lord is famous for the way he punishes the wicked in their own snares! (Psalm 9:15, 16, Living Bible)

Our God is a consuming fire. The contrast between God's perfect self-sacrificing love and the guilt and shame of sin and selfishness would kill anyone, even Jesus, the Son of God, our Sin-Bearer. Jesus's heart ever burned with the pure, holy flame of unselfish love. Jesus never yielded to temptation and sin. Yet an ocean of sin battered Jesus everywhere he turned, but its foul waves could never cause his flame of love to wane or even to flicker. The cross proves that God does not have to physically kill the sinner. Spiritual trauma killed Jesus before the physical trauma of the cross could. Even Pilate, the Roman governor, was surprised that Jesus had died so soon:

It was towards evening when Joseph of Arimathea arrived. He was a respected member of the Council, who was waiting for the coming of the Kingdom of God. It was Preparation day (that is, the day before the Sabbath), so Joseph went boldly into the presence of Pilate and asked him for the body of Jesus. Pilate was surprised to hear that Jesus was already dead. He called the army officer and asked him if Jesus had been dead a long time. After hearing the officer's report, Pilate told Joseph he could have the body. (Mark 14:42-45, TEV)

Just as Jesus died beneath the weight of our sins, the sinner dies beneath the crushing weight of his own guilt, shame, and hatred. The fire of God that comes down from Heaven to consume the wicked is the light of his glorious character of love. The fire of God's glory contrasts, accentuates, and ignites the fire of sin, guilt, and hatred. The fire of God's glory of love comes down from Heaven in the form of the vivid portrayal, the presentation to each heart and mind, of our Saviour's struggle in Gethsemane and his death on the cross of Calvary.

Christ's death on Calvary will destroy Satan! "Forasmuch then as the children are partakers of flesh and blood, he also himself likewise took part of the same; that through death he might destroy him that had the power of death, that is, the devil" (Hebrews 2:14, KJV). Yes, Christ's death destroyed Satan's influence among the loyal heavenly beings and among those who are being saved from the Earth.

Furthermore, at the white throne judgment, when the crucifixion of Jesus Christ is portrayed before Gog and Magog, Satan will have no power to turn from the picture of his own work. Christ, through his death, destroys Satan indirectly, but literally. The crucifixion of Christ is the full demonstration of God's glory, and his wrath. Our God is a consuming fire!

> Take heed unto yourselves, lest ye forget the covenant of the LORD your God, which he made with you, and make you a graven image, or the likeness of any thing, which the LORD thy God hath forbidden thee. For the LORD thy God is a consuming fire, even a jealous God. (Deuteronomy 4:23, 24, KJV)

> And the glory of the LORD abode upon mount Sinai, and the cloud covered it six days: and the seventh day he called unto Moses out of the midst of the cloud. And the sight of the glory of the LORD was like devouring fire on the top of the mount in the eyes of the children of Israel (Exodus 24:16, 17, KJV)

The Law of Life, The Law of Death

God presented his Ten Commandments to Moses on top of the burning mountain, amidst thunder and lightning. The divine statutes can be summarized as love for God and love for others. Love brings life.

When any of God's creatures reject his law of love, they're rejecting life, liberty, and happiness. Sin is the great destroyer. Rebellion's seed grows and yields a mature fruit, the bitter harvest of the second death. This is the natural consequence of sin and selfishness. Sin is self-destructive.

Sadly, in varying degrees, even Christians have accepted some of Satan's lies as an article of faith. God has described the law of life. But because our wise and loving heavenly Father has been shielding Satan, his fallen angels and fallen humanity from the fullness of the natural consequences of selfishness, sin, and guilt, we have taken sin lightly. We do not see the immediate, destructive consequences of sin. Sin has become familiar to us. Therefore we do not think it's so bad.

Just as he did in Heaven, Satan has turned God's mercy into a lie. Satan depicts God's law and character as arbitrary and condemning. He portrays our loving Father as angrily destroying those of his children who don't repent. At the end of the age, God will allow the lost to experience the full bitterness of sin. The whole universe will see how destructive sin really is. God does not have to arbitrarily punish or destroy anyone. Sin kills.

God will allow those of his stubborn, rebellious children who have refused to let go of sin to experience the desire of their hearts. Without the shield of his love and grace that they have rejected, the desire of their hearts will turn to bitterness. Yet God loves them still. What patience! What love and mercy! What grace! The presentation of Jesus's sacrifice, contrasted with each person's vivid, self-condemning memory, vindicates our heavenly Father. The wages of sin is death. The gift of God is eternal life. God desires to consume our sin and guilt before our sin and guilt consume us, "For our God is a consuming fire" (Hebrews 12:29, KJV).

Contrast God's purifying, healing fire with sin's fire, "For wickedness burns like the fire; it shall devour the briers and thorns, and shall kindle in the thickets of the forest, and they shall roll upwards like the lifting up of smoke" (Isaiah 9:18 MKJV).

Therefore let us repent of our sin (unbelief), that we may rejoice when Jesus comes to claim his believing children.

At the second coming, Jesus's loving eyes, like flames of fire will ignite the guilty consciences of the wicked. The same principle in regard to the second coming applies to the white throne judgment presentation of Jesus on the cross. God's glorious character of love, in its infinite intensity, overwhelms any sinner who is hanging onto his sin. At the end of the thousand years of rest, the judgment presentation of Jesus on the cross vividly portrays the Son of God in Gethsemane and on Calvary. The power of God's love is clearly revealed. Self-sacrificing love is God's mightiest weapon. Jesus's sacrifice is God's method for unleashing the infinite power of his love.

Even Satan will be constrained to bow before God. David foretells this event, "All the prosperous on the earth shall eat and worship, all those that go down to the dust shall bow before Him, even he who cannot keep himself alive" (Psalm 22:29, NKJ). Satan cannot keep himself alive. Only God has immortal life within himself. Satan does not, nor do we.

God will not force anyone to confess that Jesus Christ is Lord. Nor will God force every knee to bow. God always acts based on his eternal principles. The exercise of force is contrary to the eternal principles of God's government.

At the white throne judgment, our Father presents his love as revealed by Jesus's death on the cross of Calvary to impenitent sinners in a 360 degree, 3-D, holographic, omni-vision-type experience. The presentation of Jesus's sacrifice is the glory of God. It is his character of love. This is what makes our God a consuming fire.

The contrast between God's pure, holy, unselfish love and each sinner's selfish, and rebellious heart, mind, and character is the second death experience. It is hell. This is what Christ experienced on the cross. The humanity of Christ could not survive the experience. This contrast crushed out his life. The impenitent sinner will also go through the same crushing experience of the second death. Isaiah also describes the judgment presentation of Jesus on the cross:

> For there is no other God but me—a just God and a Savior—no, not one! Let all the world look to me for salvation! For I am God; there is no other. I have sworn by my own name, and I will never go back on my word: Every knee will bow to me, and every tongue will confess allegiance to my name." The people will declare, "The LORD is the source of all my righteousness and strength." And all who were angry with him will come to him and be ashamed. (Isaiah 45:21-24, NKJ)

Paul talks about it, "For it is written, As I live, saith the Lord, every knee shall bow to me, and every tongue shall confess to God" (Romans 14:11, KJV). Again Paul describes the power of the cross causing every knee to bow:

> Who, being in the form of God, thought it not robbery to be equal with God: But made himself of no reputation, and took upon him the form of a servant, and was made in the likeness of men: And being found in fashion as a man, he humbled himself, and became obedient unto death, even the death of the cross. Wherefore God also hath highly exalted him, and given him a name which is above every name: That at the name of Jesus every knee should bow, of things in heaven, and things in earth, and things under the earth; And that every tongue should confess that Jesus Christ is Lord, to the glory of God the Father. (Philippians 2:6-11, KJV)

The beauty of Jesus's sacrifice causes all to kneel in worship before him. Saint and sinner, good and bad, righteous and wicked, none need be terrified of God. God has nothing but love for all people. That is what the cross proves.

Sin is Self-Destructive

But we should be terrified of sin. Jesus died the second death as a consequence of carrying our sins. Unrepentant sinners at the end of time also die the second death as a consequence of refusing to let Jesus carry their sins.

Just as God did not physically kill his Son, God will not physically kill the unrepentant angels or sinners. He does not have to. It is the weight of sin, guilt, and shame, the fire of a burning heart, mind, and spirit, that crush out life forever. Sin contains the seeds of its own destruction.

No sinner has ever yet been treated as he deserves, "He has not dealt with us according to our sins, nor rewarded us according to our iniquities" (Psalm 103:10, MKJ). But God will honor everyone's freedom. They will reap what they have sown at the white throne judgment.

God has shielded fallen angels and fallen humans from the full consequences of sin and rebellion. More than this, God has poured out his blessings upon the good and bad alike. But Satan has done his best to pervert God's blessings into curses.

The living wicked at the second coming of Christ will get a foretaste of the judgment. God's glory, his infinite love, contains absolutely no condemnation. Although, the contrast between God's goodness and the sinner's depravity will feel like condemnation.

The destructive power of sin has so warped the evil angels and sinful men that they cannot tolerate God's love. God's love condemns and consumes the wicked in the same way that beautiful art condemns bad art—by example.

Dear reader, join me in praying that we will allow God's love to burn in our hearts, consuming sin, day by day. Let us behold Jesus on the cross on a daily basis, allowing the fire of the Holy Spirit to cleanse us from all unrighteousness. In small, daily doses, God's glory, his consuming fire purifies, strengthens, and heals. If it is painful, ego, self, the carnal heart, is what suffers. Indeed self (selfishness) must die, "I am crucified with

92

Christ: nevertheless I live; yet not I, but Christ liveth in me: and the life which I now live in the flesh I live by the faith of the Son of God, who loved me, and gave himself for me" (Galatians 2:20, KJV). Those who do not die to self cannot live to God. Their sin, shame, and guilt will consume them:

> The way of the just is uprightness; O Most Upright, You weigh the path of the just. Yes, in the way of Your judgments, O LORD, we have waited for You; The desire of our soul is for Your name and for the remembrance of You. With my soul I have desired You in the night, yes, by my spirit within me I will seek You early; For when Your judgments are in the earth, the inhabitants of the world will learn righteousness. Let grace be shown to the wicked, yet he will not learn righteousness; In the land of uprightness he will deal unjustly, and will not behold the majesty of the LORD. LORD, when Your hand is lifted up, they will not see. But they will see and be ashamed for their envy of people; Yes, the fire of Your enemies shall devour them. (Isaiah 26:7-11, NKJ)

God has stated the point in time that Satan will be unmasked in the presence of those he has deceived. The great white throne judgment will occur after the millennium of rest. The justice of God (his love) means that God does not, indeed cannot, forcibly extend his protection to those who finally and totally reject his love. Otherwise he would become a dictator.

No Man Shall Spare His Brother

Moreover, no purpose of mercy would be served. In fact, it would be cruel to arbitrarily extend the lives of those that have formed evil habits and characters. The lost have no true joy or peace. Their hearts are filled with rage at those that have deceived them or caused them pain. Satan, his evil angels, and the lost, will turn on one another. Without God's protection, Satan will become as vulnerable as any man. Ezekiel foretold Satan's end:

See, I am sending against you strange men, feared among the nations: they will let loose their swords against your bright wisdom, they will make your glory a common thing. They will send you down to the underworld, and your death will be the death of those who are put to the sword in the heart of the seas.

Will you say, in the face of those who are taking your life, I am God? but you are man and not God in the hands of those who are wounding you.

You were in Eden, the garden of God; every stone of great price was your clothing, the sardius, the topaz, and the diamond, the beryl, the onyx, and the jasper, the emerald and the carbuncle: your store-houses were full of gold, and things of great price were in you; in the day when you were made they were got ready.

I gave you your place with the winged one; I put you on the mountain of God; you went up and down among the stones of fire.

There has been no evil in your ways from the day when you were made, till sin was seen in you. Through all your trading you have become full of violent ways, and have done evil: so I sent you out shamed from the mountain of God; the winged one put an end to you from among the stones of fire.

By all your sin, even by your evil trading, you have made your holy places unclean; so I will make a fire come out from you, it will make a meal of you, and I will make you as dust on the earth before the eyes of all who see you. (Ezekiel 28:7-18, BBE)

God makes fire come out from Satan by presenting Satan with a view of his own sins in contrast to the mercy, love, and patience of Jesus. If Jesus could not survive the cross, neither will Satan survive the white throne judgment. Jesus was res- urrected because he was holy, pure love, with no stain of sin. Satan will not be resurrected from his fate. Sin will burn itself out and never arise again:

But with an overflowing flood
He will make an utter end of its place,
And darkness will pursue His enemies.
What do you conspire against the Lord?
He will make an utter end of it.
Affliction will not rise up a second time.
For while tangled like thorns,
And while drunken like drunkards,
They shall be devoured like stubble fully dried.
(Nahum 1:8-10 NKJ)

Sin and sinners will be consumed like stubble fully dried. No fire burns hotter than a guilty conscience. "But the children of the kingdom shall be cast out into outer darkness: there shall be weeping and gnashing of teeth" (Matthew 8:12, KJV). Isaiah reaffirms this concept:

For wickedness burneth as the fire: it shall devour the briers and thorns, and shall kindle in the thickets of the forest, and they shall mount up like the lifting up of smoke. Through the wrath of the LORD of hosts is the land darkened, and the people shall be as the fuel of the fire: no man shall spare his brother. (Isaiah 9:18, 19, KJV)

Wickedness, a searing guilty conscience from a life of sin, burns out the life of the lost. God's principles of love are not compatible with torture. It is sin that burns. Each thought and act of selfishness and sin carries within itself the seeds of self-destruction. Sin and guilt will explode into fiery human rage when determined sinners burn the last bridge, beyond which our loving Father's protection will not reach, lest he become a dictator.

"No man shall spare his brother." This refers to the great battle of Gog and Magog, which will occur after the millennium of rest. The lost will turn on each other with fury. The lost multitudes will especially target those who have been influential leaders in the paths of deception.

Before the thousand years of rest, (the seventh millennium) the die has been cast; men have decided their destiny. At the second coming of Jesus, as well as at the white throne judgment it will be too late for change, because men's hearts will have been hardened by repeated rejections of God's mercy. Now, today is the time for acceptance of God's love. Jesus gives us abundant opportunity to open our hearts and choose his love. The darker the heart, the more Jesus yearns to shed his loving light into that heart.

The second coming of Jesus and the judgment of the wicked after the millennium, contain many parallel aspects. Bible writers often combine two events in a single description. Jesus combined the description of the destruction of Jerusalem with the worldwide destruction at his second coming. Bible texts about "The great day of the Lord" accurately describe the terror of the wicked at the second coming of Jesus as well as the final, white throne judgment:

> Send out a cry of grief; for the day of the Lord is near; it comes as destruction from the Most High. For this cause all hands will be feeble, and every heart of man be turned to water; Their hearts will be full of fear; pains and sorrows will overcome them; they will be in pain like a woman in childbirth; they will be shocked at one another; their faces will be like flames. See, the day of the Lord is coming, cruel, with wrath and burning passion: to make the land a waste, driving the sinners in it to destruction. For the stars of heaven and its bright armies will not give their light: the sun will be made dark in his journey through the heaven, and the moon will keep back her light. And I will send punishment on the world for its evil, and on the sinners for their wrongdoing; and I will put an end to all pride, and will make low the power of the cruel. (Isaiah 13:6-11, BBE)

All that Isaiah pronounces here is true. The day of the Lord causes the sinner's heart to be full of fear, pain, and sorrow. Then will "every heart of man be turned to water." That reminds one of the blood and water that flowed out of Jesus's heart when the soldier pierced his side. Their "faces will be like flames" expresses the burning guilt and shame caused by a life of sin. "I will put an end to all pride." In the brilliant light of the cross of Calvary, there will be no room for human pride, especially among unrepentant sinners. With our understanding of God's character of love, and our knowledge of the judgment scene, this passage should cause us to be afraid of, and hate sin and its destructive power, "The fear of the LORD is to hate evil" (Proverbs 8:13, KJV). Here is another description of the day of the Lord, the judgment scene:

> For the day of the LORD upon all the nations is near; As you have done, it shall be done to you; Your reprisal shall return upon your own head. For as you drank on my holy mountain, so shall all the nations drink continually; Yes, they shall drink, and swallow, and they shall be as though they had never been. But on Mount Zion there shall be deliverance, and there shall be holiness; The house of Jacob shall possess their possessions. The house of Jacob shall be a fire, and the house of Joseph a flame; But the house of Esau shall be stubble; They shall kindle them and devour them, and no survivor shall remain of the house of Esau," for the LORD has spoken. (Obadiah 15-18, NKJ)

God is love. We must not blame God for the consequences of sin. "Your reprisal shall return upon your own head." That is why we arc not to take our own revenge. God proclaims, "Vengeance is Mine." If we take vengeance into our own hands, we will be adding to our own mountain of guilt. Vengeance requires judgment. Jesus instructed us to avoid judging others, "Do not judge, so that you may not be judged" (Matthew 7:1, NRSV).

We must have faith that God will execute justice. He will. How he executes justice is amazing to me. I worship You, Father for bringing sin and sinners to an end without using any of Satan's evil methods. The sinner will be his own harshest judge. We're near the end of time. Now is the time to accept God's light, his glorious character of love. Mankind has suffered long enough from the darkness of Satan's subtle lies about our loving heavenly Father. We must learn to interpret, understand, and appreciate all scripture in the intense light of the glory of God's love as revealed by his Son, Jesus, on the cross.

Satan is Abaddon the Destroyer

The way God's wrath is responsible for the death and destruction recorded in the Old and New Testament can be understood in light of Christ's experience in the Garden of Gethsemane. God did not kill his Son! Our heavenly Father did not react in anger when Jesus took our sins upon himself in Gethsemane. The Father hid his face from Jesus. That is God's wrath. Even that was not an arbitrary act.

It was the cruel darkness of sin that prevented our Saviour from seeing his loving Father's face. It was Satan who cruelly tempted Christ to believe that he would never be one with the Father again. It was Satan who pointed out the apparent futility of Christ's sacrifice. It was Satan who poured all the woe of human suffering into Christ's bitter cup. It was Satan who inspired men to whip, torture, ridicule, and crucify our dear Saviour.

The relationship between Christ's experience in Gethsemane and unrepentant sinners destroyed by God's wrath now becomes simple, and clear. God's wrath means that he seems to "hide his face" from those who, because of the darkness of sin cannot see him. It is Satan who loves to tempt, discourage, and torment weak humanity. It is Satan who causes us to feel that our sins have separated us from God. It is sin that destroys. Satan has entered so fully into sin that there is nothing else in him. Satan is Apollyon, or Abaddon, the Destroyer (see Revelation 9:11). David knew who the Destroyer was, "Concerning the works of men, by the word of thy lips I have kept me from the paths of the destroyer" (Psalm 17:4, KJV).

The destruction of Sodom and Gomorrah, the flood, the death of Uzzah, Korah, Dathan and Abiram, etc., these are not angry, destructive exceptions to our otherwise merciful and kind heavenly Father's foundation principle of benevolent love! "We must not put the Lord to the test, as some of them did and were destroyed by serpents; nor grumble, as some of them did and were destroyed by the Destroyer" (1Corinthians 10:9, 10, RSV). Notice that serpents destroyed some rebellious people (serpents are a symbol of Satan). The text mentions the Destroyer, who, of course, is Satan.

Our Father does not look for ways to destroy the people that he has created. The cross overwhelmingly demonstrates how far God will go to save souls. No matter how dark and deep the rebellion and ugliness of sin, it cannot cause our loving heavenly Father to deviate from his holy character of love. No exceptions. By the rules of engagement in the war between Jesus and Satan, when cities like Sodom and Gomorrah pass the point of no return, God must allow Satan full control of those who have fully chosen his principles:

> How can I give you up, O Ephraim? How can I surrender you O Israel? How can I give you like Admah? How can I treat you Like Zeboiim? My heart is turned over within Me, together my compassions are kindled. (Hosea 11:8, NASB, Margin)

To whom would God give up Ephraim? To whom would God surrender Israel? The answer is the same being to whom God gave up Admah, Zeboiim, Sodom and Gomorrah. There are only two sides to this war: God and Satan. Remember that Satan brought fire down from heaven and destroyed Job's sheep and servants. Keep in mind also that Satan will use fire again: "He did unbelievable miracles such as making fire flame down to earth from the skies while everyone was watching" (Revelation 13:13, Living Bible). Of course, Satan can use the armies of pagan nations against Israel, as he did many times.

Nevertheless, God takes responsibility because he is the

Sovereign King. And Satan delights in blaming God for all destruction and death.

When God's rules of war constrain him to allow Satan to destroy men, Satan leaps at the chance. Satan exults to cause suffering and death. Then he blames it on God! Shall we join Satan in his evil work of blaming God? No. By the grace of God, no.

Isaiah looks ahead in time to the white throne judgment when as Jesus said "all things will be revealed." Then Gog and Magog, all the wicked will see who was the source of destruction—Satan:

> Those who see you shall stare and closely watch you, saying, Is this the man who made the earth to tremble; who shook kingdoms; who made the world as a wilderness, and destroyed its cities; who did not open the house for his prisoners? (Isaiah 14:16, 17, MKJ)

Isaiah prophesied that all humanity would discover that it was Satan who had destroyed the world's cities, not God. (That includes Sodom and Gomorrah). All will see that it was Satan who made the world a wilderness. Satan "made the earth to tremble." That refers to earthquakes, as well as to making people fearful. Indeed, Satan holds the dead as his prisoners, but only until Jesus's mighty voice calls them from the grave!

> For we say this to you by the Word of the Lord, that we who are alive and remain until the coming of the Lord shall not go before those who are asleep. For the Lord Himself shall descend from Heaven with a shout, with the voice of the archangel and with the trumpet of God. And the dead in Christ shall rise first. Then we who are alive and remain shall be caught up together with them in the clouds, to meet the Lord in the air. And so we shall ever be with the Lord. (1Thessalonians 4:15-17, MKJ)

Satan seeks to punish and destroy sinners. He keeps track

of our sins and accuses us before God. Our Father doesn't keep track of our sins, at least not for the purpose of punishment. God looks for ways to rescue us from sin:

> Anyone who is joined to Christ is a new being; the old is gone, the new has come. All this is done by God, who through Christ changed us from enemies into his friends and gave us the task of making others his friends also. Our message is that God was making the whole human race his friends through Christ. God did not keep an account of their sins, and he has given us the message which tells how he makes them his friends. Here we are, then, speaking for Christ, as though God himself were making his appeal through us. We plead on Christ's behalf: let God change you from enemies into his friends! Christ was without sin, but for our sake God made him share our sin in order that in union with him we might share the righteousness of God. (2Corinthians 5:17-21, TEV)

Jesus died to win our friendship. God's way of eliminating his enemies is to win their hearts, that is to make them his friends. God does not keep an account of our sins. Still, unrepentant sinners face the second death. At first glance these two Biblical truths would seem to contradict one another. If God does not keep an account of our sins, how are unrepentant, rebellious sinners to be judged and cast into hell?

Casting Out Satan

Whenever we see an apparent contradiction in the Bible we should rejoice because the Holy Spirit is preparing our hearts and minds to receive a deeper truth. The contradiction is not in the Scriptures themselves, but in our misunderstanding of Biblical terms, concepts, and principles.

As honest searchers for truth, we must be willing to let go of preconceived assumptions about God, his sovereignty, the law, the judgment, and the second death, which is hell. We must be willing to test our Bible truths in the light that streams

101

from the cross of Calvary.

For example, in the chapter *War in Heaven*, we discussed how Satan was cast out of Heaven. Through Jesus's sacrifice on the cross, God revealed to all Heaven and Earth the beauty of his character of love, the destructiveness of sin, and the ugliness of Satan's character. Satan was cast out of the hearts and minds of all heavenly beings.

Let us join the heavenly beings, and by looking to Jesus's sacrifice on the cross, cast Satan out of our hearts and minds. This process will involve casting down pride of opinion and letting go of long-held beliefs.

God is sovereign. We are mortal humans. Humbly, carefully comparing Scripture principle with Scripture principle, checking our interpretation in the light of the cross of Calvary, we should try to grasp how God will use the same method to cast sinners into hell as he did to cast Satan out of Heaven.

God has chosen to accomplish these things by the powerful revelation of his character of love through Jesus's death on the cross of Calvary.

The powerful revelation of Jesus's death highlights the contrast between God's unselfish love and the hideous, destructive nature of sin and rebellion. The war between God and Satan is a spiritual war, fought on the battlefield of the hearts and minds of all God's created beings. All of Heaven has chosen God's law of unselfish love as demonstrated by the life and death of Jesus. How about you? Who will be the sovereign of your heart?

Babylon, the Cross, and Unity

It is only on Earth that the dark destructive plague of sin remains. Satan cannot undo the fact, the victory of Jesus's life and death. But he can misrepresent the issues, and cause confusion. That is why hundreds of widely different churches all claim to rightly interpret the Scriptures and yet differ in many important teachings.

The apostle John used the word "Babylon," which means confusion to describe end-time Christianity. Satan is a counterfeiter. He subtly twists and perverts our understanding of the character of God. One way that Satan causes confusion is to cause us to look at Jesus's suffering and death on the cross on only a physical, surface, level.

The physical level is a good place to start. The astonishingly successful movie, "The Passion of the Christ," vividly, graphically, portrayed Jesus's physical suffering and death. Jesus did suffer physically. Mel Gibson did a great job of portraying the physical sufferings of Jesus. Yet Jesus's mental, emotional, and spiritual suffering were infinitely deeper and broader than his physical suffering. However, it is difficult, if not impossible, to give even the smallest idea of Jesus's infinite mental anguish through the finite medium of cinema.

It is good to visualize and appreciate Jesus's physical suffering. However, we need to look beyond the literal blood and gore, keeping in mind, the core issues of Jesus's mental, emotional, and spiritual suffering. None of the Bible writers record Jesus complaining about, or even mentioning the physical pain of the crucifixion. All Jesus's recorded words evidenced intense spiritual, emotional and mental suffering. Jesus cried out, "My God, my God, why have you forsaken me?" This indicates intense spiritual pain. Jesus also prayed that his Father forgive his tormentors. Again, this is a spiritual concern. Jesus would rather suffer the horrors of the second death than leave his precious children to experience it. What love! What tenderhearted courage! Truly, Jesus is the Lamb of God. He shows us that our Father is gentle and kind.

Our loving heavenly Father is not a destructive tyrant. Satan is a destructive tyrant. Satan uses trickery, lies, and half-truths, as well as enticement, coercion, jealousy, and human rage as weapons of destruction. Our Father is the Creator-God, the Giver, and Sustainer of life. God is love. In him is light and no darkness at all!

---

1 McElroy, Susan Chernak (2002). HEART IN THE WILD. New York: Random House Publishing Group.

Therefore my heart shall sound
for Moab like flutes,
and my heart shall sound like flutes
for the men of Kirheres...
(Jeremiah 48:36, NKJ)

In all their affliction he was afflicted...
in his love and in his pity he redeemed
them; and he bare them,
and carried them all the days of old.
(Isaiah 63:9, KJV)

The LORD hath appeared of old
unto me, saying, Yea, I have loved thee
with an everlasting love: therefore with lovingkindness have I drawn thee.
(Jeremiah 31:3, KJV)

5

Our Suffering Father

Now is the Time

The last time that Mike could remember seeing his parents together, he was sitting in his high chair eating dry cereal, with his mom standing on one side and his dad on the other side, screaming back and forth. His parents divorced soon after.

As Mike grew up, his father never visited, even though he only lived five minutes away from Mike, in a very small town. He never called Mike. Mike never got birthday cards or gifts. Mike's mother would ask him, "What kind of a father do you have? He never visits. He could at least call or write when he lives so close." As Mike grew a little older, his mother also told him that his father never sent child support. Mike grew up knowing that his father did not love him. He wondered why.

When Mike became a teenager, he would, from time to time, visit his father, motivated by a combination of a sense of duty and curiosity. Mike often wondered to himself, "What kind of a man would abandon his son like that?" Yet Mike felt that he should get to know him at least a little bit, after all he was his biological father. But Mike found it difficult to visit him. He always felt uncomfortable in his presence. Though his father always seemed pleasant and took an interest in him, Mike just could not accept him as sincere. Where had his father been when he was growing up? He just could not respect such

105

a man. He wanted to love him. He felt a duty to love him. Mike even felt just a little guilty that he did not love him. But how could he?

Then Mike met Misty. She was gorgeous. The first time Mike saw Misty he knew that he wanted to marry her. The first time that Misty saw Mike, she knew that too—that he wanted to marry her. They started dating. Over time, the relationship deepened, and Misty knew that Mike would soon ask her to marry him.

Misty told Mike that if he wanted to marry her that he would have to reconcile with his father. Mike already felt the pressure of duty and guilt to spend time with his father. But now! Now Misty added more pressure to an already stressed situation. Mike visited his father more often. But he could not get past the feeling of distance and disrespect.

One day Mike was visiting his father. They were sitting in the living room talking. Mike just could not take pretending any more. With all the intensity that had been simmering over the years, Mike boiled over, revealing to his father how he truly felt. Expressing his bitterness and pain with a quaver in his voice, Mike asked him why he had never visited, sent cards, called, or even sent child support. His father nodded and waited until Mike had finished. Then he said, "Mike there is something I want to show you." He led Mike to the den. He opened a file cabinet and pulled out a stack of canceled checks. He said, "I did send the child support every month. I was never late." As Mike looked through the checks, he was stunned. What his father said was true.

Mike's mind reeled; he wondered why his mother had bitterly told him that his father had never sent any of the required child support. Then his father said, "Mike, I have not wanted to interfere with your relationship with your mother. There are some things that I have not told you. But I think now is the time." Then Mike's father explained that there had been a fiercely contested custody dispute. His mother had won sole custody. The ruling had forbidden him to contact Mike in person, or even by phone. That's why, even though he lived close by, he had never visited or called Mike when he was growing up. He had sent birthday cards and gifts, and Christmas cards and gifts to Mike every year. The cards and gifts had always been returned, marked refused. He had wanted to spend time with Mike, to guide him while he grew up, to teach him to throw and catch a ball. But the court ruling had forbidden him to do these things.

Instantly, Mike's feelings changed. His disrespect and bitterness melted away. Bitterness gave way to understanding and sympathy. Spontaneously, Mike felt, for the first time, warm love for his father. For the first time, Mike gave his father a great big hug. And he meant it with all his heart.

Notice that Mike's father hadn't changed. He was the same person. What had changed was how Mike thought about his father. Mike had been given some bad information. As soon as the lies were swept away, the relationship was restored.

Could we face the same situation with our heavenly Father? I believe that we do. We've been given some bad information about our Father. When the lies about our Father are swept away, we will find that it is easy, even natural to love him. Our feelings will change. Our Father has been patiently waiting until we are ready to learn the truth about him. I think now is the time. He has suffered enough. And so have we.

The Truth Shall Set You Free

I grew up thinking that the only time that God had suffered was when Jesus became a man and died for our sins. But, rather than describing the limits of God's suffering, the cross provides a window into the heart of our Father. Every act of cruelty, every twinge of pain, every pang of guilt reaches and grieves our tenderhearted Father. When Israel suffered the troubles that were the inevitable result of turning away from God, "…his soul was grieved for the misery of Israel" (Judges 10:16, KJV). The greater one's love, the greater one's potential for suffering.

God the Father suffered equally with Jesus on the cross, for Jesus proclaims to us that, "I and my Father are one" (John

107

10:30, KJV). When Jesus was crucified, the Father was right there with him. Jesus felt separated from God the Father. This sense of separation caused him to cry out "My God, my God, why have you forsaken me?" But we know that our loving heavenly Father never deserted his beloved Son, "For God was in Christ, reconciling the world to himself, not counting people's sins against them, and has committed to us the word of reconciliation" (2Corinthians 5:19, A blend of the NLT and the KJV). Whenever, wherever anyone suffers, Jesus and our heavenly Father are there sharing in their suffering, "And the King shall answer and say to them, Truly I say to you, Inasmuch as you did it to one of the least of these My brothers, you have done it to Me" (Matthew 25:40, MKJ). "In all their affliction he was afflicted, and the angel of his presence saved them: in his love and in his pity he redeemed them; and he bare them, and carried them all the days of old" (Isaiah 63:9, KJV).

All humans are God's children, because he created them, and furthermore because he has redeemed them. Each soul is precious in our Father's sight. Our heavenly Father is not an impersonal, powerful, *force* as portrayed in *Star Wars*. Our Father is a Person. He has a character and a personality. He has feelings, "In the same way, the Spirit helps us in our weakness. We do not know what we ought to pray for, but the Spirit himself intercedes for us with groans that words cannot express" (Romans 8:26, NIV).

Our loving, tenderhearted, heavenly Father, through the Holy Spirit, is interceding, yes, even pleading with us, with groans that words cannot express! He longs to rescue us from the degradation, destruction, and pain of sin, "As surely as I live, says the Sovereign Lord, I take no pleasure in the death of wicked people. I only want them to turn from their wicked ways so they can live. Turn! Turn from your wickedness, O people of Israel! Why should you die?" (Ezekiel 33:11, NLT). God does "not willingly afflict or grieve anyone" (Lamentations 3:33, NRSV).

Ask any loving parent that has gone through the experience; he or she will express to you that few things can cause more pain than the suicide of a favorite child. The greater the love, the greater the pain, and the loss! God's love for each of us is infinite. His suffering is also infinite! God knows that he is the only source of life, happiness, peace, meaning, and love. It hurts our Father when one of his children refuses to turn from the suicidal poison of sin and rejects his antidote of unselfish love!

Not a sigh is breathed, not a pain felt, not a grief pierces the soul, but the throb vibrates to the Father's heart. The Almighty God, the King of the universe, the Creator-God, is kind and sympathetic. He is all-knowing and all-feeling. Let us, through the sacrifice of Jesus, the Son of God, look into the heart of God. The cross shows selfish, sinful humanity the depths of the totally unselfish love that fills the heart of our God.

Jesus, one with God, hanging on the cross, shows us that the sovereign God of the universe would withhold nothing in order to rescue even one sinner from destruction, even if that meant losing his own life. Amazing love! Incredible love! Pure, holy, self-sacrificing, love!

The Power of Foolish Love

To our natural, self-centered hearts, God's love sounds a bit extreme, even crazy. The apostle Paul captures this thought, "For the preaching of the cross is to them that perish foolishness; but unto us which are saved it is the power of God" (Corinthians 1:18, KJV). God's holy love certainly does appear foolish to selfish hearts, warped and degraded by sin.

Born sinful and selfish as we are, our natural tendency is to "look out for number one." We get angry when someone cuts us off on the freeway. We may honk our horn or even make an angry gesture to show how we feel. It makes us mad to think that someone got ahead of us and caused us a few seconds delay. Then we justify our anger by muttering, "They could've caused an accident."

Our time, our happiness, and our possessions, are important to us. When someone wrongs us, what is it that naturally flows from our hearts and mouths? Angry thoughts, words, and actions are our natural, selfish response. When someone does us wrong, the natural response is to "get even," or to "teach them a lesson."

As we pray and meditate about God's infinite sacrifice on the cross of Calvary, we will begin to experience "the power of God." The Holy Spirit will change us "from glory to glory." By beholding we become changed. When we accept Christ, we accept God as our Father. When we call God our Father, we accept all his children as our brothers and sisters.

Our Sins Pierce God's Heart

I pray that each day we will spend time gazing at the beauty of God's love as displayed by Jesus on the cross of Calvary. Even if we walk daily with our God, we will never fully comprehend the infinite love and suffering of our dear Heavenly Father. Every time that we hang onto selfishness (sin) we pierce the heart of God. Let us look at a prophecy that describes our reaction when we see Jesus as he truly is at the second coming:

> And I will pour upon the house of David, and upon the inhabitants of Jerusalem, the spirit of grace and of supplications: and they shall look upon me whom they have pierced, and they shall mourn for him, as one mourneth for his only son, and shall be in bitterness for him, as one that is in bitterness for his firstborn. In that day shall there be a great mourning in Jerusalem, as the mourning of Hadadrimmon in the valley of Megiddon. And the land shall mourn, every family apart…(Zechariah 12:10-12, KJV)

> But He was pierced through for our transgressions, crushed for our iniquities. (Isaiah 53:5, NKJ Margin)

The house of David represents the rulers of God's people, the church leaders. The inhabitants of Jerusalem represent God's people, church members, Christians. When we, for the very first time, see God as he truly is, infinitely kind and loving, sympathetic and tenderhearted, we will indeed "mourn for him" whom we have pierced. Jesus on the cross shows us that our sin and selfishness pierce the heart of God. When Jesus comes and we look into his eyes for the first time, we will begin to realize more fully that our heavenly Father's infinite, sensitive love expose him to infinite suffering. Jesus alluded to this same scripture passage when he foretold the same reaction of mourning at his second coming:

> Then the sign of the Son of Man will appear in heaven, and then all the tribes of the earth will mourn, and they will see the Son of Man coming on the clouds of heaven with power and great glory. And He will send His angels with a great sound of a trumpet, and they will gather together His elect from the four winds, from one end of heaven to the other. (Matthew 24:30, 31, NKJ)

> Behold, he cometh with clouds; and every eye shall see him, and they also which pierced him: and all kindreds of the earth shall wail because of him. Even so, Amen. (Revelation 1:7, KJV)

The reason "all the tribes of the earth will mourn" when Jesus comes, is the same reason that God inspired Zechariah to share with us. The good and bad alike, the saved and the lost, all tribes will mourn when they see "the glory of God" which is his character of love.

We have all pierced the heart of Jesus and our loving heavenly Father by our self-centered, hardhearted, and rebellious ways. Our Father sympathizes with us in our weakness. God truly feels our pain. Isaiah reveals God's love, care, and concern for us in this prophecy about the ministry of Christ. Can you sense how God longs to relieve our suffering?

> The Spirit of the Lord GOD is upon Me, Because the LORD has anointed Me To preach good tidings to the poor; He has sent Me to heal the brokenhearted, To pro-

claim liberty to the captives, And the opening of the prison to those who are bound; To proclaim the acceptable year of the LORD, And the day of vengeance of our God; To comfort all who mourn, To console those who mourn in Zion, To give them beauty for ashes, The oil of joy for mourning, The garment of praise for the spirit of heaviness; That they may be called trees of righteousness, The planting of the LORD, that He may be glorified. (Isaiah 61:1-3, NKJ)

God Mourns for Moab

God spoke through his prophet Jeremiah to Israel and many of the surrounding nations. Jeremiah has often been called the weeping prophet. Remember that a prophet is a spokesman for God. Jeremiah's tears trickling down his cheeks are only a faint reflection of God's tears of sorrow. In the Old Testament times, Israel was God's chosen nation. Yet God did not love Israel instead of the other nations; he had chosen to love the other nations through Israel. Israel, though, often hated her neighbors, but God loved them. Listen as God mourns over the arrogance, pride, and ignorance (about God's love) that kept Moab from a saving relationship with him:

> We have heard the pride of Moab (He is exceedingly proud), Of his loftiness and arrogance and pride, And of the haughtiness of his heart." "I know his wrath," says the LORD, "But it is not right; His lies have made nothing right. Therefore I will wail for Moab, and I will cry out for all Moab; I will mourn for the men of Kir Heres. O vine of Sibmah! I will weep for you with the weeping of Jazer.... Therefore My heart shall wail like flutes for Moab, and like flutes My heart shall wail For the men of Kir Heres. Therefore the riches they have acquired have perished. (Jeremiah 48:29-36, NKJ)

Can you imagine the heart of God wailing like flutes for the people of Moab? Our Father is not cold and remote, or arbitrary and harsh, but rather he is warmhearted and compassionate. We know that God is present everywhere, God is all-powerful, and that God is all-knowing. God is also all-feeling.

While we can never plumb the depths of this infinite attribute of our heavenly Father, we can certainly examine some of its basic implications. God's feelings, his capacity for joy, sorrow, compassion, anger, patience, serenity, and eagerness soar infinitely high, dive infinitely deep, and are infinitely broad. "Therefore My heart shall wail like flutes for Moab." God cried out for the people of Moab. Arrogance and pride were destroying Moab. In the unfathomable depths of his being, God's heart throbbed in sympathetic pain for Moab, resonating like the funereal tones of a mournful flute. Again let us consider what Jeremiah reveals about the heart of our heavenly Father:

> My people are crushed, and so is my heart. I am horrified and mourn. If medicine and doctors may be found in Gilead, why aren't my people healed? I wish that my eyes were fountains of tears, so I could cry day and night for my people who were killed. (Jeremiah 8:21, 22; 9:1, CEV)

"My people are crushed, and so is my heart." It is time to turn away from Satan's lies about God (Repent). Satan has presented God as a cruel, arbitrary, and heartless tyrant. In fact, it is Satan that is a cruel, arbitrary, and venomous tyrant. God and Satan are waging a war to capture the hearts and minds of the entire universe. God won the war in Heaven by revealing his infinite love when Jesus died on Calvary's tree. The cross unmasked Satan as nothing else could.

Good and evil, love and hate, selfishness and unselfishness were contrasted as never before or since! Jesus won the decisive battle at the cross. However, the battle rages on in our hearts and minds. By the grace of God we can have a part in bringing this six-thousand-year-long war to a triumphant conclusion. Behold your God. Allow the cleansing power of his unselfish love to create a new heart within you. Heavenly Father, fill us with your love that we may let go of sin and self, and allow the healing springs that flow from Calvary to

113

wash us clean of sin and self, in Jesus's name, and for his sake, amen.

Human Suffering and the Cross

As Christians, we look to the cross as the place of infinite suffering. During WWII, the Holocaust claimed six million victims. The communist regime during the time of Stalin wiped out 60 million people. Idi Amin tortured unnumbered victims. During the dark ages, the Office of the Inquisition and papal directed armies tortured and murdered an estimated 200 million "heretics." The American Civil war and the two World Wars brought suffering and death to millions. More recently Cambodia's innocent people endured the Killing Fields. Consider the genocide of Rhodesia. Currently, the people of Somalia suffer from famine and genocidal atrocities.

Do not forget all the personal tragedies and sufferings too numerous and "ordinary" to include in any history or encyclopedia. All this Christ experienced on Calvary! He experienced the suffering of each innocent victim. He also experienced the guilt, shame, and self-condemnation of each guilty perpetrator. The vastness of pain, suffering, and guilt boggles the heart, mind, and soul.

I feel that I must try to understand some of the enormity of Christ's suffering, but my heart stands trembling at the edge of the endless, dark abyss of suffering that Jesus experienced for all of us. As my heart gazes into the murky depths, mercifully I find that God has shrouded most of it in impenetrable darkness. I know that it is beyond the capacity of my heart to grasp it. Yet the infinite suffering of God did not begin or end at the cross of Calvary. Our Saviour's unfathomable suffering on Calvary's tree is a window into the heart of our heavenly Father:

But now, at the end of these days, it has come to us through his Son, to whom he has given all things for a heritage, and through whom he made the order of the generations; Who, being the outshining of his glory, the true image of his substance, supporting all things by the word of his power, having given himself as an offering making

114

clean from sins, took his seat at the right hand of God in heaven; (Hebrews 1:2, 3, BBE)

Jesus is the "image of his substance," which means if we want to know about the Father we can look to the Son. Jesus is the outshining of his Father's glory. Jesus Christ is "… the Lamb slain from the foundation of the world" (Revelation 13:8, KJV). The blood of the slain Lamb is a symbol of God's suffering on account of sin. Jesus and the Father are one. Since the very beginning of the rebellion, sin has caused our God unimaginable suffering. Even now each person's sorrow vibrates in the heart of God with a deeper resonance than we, as humans can know. However, God endures all this for the prospect of the triumphant rejoicing that each redeemed soul brings. Behold God's amazing, self-sacrificing love, and patient endurance.

The physical sufferings of Jesus ended with his death on the cross. On the other hand, God's mental and emotional vulnerability continues unabated. The apostle Paul addresses this issue, "…seeing they crucify to themselves the Son of God afresh, and put him to an open shame" (Hebrews 6:6, KJV). When any precious soul turns away from our loving heavenly Father, it causes him infinite heartache. Jesus would much rather endure the cruel spikes of the cross and the soldier's vicious scourge than the mental and emotional suffering that our world of sin still causes him. Christ's physical sufferings on the cross are full of meaning. Nonetheless, his physical suffering cannot express the immense abyss of mental, spiritual, and emotional suffering that he endured on the cross, and that on account of his strong, sympathetic love, he continues to endure to this day.

If you have never given your heart and mind to Jesus, picture our tenderhearted Father as he cries out in anguish for you; "Turn, turn from your self-centered, self-destructive sin; And I will heal you. Why will you die?" See him rejoice over your soul as you see him as he is and fall in love with him!

Awake, O sword, against my shepherd,
and against the man that is my fellow,
saith the LORD of hosts.
(Zechariah 13:7, KJV)

6

The Cross and Beauty

Is Your Love Greater Than Mine?

My friend, Timmy, is a big-boned, man's man about six foot seven inches tall. He is one of the most sensitive and intense people that I know. God had rescued him from a harsh, self-destructive life. Like Mary Magdalene, Timmy responded wholeheartedly to Jesus's restoring love. Timmy came from a rough background and felt comfortable talking with the gang members and drug addicts on the toughest streets of East L.A. His favorite topic was Jesus.

The Holy Spirit worked through Timmy in a powerful way. God used Timmy's commanding presence, intense love, and his firsthand street knowledge to draw many people to Jesus. The Holy Spirit would often give Timmy specific directions. He would go to a specific street corner and find people that had been told to expect him, and were eager to hear about Jesus. Timmy's spirit would dance with exuberant joy each time someone accepted Jesus. His spirit soared higher than the strongest eagle can fly.

Like Mary Magdalene, Timmy fell back into the dark depths of sin. He says that he returned to the vomit. Recently, Timmy has been struggling to regain his close walk with God. From time to time the Holy Spirit has been using Timmy, but he still struggles to regain the intensity and warmth of his first

117

love.

Doubts and anxieties about his salvation sometimes harass Timmy. One day, the dark shadows of doubt enshrouded him. He decided to drive up into the mountains. Timmy loves to commune with God in nature. The gentle flow of a mountain stream helps bring peace to his soul.

Timmy cried out loud to God, "Have I gone too far, am I lost forever? Lord, are You just going to use me for a while and then throw me away into hell?" God answered Timmy with a question, "Timmy, is your love greater than Mine?" Surprised, Timmy responded, "No Lord, You are the Master of love; my love could never be greater than Yours." God asked Timmy another question, "Timmy, would you throw me into hell?" Shocked at the idea, Timmy responded, "No Lord, I would never do that to You!" God said, "Then why do you think I would do that to you? Is your love greater than Mine?"

Our love is not greater than God's love. Through the revelation of the cross, our Father gently leads us away from a relationship based on misunderstanding and fearfulness, to one based on the beauty and attractiveness of his character of love. The King of the Universe, the Almighty Creator-God wants a marriage-type relationship with us. In the past we have worshiped God as "Lord and Master." Now the Creator-God yearns for a relationship with us where we relate to him as a wife would to her husband:

> "And it shall be, in that day," Says the Lord, "That you will call Me 'My Husband,' And no longer call Me 'My Master,' "For I will take from her mouth the names of the Baals, And they shall be remembered by their name no more." (Hosea 2:16, 17, NKJ)

Master or Husband?

Nearly two thousand years ago, God's bride, his special people Israel, rejected him as her Husband in the person of Jesus. Israel was looking for someone to call *my Master*. Jesus Christ is the way, the truth, and the life. To reject the truth is to reject Christ.

All throughout their history, the children of Israel desired and prayed to God for vengeance upon their enemies. Israel rejected her Messiah because he did not conform to her preconceived opinions and her desire for a powerful, forceful commander to lead her nation's armies to victory over, revenge upon, and annihilation of her enemies.

Most Israelites hated Rome. Many Jewish leaders argued that Jesus couldn't be the promised Messiah because he refused to take political leadership. Jesus's life and words contradicted their arguments. He showed them, and us that the only true way to conquer one's enemies is to love them. The Israelites' rejection of Jesus and hatred of Rome sowed evil seed that led to the eventual destruction of Jerusalem in A.D. 70.

The special, chosen people, the organized church of Christ's time, desired a God that was a mixture of good and evil, love and hate, mercy and revenge. The religious leaders preferred and chose self-seeking Satan, in the person of Barabbas, over the humble, loving, and self-sacrificing Jesus.

If Israel had accepted Jesus and his principle of unselfish, unconditional love, the Israelites would have learned to love the Roman people. Rather than being destroyed in A.D. 70, Jerusalem would have been established forever. Through the awesome power of God's love, Israel could have conquered Rome and the world. If only Israel had accepted God's principle of self-sacrificing love! The world would be a much different and better place.

God's incredibly difficult challenge, throughout history, has been to reveal his glorious character of love to his chosen people without alienating them. God faces the same challenge today!

We view God through our sin-warped eyes. We want to live in our sins and yet be forgiven and resurrected with a Christ-like character. We still hate our enemies. I have heard Christians shriek with demonic joy when CNN showed live coverage of missiles and bombs killing Iraqi soldiers fleeing the battlefield. These Christians don't know Jesus.

119

Jesus is More than a Name

Imagine that two identical, beautiful beings, clothed in brilliant white light are sitting in your living room. Both claim to be Jesus. Both can work mighty miracles. One of them is Jesus, while the other is Satan, impersonating Jesus. With powerful, musical voices, both speak lovely truths from the Holy Scriptures.

Do you know Jesus's character and the principles of the Bible well enough to be able to distinguish between them? What questions would you ask? Remember that when it suited him, Satan would at times quote the Scriptures. For example, after Jesus's forty-day fast in the wilderness, Satan came to tempt Jesus, quoting scriptures. At other times he would mix just a little error with the truth. Keep in mind that Satan's deceptions will be so subtle that if it were possible, the very elect would be deceived (see Matthew 24:24). I invite you to get to know Jesus's character and personality better so that you can discern the imposter.

Satan will impersonate Jesus in a forceful way, "I have come in My Father's name [Character of love], and you do not receive Me. If another shall come in his own name [Mixed character of love and force] , him you will receive" (John 5:43, MKJ, brackets mine).

Some people desire a strong, vengeful God, who will quickly and forcefully put an end to sin and sinners. These people desire and will follow the imposter. Some want God to punish the wicked people who have caused righteous people so much grief and sorrow. How much value do we place on a sinner's soul? Our heavenly Father loves the vilest sinner to the very depths of his infinitely deep heart. Jesus's sacrifice proves that.

Only by meditating on and studying God's sacrifice on the cross of Calvary can we begin to understand God's infinite love that gives infinite worth to each individual human being. Should we grieve our Father's heart by praying for anyone's destruction? We should not even pray for the destruction of our nation's "enemies."

Let us truly pray, "in Jesus's name," by praying for our enemies. Let us pray and act in harmony with the brilliant light of God's love, his law of love that has remained unchanged from the deepest eternity. Then God's work of redeeming precious souls from sin and selfishness will yield a fruitful harvest.

God loves his enemies. He wants us to do the same. However, God's love is also just. God's mercy does not cancel out his justice. But remember, God's justice has little or nothing in common with human justice:

God's Justice

Let the wicked leave their way of life and change their way of thinking. Let them turn to the Lord, our God; he is merciful and quick to forgive. "My thoughts," says the Lord, "are not like yours, and my ways are different from yours. As high as the heavens are above the Earth, so high are my ways and thoughts above yours." (Isaiah 55:7, 8, TEV)

Man's idea of justice is an "eye for an eye" and a "tooth for a tooth." But God became a man in order to suffer the full consequences of our sins so that we would not have to. That ought to make it very clear that God's idea of justice and ours are so different as to be pretty much opposite.

If God hadn't forgiven sinners, we'd all be dead. Jesus's sacrifice proves that God had already forgiven us. Jesus didn't die in order to convince the Father to forgive us, but because he already had. Jesus's sacrifice convinces us that God forgives our sins. Remember, Jesus took our punishment, "Awake, O sword, against my shepherd, and against the man that is my fellow, saith the LORD of hosts: smite the shepherd, and the sheep shall be scattered" (Zechariah 13:7, KJV). Our heavenly Father is a God of terrible majesty and justice. Consider Calvary. In his wrath against sin, God unsheathed his sword of justice. With that sharp sword, God the Father pierced the heart of his Son, Jesus!

This is the same sword that God uses against all his enemies. God's sword of wrath is to allow the sinner, or in this case the sinless Sin-Bearer, to experience the horror of the full weight, the burning guilt, shame, condemnation, fiery indignation, and wrath of sin. The unrepentant sinner at the final judgment will experience his own guilt. Jesus experienced the total sin and guilt of the whole world. Indeed, that is a terrible sword!

The unrepentant sinner, warped and degraded by sin and guilt, would find the presence of Christ unbearable. To such a person the presence of Jesus would not be Heaven, but hell. Our God is a consuming fire. To the completely selfish person, the presence of our perfectly unselfish and loving Jesus would ignite their guilty conscience to burn with a white-hot flame. This is no arbitrary law of God. No. It is the inevitable consequence of hanging on to sin and guilt. In Heaven, Satan had claimed that God's law was arbitrary and unnecessary. On Earth, Satan continues to tell these same lies. Some Christians have been duped into helping promote Satan's lies in the name of God's grace.

In order to uphold, to fulfill, to magnify God's law of love, Jesus Christ had to accomplish the seemingly impossible. He had to demonstrate two apparently opposite and contrary things.

1. He had to demonstrate God's unchangeable, self-sacrificing, unconditional, infinite law of love, which describes his character, the foundation of his government.

2. He had to also demonstrate the inevitable, destructive, and everlasting consequences of sin.

Only as the eternal Son of God could Jesus reveal the height and depth of God's law of unselfish, unconditional love! Only as the Son of Man could he reveal the dense darkness and depth of sin! Behold the Man! Behold our God! Behold Jesus on the cross!

Force Cannot Change the Human Heart

Only by love is love awakened. God does not use, and does not need to use force, fear, or coercion. Indeed God cannot use force to make us love him. Sowing seeds of fear cannot yield a harvest of love.

Fear and coercion produce resistance and hatred. For God to try to force or coerce us into loving him would, in principle, be analogous to rape. These are not our heavenly Father's methods. God relies on the beauty of his character of love to win our hearts.

His kingdom is ruled and guided by love. Our Father has one mighty weapon, namely the presentation of the principle of unselfish, unconditional, self-sacrificing love. It just happens to be the most powerful weapon in the universe! Remember, God wants us to love him. To the degree that God's self-sacrificing love fills our hearts, God will be able to use his powerful weapon of love through us to reach the hearts of those around us. We are God's chosen instruments of war.

Love and freedom are inseparable. Fear and force cannot produce a harmonious, happy society. Heaven's foundation is only as secure as the strength of each person's loyalty. If any person were to doubt the goodness of the King, sooner or later Heaven's harmony would disintegrate.

As many an earthly tyrant could testify, fear and force can never bring true loyalty! During WWII, Hitler was the undisputed leader of Germany. He was an absolute dictator. Yet many of Germany's top leaders wanted to assassinate Hitler. Force cannot win loyalty. A true king leads by serving. Nor can money, material rewards, or the promise of streets of gold win or change our hearts. Only love can win our hearts. Only God's perfect love can win our complete loyalty.

Our Father's love is holy and pure. It is untainted by unwise human ideas, "In Him we have redemption through His blood, the forgiveness of sins, according to the riches of His grace which He made to abound toward us in all wisdom and prudence" (Ephesians 1:7, 8, NKJ). God, in His wisdom and prudence, decided that His grace could overcome our rebellion and sin. God's grace is the outpouring of His love through Jesus Christ, His Son, "This is how we know what love is: Christ gave his life for us. We too, then, ought to give our lives for our brothers and sisters!" (1John 3:16, TEV).

In order to see the full contrast between the Prince of light and the Prince of darkness we must distinguish which character attributes belong to which prince. Lucifer has made this as difficult as he possibly can. In Heaven, Lucifer subtly sowed the seeds of discontent. He then presented himself as trying to reconcile the discontented angels and the heavenly Father. Satan was a liar from the beginning.

Continuing the same policy today, Satan lies about the character of our heavenly Father. Some of his lies are very subtle and are very difficult to discern, "For false messiahs and false prophets will rise up and perform great miraculous signs and wonders so as to deceive, if possible, even God's chosen ones. See, I have warned you" (Matthew 24:24, 25, NLT).

Where he can get away with it, though, his lies are blasphemously blatant. Even insurance companies have policies that call certain natural disasters, such as lightning and earthquakes, "Acts of God."

Bible Interpretation In the Light of the Cross

However, Satan has focused his greatest attacks on the Christian church. The vast majority of Christians are entrenched in one of many denominations, with a set of creeds that depend on human tradition for interpreting the Bible. We look at Bible terms and define them using man's wisdom. We need to interpret and define Bible terms and concepts using the Bible itself. How can we sort out the multitude of different slants on the Bible?

The Bible is the book of truth. Yet, every denomination interprets the Bible differently. Has God left us without a standard to determine which interpretation is correct? No! Praise our heavenly Father, for he has given us a way to sort out truth from error. Praise God for the cross of Calvary! "For no other foundation can anyone lay than that which is laid, which is Jesus Christ" (1Corinthians 3:11, NKJ).

In the light of the cross, God's vengeance and wrath are far different from sinful man's anger and desire for revenge.

God's wrath is the granting of a solemn freedom, the freedom to choose Satan and his principles of selfishness, sin, and death. God's wrath against ungrateful, unrepentant sinners is to hand them over to Satan, their chosen master, who is called Abaddon, or Apollyon, the Destroyer. They are Satan's rightful prey. God must reluctantly withdraw his protection. To force his protective presence on those who have rejected him would make God a dictator. It would lend credence to Satan's charges against God.

Can you imagine how difficult it is for our loving heavenly Father to hand over his incurably rebellious children to the Destroyer? The final instance of this principle occurs as God's "strange act" (Isaiah 28:21, KJV). It takes place at the end of the seventh millennium, the millennium of rest. The relationship between the Father and his Son Jesus on the cross of Calvary gives us, with painful clarity, a preview to God's "strange act."

Remember that God does not change, "For I am the LORD, I change not; therefore ye sons of Jacob are not consumed" (Malachi 3:6, KJV). "Every good gift and every perfect gift is from above, and cometh down from the Father of lights, with whom is no variableness, neither shadow of turning" (James 1:17, KJV).

Everything that God feels, thinks, says, and does is based on principle. His principles never change. The foundation principle of God's government, indeed his very character, is self-sacrificing love. God is never confused between what is good and what is evil. Our Creator-God never bases his actions on the principles of Satan, the Destroyer. Never:

Do not keep company with those who have not faith: for what is there in common between righteousness and evil, or between light and dark? And what agreement is there between Christ and the Evil One? or what part has one who has faith with one who has not? (2Corinthians 6:14, 15, BBE)

125

Love Versus Force, Lies Versus Truth

Satan uses lies and deceit. He destroys and kills. Does God use the same methods that Satan does? Paul told us no. What does the apostle John say? "This then is the message which we have heard of him, and declare unto you, that God is light, and in him is no darkness at all" (1 John 1:5, KJV). Paul again asserts that God must be faithful to himself, "If we are faithless, he remains faithful—for he cannot deny himself" (2 Timothy 2:13, RSV). God is light. Light brings life. Darkness brings death. God has no darkness in him.

We see then, that our heavenly Father rules the universe based on principles, motives, and actions that are different, distinct, and totally opposite to Satan's principles, motives, and actions. God's government is based on benevolent love.

Our Father delights in creating, giving life, sustaining life, loving others, and being loved in return. Satan's government is based on lies, selfishness, greed, fear, hope of reward, punishment, destruction, and murder. Satan delights in promoting rebellion, sin, suffering, and death. Satan delights in killing God's beloved creatures.

Our loving heavenly Father never cooperates with Satan in his acts of destruction! God never uses the same methods that Satan does! Satan and those who subscribe to the principles of his government seek to exalt themselves by any means. Not so in God's government. The end result that God seeks is a totally free society of intelligent, loving beings living in peace and harmony.

Only by love is love awakened. That is the message of the cross of Christ. God poured out his love through his Son, Jesus. We can only love God because he first loved us. Fear, even the mortifying fear of an eternally burning hell, cannot produce love. Hope of reward, even the hope of walking streets of gold and eating from the tree of life cannot produce love. Love cannot be bought.

In his infinite wisdom, God has designed the human heart with the capacity to love and to be loved. Having designed the human heart in this way, God has chosen not to, and indeed, cannot use the threat of an eternally burning hell, or the hope of Heaven to draw us into a love relationship with him. Jesus showed us that the door to eternal life is only opened by the mighty power of self-sacrificing love that places the value of others above one's own existence. This is the message of the cross.

Precious soul, Jesus invites you to behold, to meditate on the height and depth of his self-sacrificing, infinite love for you. Choose to allow the Holy Spirit to begin to write God's law of love in your heart. Eternal life begins on Earth, here, and now, the moment that you begin to respond to the awesome beauty of God's character, his principle, his law of unconditional, self-sacrificing love.

That response to God's love is called faith. It is the only kind of faith that will save. Pray with me. Heavenly Father, I bow before you in awe of the mighty power of your self-sacrificing love! Oh Father, soften my sin-hardened, selfish heart; pour your love into my heart until love for you and your children fills me, leaving no room for bitter self-centeredness. Thank you, Father, for answering my prayer in the name of Jesus, amen.

Love that Would Die for an Enemy

Our God is not like Dr. Jekyll and Mr. Hyde, kind, and full of goodness and light during the day of the proclamation of the gospel, but turning into a destructive monster, throwing sinners into the fires of hell when the night of human probation closes! The Roman god Janus is portrayed as a two-faced god. Our Father is not like that. The King of the universe does not have multiple personalities. God's love and kindness flow out from his heart equally to the good and bad alike:

> But I say to you, Do not make use of force against an evil man; but to him who gives you a blow on the right side of your face let the left be turned. (Matthew 5:39, BBE)

> But I tell you to love your enemies and pray for anyone

who mistreats you. Then you will be acting like your Father in heaven. He makes the sun rise on both good and bad people. And he sends rain for the ones who do right and for the ones who do wrong. If you love only those people who love you, will God reward you for that? Even tax collectors love their friends. If you greet only your friends, what's so great about that? Don't even unbelievers do that? But you must always act like your Father in heaven. (Matthew 5:44-48, CEV)

"But I tell you to love your enemies...Then you will be acting like your Father in heaven." God loves his enemies. God is no respecter of persons. God loves the sinner and the righteous equally. God is love. God does not change. When the sinner crosses the point of no return, God's love for him remains unchanged. It is the sinner's heart that has closed itself to God's love, but God loves him still. In the Bible, Jesus clearly reveals God's love for a sinful, rebellious, and dying world, "For God so loved the world, that he gave his only begotten Son, that whosoever believeth in him should not perish, but have everlasting life" (John 3:16, KJV). Paul restated the same everlasting principle:

> For when we were still without strength, at the right time Christ gave his life for evildoers. Now it is hard for anyone to give his life even for an upright man, though it might be that for a good man someone would give his life. But God has made clear his love to us, in that, when we were still sinners, Christ gave his life for us. (Romans 5:6-8, BBE)

God loves sinners. The deeper their darkness and rebellion, the stronger his yearning to rescue them. Perhaps the most striking example of God's love for his enemies is Jesus's treatment of Judas:

> And as He was yet speaking, behold, Judas came, one of the Twelve. And with him came a great crowd with swords

and clubs, being sent from the chief priests and elders of the people. And he who betrayed Him gave them a sign, saying, Whomever I shall kiss, He is the one, lay hold on Him. And coming up to Jesus immediately, he said, Hail, Master! And *he* kissed Him. And Jesus said to him, Friend, why are you here? Then they came and laid hands on Jesus and took Him. (Matthew 26:47-50, MKJ)

Jesus called Judas, the betrayer, *friend.* In this world, trust and friendship must be earned. Jesus showed us that in the kingdom of Heaven, friendship is a gift that is freely given to all, even to the man who betrayed him to death. Jesus did not condemn or in any way punish Judas. Jesus loved Judas and called him friend.

The Power of Love

If we wish to become part of the kingdom of Heaven, we too must treat others as friends. We mustn't demand that people earn the right to be treated as friends. We will get hurt and meet with disappointment. But never more than Jesus did! While, Jesus's infinite love opened his heart to greater pain that any other person, it has also given him greater joy.

Your throne, O God, is forever and ever; the scepter of Your kingdom is a scepter of uprightness. You love righteousness and hate wickedness; on account of this God, Your God, has anointed You with the oil of gladness more than Your fellows. (Psalm 45:6, 7, RSV)

The sacrifice of Jesus upon the cross reveals the strength, the depth, and the power of God's love. Behold the Son of God. Part of Jesus's suffering on the cross came from his knowledge of the malignant power of sin. He knew that through constant exposure to it, humanity had become ignorant of its destructive power. We are Jesus's brothers and sisters. He loves us. He doesn't want to see sin destroy our souls.

For months, I struggled and prayed daily, asking God,

"How did Jesus become our Sin-Bearer?" It took time, but the Holy Spirit, through scripture, showed me that the answer must be understood through his love. The stronger, deeper, and purer the love for a family member, the more intense the anguish when watching them slip away into death. Jesus's love for us was, is, and will always be infinitely deep, strong, and pure. It was Jesus's incredible love that opened his heart to the depths of suffering. That is how he became our Sin-Bearer.

The interaction between the Father and the Son on the cross illustrates how God brings an end to sin. Christ felt the despair and agony that unrepentant sinners will feel when God reveals to them that they have irrevocably hardened their hearts against his mercy. On the cross, Christ felt the same destructive anguish and guilt that sinners resurrected in the second resurrection will feel when they face their life's record in contrast with the record of Christ's life and death.

Christ asserts that which you sow you will also reap. God's justice is like the cycle of the seasons. Rain falls, enters the river, flows to the ocean, evaporates, and forms clouds, and falls as rain again. What goes around, comes around. Be sure your sins will find you out. The wages of sin is death. Sin is more destructive than most realize. But familiarity with sin makes us comfortable with it. As humans, we have gotten used to, familiar with sin. We deceive ourselves supposing that sin is not really that bad. It is that bad. In fact, it's even worse. Sin is horrendously self-destructive. If God the Father hadn't stepped in to shield Lucifer and his angels from the natural consequences of sin, they would have self-destructed long ago. After the sabbath millennium of rest, the wicked angels and unbelieving humans will experience the full destructive power of sin.

God will perform this strange act by allowing his beloved, lost children to step beyond his shielding love and experience the natural results of their determined, rebellious, and self-destructive course of sin. They will reap what they have sown. They have rejected the law of life. The lost have formed habits, thought patterns, feelings, and actions that have resulted in a character that cannot survive. They have chosen the law of sin and death. God visits his wrath on rebels by allowing each lost angel and person to judge himself.

God is loving and wise. From the depths of eternity he saw the natural consequences of rebellion against his law of life. Christ on the cross of Calvary shows us the root cause and the horrible end results of the malignant cancer of sin. At the same time he provides the only cure for the plague of sin, and shows us how to apply it. Only when we rest on God's love as Christ did, can our Father rescue us from sin and death.

The wrath of God, his law, and justice must be studied in the beautiful light that streams from the cross of Calvary. If there is any apparent contradiction, discrepancy, or tension between the cross of Calvary and our understanding of any idea, doctrine or teaching, principle or story in the Old or New Testament, we must change our understanding of these until there is perfect harmony between them and the truth of the love of God as displayed by Jesus on the cross.

God has not destroyed Satan and his sympathizers. God does not destroy, compel, nor coerce anyone. The continued existence of sin for six thousand years is strong evidence for God's patience, mercy, wisdom, and hatred of force and coercion. Force is contrary to, and in fact, the opposite of, his glorious character of love. God has written, with his own finger, on stone tablets, the foundation principles of his government and his glorious character of love. The life and death of Christ exemplified, honored, and expanded our understanding of the Ten Commandments. His throne, his authority rest upon our understanding of his goodness, mercy, and love. The demonstration of these principles is God's mighty weapon, one edge of his sword of truth. God's unselfish love is the very foundation of his throne.

*Don't suppose that
I came to do away with the
Law and the Prophets.
I did not come to do away with them,
but to give them their full meaning.*
(Matthew 5:17, CEV)

*The law of the Lord is perfect,
converting the soul.*
(Psalm 19:7, KJV)

7

God's Law of Love

The Laws of Physics and the Law of God

The bright spring sun casts a rosy glow as it streams through the tinted windows of Tom's new luxury car. He is a new Christian, a new member of Bill's steadily growing, small-town church. Bill has been explaining to him his understanding that the law was nailed to the cross. We are not under the law, but grace, Bill informs him. Christ kept the law so that we don't have to.

Just then they hear a brief siren and see flashing red lights behind them. They both get that sinking feeling in their stomach. Bill asks Tom, "How fast are you going?" "Forty" he says. Bill groans, "Forty? Oh no, and this is a school zone." As Tom pulls to the side of the road, Bill silently prays. To Bill's relief and slight embarrassment the police officer turns out to be Jessica, a Tuesday-night Bible-study partner that they both know.

Tom lowers the window as Jessica approaches the car. The three of them exchange greetings. Then Jessica crosses her arms and asks, "Tom, did you realize how fast you were going?" "No," Tom responds, "I just got this car and it's a little quieter and smoother riding than what I'm used to. Also, I was a little distracted by our conversation. We were talking about being under grace and not having to keep the law." Bill's face begins to feel a bit warm and he knows that his cheeks match

133

the glow from the tinted windows.

Jessica frowns and smiles, "Hmmm, as an officer of the law I do not agree with that! But I'm sure that a verbal warning will be sufficient. Please be more careful." "Thank you, I certainly will," Tom responds, "and by the way, we're going to continue this conversation at that new café, just down the street from the church. Would you like to join us before the study this evening?" Her eyes sparkling her interest, Jessica agrees, "I can be at the Half-Moon Café about 5:30." Bill and Tom nod their agreement.

The three of them choose an outside table, and place their orders. "Judging by the smells coming from the kitchen this café is going to be a success," Bill quips. Tom and Jessica laughingly agree. Bill has prayer for the conversation and study. Jessica mentions that she has been reading about cosmology recently. She feels that some of the things she has been learning have given her a new perspective on the law of God. Curious, Bill asks Jessica to share what she has learned.

Jessica pauses to collect her thoughts and then begins, "The sun, planets, moons, comets, and asteroids in our solar system follow God's laws of gravity, inertia, etc. The billions of stars in our Milky Way galaxy, the billions of other galaxies (each containing billions of stars), all these follow the laws that God has established. God has delicately and precisely balanced the laws that govern the incomprehensibly massive galaxies and the tiny atoms." Bill and Tom both nod in agreement.

"One of the books I have been reading is *A Brief History Of Time* by Stephen Hawking. Listen to what I found starting on page 129:

'The laws of science, as we know them at present, contain many fundamental numbers, like the size of the electric charge of the electron and the ratio of the masses of the proton and the electron.
The remarkable fact is that the values of these numbers seem to have been very finely adjusted to make possible the development of life. For example, if the electric charge

of the electron had been only slightly different, stars either would have been unable to burn hydrogen and helium, or else they would not have exploded... it seems clear that there are relatively few ranges of values for the numbers that would allow the development of any form of intelligent life... One can take this... as evidence of a divine purpose in creation..."'[1]

Jessica continues, "I see you brought your Bibles. Lets hear David's song about the glory of God's laws that govern his creation. First he praises God's natural laws, the laws of physics. Tom, would you read the first six verses of Psalm 19?" Tom opens his brand-new *New Living Translation* and begins:

"The heavens tell of the glory of God. The skies display his marvelous craftsmanship. Day after day they continue to speak; night after night they make him known. They speak without a sound or a word; their voice is silent in the skies; yet their message has gone out to all the earth, and their words to all the world.
The sun lives in the heavens where God placed it. It bursts forth like a radiant bridegroom after his wedding. It rejoices like a great athlete eager to run the race. The sun rises at one end of the heavens and follows its course to the other end. Nothing can hide from its heat."

"Thank you, Tom," Jessica smiles and then explains, "Psalm 19 is a poetic parable. The sun, moon, and stars unerringly follow Gods physical laws, bringing us light, warmth, ocean tides, as well as joy, and a sense of awe."
Tom interjects, "Yes, God has designed the laws of physics that govern the universe to support life. So, Jessica," Tom asks, "How does this relate to the Ten Commandments?" "Well," she answers, "If the physical laws were even slightly different the universe would be unable to support life. Any change from God's laws would bring death.
For example, if the force of gravity were stronger by the

smallest amount, the universe would have rapidly collapsed upon itself and life couldn't exist. If the force of gravity were weaker by the most minuscule amount, the environment of the universe would not be suitable for life. If the strong and weak forces that govern the nucleus of atoms were different by the tiniest amount, the universe would be left with only hydrogen atoms, or conversely, only extremely massive atoms. The proton and the electron have the same amount of, but opposite charge. Yet the proton is 1836 times more massive than the electron. Were this ratio any different, there would be few or no elements and therefore no life.

Our kind, loving, and wise heavenly Father delicately and precisely designed the laws of physics to support life. As far as humans have been able to observe, these intricate, finely balanced laws are perfect and unchanging. What a testimony for our Creator-God! He is perfect and he never changes. When he establishes something, it will stand. Praise God, his laws are unchanging! Our heavenly Father designed the universe and it's laws perfectly.

If any scientist were to claim that the laws of physics were no longer necessary for life, no one would believe him. In any case, whether or not a person is aware of the laws, or principles of physics, one's life and happiness depend on them. In Psalm 19, David makes the case that the Ten Commandments are just as important for life and happiness as the laws of physics that govern the universe. To more specifically answer your question, God's grace does not extinguish his law, but rather puts it in its proper perspective."

"Bill," Jessica asks, "Would you read the rest of Psalm 19?" Bill puts on his glasses, opens his well-used King James Bible, and begins to read:

"The law of the LORD is perfect, converting the soul: the testimony of the LORD is sure, making wise the simple. The statutes of the LORD are right, rejoicing the heart: the commandment of the LORD is pure, enlightening the eyes. The fear of the LORD is clean, enduring for ever: the judgments of the LORD are true and righteous altogether. More to be desired are they than gold, yea, than much fine gold: sweeter also than honey and the honeycomb. Moreover by them is thy servant warned: and in keeping of them there is great reward. Who can understand his errors? cleanse thou me from secret faults. Keep back thy servant also from presumptuous sins; let them not have dominion over me: then shall I be upright, and I shall be innocent from the great transgression. Let the words of my mouth, and the meditation of my heart, be acceptable in thy sight, O LORD, my strength, and my redeemer."

"Thank you, Bill," Jessica said, her eyes sparkling, "David uses the sun as an illustration, an analogy to show the parallels between God's laws governing the physical world and his Ten Commandments governing our spiritual and relational life. Just as there is an underlying principle that can describe each of the four basic forces of physics, so also, there is an underlying principle that describes each of the Ten Commandments."

Tom's face brightens as he catches the direction Jessica is heading and he interjects, "I see, you are talking about the Grand Unifying Theory that would explain, or unify the basic forces, the force of gravity, the electromagnetic force, the strong nuclear force, and the weak nuclear force. You are pointing out that as Christians we also should examine the spiritual laws of God to see if we can find the grand unifying law or principle of the Ten Commandments."

"Yes." Jessica confirms, "Look at what James declares, 'For whoever shall keep the whole law, and yet stumble in one point, he is guilty of all' (James 2:10, NKJ). The Holy Spirit has led me to understand this principle to be self-sacrificing love. Jesus summarizes the Ten Commandments:

Jesus said to him, "'You shall love the Lord your God with all your heart, with all your soul, and with all your mind.' This is the first and great commandment. And the second is like it: 'You shall love your neighbor as yourself.' On these

137

two commandments hang all the Law and the Prophets."
(Matthew 22:37-40, NKJ)

Unselfish love is the foundation principle that governs all healthy, successful relationships. Our kind, loving, heavenly Father has delicately designed the laws that govern our interaction with him and with each other, for the purpose of nurturing happy, loving relationships.

Any deviation from God's Ten Commandments is sin and leads inevitably to unhappiness and death. As far as humans have been able to observe, these intricate, finely balanced laws are perfect and unchanging. What a testimony for our Creator-God! He is perfect and he never changes. When he establishes something, it will stand forever. Praise God, his laws are unchanging!"

Jessica continues, "The light of God's character of love, his 'Ten Words' shed light and joy to all who understand and obey the deep spiritual principle found in them. Jesus, through his life and death demonstrated and confirmed the unchanging, the eternal beauty of God's Ten Commandments, his law of love." Then Jessica muses, "I wonder if Jesus had Psalm 19 in mind when he said, 'For assuredly, I say to you, till heaven and earth pass away, one jot or one tittle will by no means pass from the law till all is fulfilled'" (Matthew 5:18, NKJ).

Bill looks up from his Bible and responds, "I think you might have something there."

The physical food arrives and the conversation changes to Tom's search for a house.

I invite you, dear reader, to join me in continuing to search the laws that govern our heavenly Father's universe, keeping in mind the message of Christ's sacrifice on the cross of Calvary.

The Ten Commandments, God's law, also called the tables of the testimony, express the principle of altruistic love, the essence of God's holy character, the law of life, the very foundation of his government. The letters, the words of the Ten Commandments, are only a beginning point in understanding our heavenly Father's holy character, his law of love.

Jesus, the Law Unfolded

The law of God is the written expression of his character of love. God is love. God wrote the Ten Commandments with his own finger, on tables of stone. God keeps his own law, "If we are not faithful, he remains faithful, because he cannot be false to himself" (2Timothy 2:13, TEV).

The cross proves that God would rather die than set aside his law of self-sacrificing love. The principles of God's law extend beyond the heights and depths of infinity. Jesus Christ, the Son of God, in his life and especially in his sacrifice, reveal and demonstrate the deeper things of God's law. Christ showed that in order to keep the law we must be willing to value the salvation of others more than our own eternal life:

> Then Jesus said to the disciples, "If any of you wants to be my follower, you must put aside your selfish ambition, shoulder your cross, and follow me. If you try to keep your life for yourself, you will lose it. But if you give up your life for me, you will find true life. (Matthew 16:24, 25, NLT)

Those who have God's law of love written in their hearts and minds will follow in Christ's footsteps. As Christ was willing to die the death that sinners deserve, those who know God well are also willing, even eager, to trade places with perishing sinners.

Listen to Jesus, "I have a baptism to be baptized with; and how I am constrained until it is accomplished!" (Luke 12:50, RSV). The apostle Paul understood the message of the cross. Paul too, loved his fellow Israelites, even the ones who were trying to kill him. He loved his enemies more than his own life, even more than his own soul:

> In the presence of Christ, I speak with utter truthfulness—I do not lie—and my conscience and the Holy Spirit confirm that what I am saying is true. My heart is filled with bitter sorrow and unending grief for my people, my Jew-

ish brothers and sisters. I would be willing to be forever cursed—cut off from Christ! —if that would save them. (Romans 9:1-3, NLT)

Moses knew God as his personal friend. Moses had spent so much time with God that his feelings and thoughts came to resemble God's thoughts and feelings, "Inside the Tent of Meeting, the Lord would speak to Moses face to face, as a man speaks to his friend" (Exodus 33:11, NLT). Moses knew God well and understood his law of self-sacrificing love:

The next day Moses told the people, "This is a terrible thing you have done. But I will go back to the Lord to see if I can do something to keep this sin from being held against you." Moses returned to the Lord and said, "The people have committed a terrible sin. They have made a gold idol to be their god. But I beg you to forgive them. If you don't, please wipe my name out of your book." (Exodus 32:30-32, CEV)

Moses had spent so much time talking with God that his character had become changed into the image of God's character. Like God, Moses loved his rebellious, sinful brothers and sisters so much that he was willing to be cut off from life, to be blotted out from God's book of life! Moses was not more loving than God! Moses' love was a gift from God. God too, loved Israel more than his own life.

God's Law, his Ten Commandments, have a deeper spiritual meaning than most religious people have begun to appreciate, "For we know that the law is spiritual, but I am carnal, sold under sin" (Romans 7:14, NKJ). Our self-centered, carnal nature cannot by itself ever hope to come into harmony with God's law of love. Still, we are instructed to keep the law, not the mere letter of the law, but rather the deep spiritual principles of the law of love.

The gospel without the law is just as meaningless as the law of God without the gospel. The gospel is the law lived out

140

in the life and sacrifice of Jesus, and the law is the gospel (the life of Jesus), in written form. If God's law, the law of Heaven could have been changed, Jesus would not have had to die. Jesus did not die to set aside or diminish the claims of God's law, but to reveal it more fully. Even here on Earth one can see the importance of the rule of law.

The U.S. Constitution and God's Law

God has richly blessed the United States. It is a democratic, constitutional republic. The actions of our nation and its government are guided and constrained by a body of law. The foundation, the cornerstone of that body of law is the constitution. The constitution recognizes and guarantees certain God-given rights and freedoms, such as freedom of speech and the freedom of religion. Our republic, based on the rule of law, is far superior to a pure democracy.

In a pure democracy a mere 51% of the people could trample on the freedoms, rights, and privileges of the other 49% of the people. A pure democracy is a dangerous and potentially tyrannical form of government. Our republic, on the other hand, is constrained, required by the constitution to protect the weak from the strong, the poor from the rich, and the minority from the majority. In theory, all receive equal protection under the law. Praise God for our republican form of government!

Praise God for inspiring our founding fathers to create our noble and beautiful constitution. As long as our great country conforms to the grand principles of liberty and justice for all, it will continue to receive God's blessings; religious liberty is most important in our Father's eyes.

The government of Heaven is a monarchy with a republican form of government. Heaven too, is governed by the rule of law. Heaven too, has a constitution—the law of unconditional, unselfish, noble, self-sacrificing love. God himself designed the constitution of Heaven. It is a description, an expression of his nature, his character, and his personality.

God shared the constitution of Heaven with humans. He wrote Heaven's constitution with his own finger, on tables of stone, and gave them to Moses. Through his life, death, and resurrection, Jesus Christ, the Son of God, expresses, demonstrates, fulfills, and establishes the eternal law of God. Jesus, on the cross of Calvary ushered in, proclaimed, and established the grace of God. The grace of God is an expression of the saving power of God's character of benevolent love, his law.

God's grace through the death of Jesus elaborates and clarifies his eternal law, his unchanging character of unselfish love. God's grace and God's Law are not antagonistic, opposite, or contrary to one another. Rather, they are different modes of expression of the same principle, which is an expression of the nature, the eternal character of God, which is self-sacrificing love.

Jesus's life and death displays God's love for humanity. It is the means of restoring his kingdom on this Earth. Our Creator, Jesus, the King of Heaven, became a Man to plant this seed of love, to reclaim his children. How he longs for his commandment to be fulfilled, "This is My commandment, that you love one another as I have loved you" (John 15:12, MKJ).

When we love people as Jesus loves them, then his image will be restored in us. Then his kingdom will be established. Then all things will be accomplished. We will have entered into eternal life. We will be ready for Heaven, for we will have heaven's eternal principles in our hearts.

In the light of God's self-sacrificing love, the dry, dead, letter of the law, written in stone, shines as a precious gem of great spiritual brilliance and beauty. May the Holy Spirit open to our hearts and minds a broader view of our gracious heavenly Father's law of love.

God's Law of love, the truth, the beauty of Jesus can be partially experienced. But words cannot fully capture this experience. Its height soars past our ability to express it. Its breadth exceeds our intellectual capacity to categorize it. Our imagination can only dimly visualize the shadowy forms of a love that is infinite and beyond the reach of mere words:

Let the wicked leave their way of life and change their

way of thinking. Let them turn to the Lord, our God; he is merciful and quick to forgive. "My thoughts," says the Lord, "are not like yours, and my ways are different from yours. As high as the heavens are above the earth, so high are my ways and thoughts above yours." (Isaiah 55:7-9, TEV)

The Ten Commandments Written in our Hearts

Our heavenly Father longs to re-create his beautiful, holy, merciful, self-sacrificing love within each of his rebellious children. If we give him permission, the mighty Creator-God will write his eternal law of love in our hearts and minds:

And I will also give you a new heart, and I will put a new spirit within you. And I will take away the stony heart out of your flesh, and I will give to you a heart of flesh. And I will put My Spirit within you and cause you to walk in My statutes, and you shall keep My judgments and do them. (Ezekiel 36:26, 27, GLT)

I will run the way of thy commandments, when thou shalt enlarge my heart. (Psalm 119:32, KJV)

Give me understanding, and I shall keep thy law; yea, I shall observe it with my whole heart. (Psalm 119:34, KJV)

We cannot give God our permission with a mere set of words. Our permission must come from a deep desire in our hearts and minds, which can only happen as we see the beauty of Jesus's character of self-sacrificing love, fall in love with him, and long to be like him. By beholding we become changed.

When from the heart, we desire to be like Jesus, our mighty Re-creator God, through the power of his Holy Spirit, will begin to change us into his image. That is how God writes his law in our hearts. In our character we will begin to resemble, to imitate God. Imitation is the highest, the sincerest form of praise and worship. It is worship acceptable and pleasing to our Father.

Worship can only come from a heart changed by the Holy Spirit to become more like God. All else is an empty form; it is not of faith, but has slipped into presumption. Presumption gloats, "God, I'm so glad that You have decided to save me as I am, but I can never be loving, forgiving, merciful, kind, and unselfish as You are." Faith sighs, "Father, thank You for showing me your incredible love, save me, heal my self-centered, sinful heart; empower me to love and forgive others as You do."

Although we are finite humans, we can grasp the underlying principles, the beauty of God's law, his character of love. From experience I can relate to you that God knows how to exchange the bitter tears of contrition and sorrow on account of self-centeredness and sin for the soaring sweetness, the soft peace, the bright joy of entering into the presence of the One altogether lovely.

The Holy Spirit will give us an understanding of the right relationship between the law of love and the gospel of salvation only as we more deeply appreciate Jesus's sacrifice and the reasons for it. And only as we choose to follow in Jesus's footsteps.

As we humbly study and meditate, searching the Bible for an understanding of the glorious theme of salvation, the Holy Spirit will open our hearts and minds. Wise King Solomon points out to us that "The way of the righteous is like the first gleam of dawn, which shines ever brighter until the full light of day" (Proverbs 4:18, NLT).

I urge you, dear reader, stretch your heart and mind, seek to expand your understanding of the height and depth of God's self-sacrificing love. Do not let the things of this world distract you. The foundation of Heaven, God's law, the principle of self-sacrificing love is the mystery of God; it is the truth, the plan of salvation. Please do not be satisfied with a shallow understanding of salvation, but seek to behold it in all its greatness. Behold the love of God.

They Shall not Hurt or Destroy

In our search for a deeper, purer understanding of the principles of God's law of love, let us consider the order of things in the new Earth. Isaiah gives us a lovely vision of what God has in mind for us:

Also the wolf shall dwell with the lamb, and the leopard shall lie down with the kid; and the calf and the cub lion and the fatling together; and a little child shall lead them. And the cow and the bear shall feed; their young ones shall lie down together; and the lion shall eat straw like the ox. And the suckling child shall play on the hole of the asp, and the weaned child shall put his hand on the adder's den. They shall not hurt nor destroy in all My holy mountain; for the earth shall be full of the knowledge of the LORD, as the waters cover the sea. (Isaiah 11:6-9, MKJ)

The reason that nothing will "hurt or destroy on all my holy mountain…" is because in the new Earth everything and everyone will know God and his perfect law of love! Everyone will live in God's law of love. Far from doing away with God's law, grace honors, and expands our understanding of it. Grace enables God's law of love to be written on our hearts.

Humanity's dominion over the Earth will be fully restored. Animals will respect and trust us, lions will be gentle, hummingbirds will delight to be near us, and skunks won't stink! Everything that smells bad is a result of sin; it is Satan's doing. All parasites, all molds, all decay, disease, death, destruction, and damnation are perversions, a departure from God's design, a result of sin. All these are part of Satan's supposed improvements on God's perfect, orderly, and loving plan.

God is King, but he is not a dictator. All humanity must be free to choose between God's law of love and Satan's perverted law of selfishness. In order for that to happen, God must allow humanity to see and experience the ugly, deceptive, and destructive results of Satan's rebellion in full contrast with the principles of Heaven, which are harmony, peace, mercy, and

145

justice, all springing from the pure fountain of self-sacrificing love.

God's Eternal Law of Love

In the first chapter, "War in Heaven," we saw how Lucifer tried to force God to change his law, the foundation of his throne. Lucifer, having fallen, has become Satan, the Adversary. He still attacks the law of God. If Satan can convince Christians that the law of God has been changed or set aside, he will have won a great victory. Even so, God through Christ fulfilled and established the eternal nature of his law. Mere man cannot change God's eternal law, "Concerning thy testimonies, I have known of old that thou hast founded them for ever" (Psalm 119:152, KJV).

God's grace is a living expression of his character of self-sacrificing love. God's law is a written expression of his righteous character of self-sacrificing love, "Thy righteousness is an everlasting righteousness, and thy law is the truth" (Psalm 119:142, KJV). The Ten Commandment laws are truth. Grace would never set the truth aside. "My tongue shall speak of thy word: for all thy commandments are righteousness" (Psalm 119:172, KJV). Grace delights in and establishes righteousness; it would never set righteousness aside. Jeremiah proclaims God's righteousness:

> Behold, the days come, saith the LORD, that I will raise unto David a righteous Branch, and a King shall reign and prosper, and shall execute judgment and justice in the earth. In his days Judah shall be saved, and Israel shall dwell safely: and this is his name whereby he shall be called, THE LORD OUR RIGHTEOUSNESS. (Jeremiah 23:5, 6, KJV)

Paul continues the same theme:

> But of him are ye in Christ Jesus, who of God is made unto us wisdom, and righteousness, and sanctification, and

redemption. (1Corinthians 1:30, KJV)

How could God's righteousness be contrary to the gospel? It is impossible! The law and the gospel are different facets of the same gem. That gem is God's character, his heart of love. Man's keeping the law of God has never been a means of salvation. Though perfect and beautiful, God's law, in its written form, cannot save us. Yet God's law, expressed through the life, death, and resurrection of Jesus Christ does have saving power. Beholding the power of God's benevolent love, our faith rests securely on Jesus. Our faith in Jesus is the means that God uses to pour out his saving power, his grace. Faith is not our Savior, Jesus is. He saves us from both the guilt and the power of sin.

Paul informs us in Hebrews, chapter 11, that Enoch, Noah, Abraham, Sarah, Isaac, Jacob, Joseph, and Rahab were all saved by faith, faith that looked forward to Christ's sacrifice. Remember that these all lived before the law was given in its written form. Moses, Gideon, Barak, Samson, Jepthah, David, Samuel, and unnumbered others, lived after the law was given, but before the time of Christ. Nevertheless, all were saved by faith alone.

The works of the law saved none of these! Animal sacrifices saved no one, "Neither is there salvation in any other: for there is none other name under heaven given among men, whereby we must be saved" (Acts 4:12, KJV). To be under the law does not mean to be saved by works, for no one has ever been saved by their works. Faith in Jesus Christ is the only path of salvation for any human being that has ever lived, or ever will live.

A Two-Part Harmony

Jesus kept the Ten Commandments perfectly. Our Saviour gave us beautiful insights into the two-part divine harmony of his Father's law:

Master, which is the great commandment in the law? Jesus said unto him, Thou shalt love the Lord thy God with all

147

thy heart, and with all thy soul, and with all thy mind. This is the first and great commandment. And the second is like unto it, Thou shalt love thy neighbour as thyself. On these two commandments hang all the law and the prophets. (Matthew 22:36-40, KJV)

Jesus here explains that the first four of the Ten Commandments are summed up by "Thou shalt love the Lord thy God with all thy heart, and with all thy soul, and with all thy mind." Love for God is an everlasting principle. The cross of Christ did not do away with that principle. No. The cross established, or fulfilled that principle. The Ten Commandments guide and direct us in establishing a good relationship with our heavenly Father. The Father and the Son are one; they are in harmony, "I and my Father are one" (John 10:30, KJV). The Father did not establish the law in order for the Son to do away with it, "Think not that I have come to abolish the law and the prophets; I have come not to abolish them but to fulfil them" (Matthew 5:17, RSV).

The second part of the law is "Thou shalt love thy neighbour as thyself." The last six of the Ten Commandments focus on the principles of human relationships and interaction. These principles will never pass away. The apostle Paul uses different words to restate the same principle:

Love one another; for he who loves his neighbor has fulfilled the law. The commandments, "You shall not commit adultery, You shall not kill, You shall not steal, You shall not covet," and any other commandment, are summed up in this sentence, "You shall love your neighbor as yourself." Love does no wrong to a neighbor; therefore love is the fulfilling of the law. (Romans 13:8-10, RSV)

Christ's life and death unfolded the beautiful principle of benevolent love that is the essence of God's Law of life, his "Ten Words." Jesus went from place to place healing all who came to him. He raised the dead. He fed the hungry.

The people were attracted to Jesus because he showed as well as told them that their heavenly Father loved them. Today, we as Christians will find our witness more effective if we can demonstrate God's love in real, practical ways. Religion is more than learning and speaking the right words and doctrines; it is living out the principle of self-sacrificing love that gives life to our profession of faith.

Jesus Lived the Law, He Didn't Condemn

Jesus explained that he had not come to condemn the world, but to save it. Prostitutes, thieves, murderers, sinners of all classes, and innocent little children, felt loved and comfortable in his presence. Jesus's eyes and words revealed to those around him that he could read their heart and soul. His eyes also revealed that he loved them, and did not condemn them. Consider the woman at the well. Jesus told her that she was living in sin, yet she knew that he loved her. She called the whole town to come and hear him (see John 4:4-42).

Jesus's life, work, teaching, death, and resurrection broaden, deepen, and correct our understanding of God's law of love, "For God sent not his Son into the world to condemn the world; but that the world through him might be saved" (John 3:17, KJV). Jesus did not, does not, and will not condemn the world. Nor does God the Father or his law condemn. Jesus is the unfolding of the written law, the law of love, "I delight to do thy will, O my God: yea, thy law is within my heart" (Psalm 40:8, KJV).

Many of the scribes and Pharisees felt condemned by Jesus's presence, but Jesus did not condemn them. Their sense of condemnation came from their love of sin and darkness, their refusal of Christ's forgiveness. Jesus spoke in sorrowful tones when he gave the church leaders of his time these powerful rebukes:

Woe to you, scribes and Pharisees, hypocrites! For you pay tithe of mint and anise and cummin, and have neglected the weightier matters of the law: justice and mercy and faith. These you ought to have done, without leaving the others undone. (Matthew 23:23, NKJ)

Therefore you are witnesses against yourselves that you are sons of those who murdered the prophets. Fill up, then, the measure of your fathers' guilt. Serpents, brood of vipers! How can you escape the condemnation of hell? Therefore, indeed, I send you prophets, wise men, and scribes: some of them you will kill and crucify, and some of them you will scourge in your synagogues and persecute from city to city, that on you may come all the righteous blood shed on the earth, from the blood of righteous Abel to the blood of Zechariah, son of Berechiah, whom you murdered between the temple and the altar. Assuredly, I say to you, all these things will come upon this generation. O Jerusalem, Jerusalem, the one who kills the prophets and stones those who are sent to her! How often I wanted to gather your children together, as a hen gathers her chicks under her wings, but you were not willing! See! Your house is left to you desolate; for I say to you, you shall see Me no more till you say, "Blessed is He who comes in the name of the LORD!" (Matthew 23:31-39, NKJ)

In these passages Jesus is not seeking to condemn the church leaders of his time, the scribes and Pharisees. But he does reveal to them their lost condition and the horrible fate that awaits them. Jesus's loving motive is to awaken these leading men to their true need. Jesus's lament is not so much for any specific evil deed of these leaders, as it is for their refusal, their unwillingness to accept him, their only hope. They would not believe. Jesus also showed them that they did not understand that the deep spiritual principles, the essence of the Ten Commandments, "mercy and justice" form the heart of the law of God. Keeping the letter of the law of God entitles no one to Heaven. But, no one will enter Heaven who willfully disregards the Ten Commandments:

An Enemy of the Law

So then, whoever disobeys even the least important of the commandments and teaches others to do the same, will be least in the Kingdom of heaven. On the other hand, whoever obeys the Law and teaches others to do the same, will be great in the Kingdom of heaven. I tell you, then, that you will be able to enter the Kingdom of heaven only if you are more faithful than the teachers of the Law and the Pharisees in doing what God requires. You have heard that people were told in the past, "Do not commit murder; anyone who does will be brought to trial." But now I tell you: whoever is angry with his brother will be brought to trial, whoever calls his brother "You good-for-nothing!" will be brought before the Council, and whoever calls his brother a worthless fool will be in danger of going to the fire of hell. (Matthew 5:19-22, TEV)

But the children of the kingdom shall be cast out into outer darkness: there shall be weeping and gnashing of teeth. (Matthew 8:12, KJV)

"Least in the Kingdom of heaven" means least in Heaven's opinion. Therefore, those who teach that the law has been done away with will be viewed as enemies of God and his law. Lucifer tried to change God's law in Heaven. Being confined to the Earth, he now tries to enlist men on his side to battle against God's perfect law of unselfish love. Satan subtly attacks God's law. He clothes his deceptions in lofty, grace-filled words. He twists the concept of God's grace to thwart its very purpose.

Satan has won the hearts of untold millions in this manner. Some Christians will argue that they are under grace and that the law has been done away with. However, God's law of love is from everlasting to everlasting. No matter how slick Satan's arguments, he cannot change or annul God's law. God is the rock of our salvation; the stone tablets, the table of the testimony; the Ten Commandments are a written description of God's character, the constitution of Heaven, and the foundation

151

principle that grace builds upon.

Before the end of the world all people will be brought to the point of decision; all will have to choose between the law of God and the laws of men, "It is time for thee, LORD, to work: for they have made void thy law" (Psalm 119:126, KJV). Those who choose man's laws over God's laws will receive the mark of the beast. All will have to choose between light and darkness, selfishness and unconditional love, eternal life, and eternal death. This decision will not be made with mere words. Those who worship God will reflect his character. Our words and deeds flow from our character. We are saved by grace that changes our character. Our works, works that flow from a heart of love, will judge us. Those who reject God will reflect Satan's character. Sinners will be judged by their works:

And I saw the dead, small and great, stand before God; and the books were opened: and another book was opened, which is the book of life: and the dead were judged out of those things which were written in the books, according to their works. (Revelation 20:12, KJV)

God's Ten Commandments describe the path of life. All other paths lead to death. God's law is pure, holy, beautiful, eternal, and practical. Our loving heavenly Father is not like a spoiled child who demands that all others play by his rules or else. God does not say that it's my way or the highway. Our Father gently, humbly, but firmly and clearly points and leads each of his beloved children to the path of life.

His Son, Jesus, is the only man that fully walked the path of life, that is, he obeyed the Ten Commandments. The life of Christ is our example. We must walk even as he walked. The death of Christ reveals God's forgiveness of sin; it also provides the power and the grace to overcome sin. We may be weak, we may falter, stumble, and fall into sin, but as Christians we must not excuse sin. To excuse sin would be to join with Satan in alleging that God is unjust.

God is just. His character of love is the foundation, the

very structure, and substance of law in Heaven. He never changes, "Every good and perfect gift comes down from the Father who created all the lights in the heavens. He is always the same and never makes dark shadows by changing" (James 1:17, CEV).

God's character is the law of Heaven. It cannot be changed, set aside, or safely ignored. Jesus's death on Calvary shows us that sin (transgression of the law) leads to death. Jesus did not die so that God's law of life could be set aside. No, Jesus died to reconcile us back to God and his law of life. If the law of life, God's character, the law of Heaven, could have been set aside, Jesus would not have had to die. It is because God's law of love and life cannot be changed that Jesus had to die in order to rescue us from Satan's dominion of sin, selfishness, and death. God is love. Love is not arbitrary, but practical. Love does not look for a way to punish, but to restore.

Our heavenly Father is not an arbitrary dictator. He grants freedom of choice to all his creatures. He reaches out to each individual, giving each person light and opportunity, warning and encouragement. But those who persistently harden themselves in unbelief and disobedience, he will give over to the inevitable results of their solemn decision. The wages of sin is death, eternal death.

The Law is Life, Sin Brings Death

Nevertheless, it is not God's law that brings death. No. God's law of love describes the path, the way of eternal life. All other paths, even though they may seem right to a man, lead to eternal death. Paul shows that God's law is not responsible for death:

Wherefore, as by one man sin entered into the world, and death by sin; and so death passed upon all men, for that all have sinned: (For until the law sin was in the world: but sin is not imputed when there is no law. Nevertheless death reigned from Adam to Moses, even over them that had not sinned after the similitude of Adam's transgression, who

153

is the figure of him that was to come. (Romans 5:12-14, KJV)

Adam brought sin into the world. Sin brought death into the world. Death does not come from God or his law, but rather from sin. "Sin is not imputed [counted] when there is no law." Paul reasons that God did not count men's sins against them before the written law was given through Moses. "Nevertheless death reigned from Adam to Moses."

Paul's reasoning further implies that the letter of God's law did not bring death, as death reigned before the letter of the law was given. Trying to earn salvation by keeping the letter of the law results in death. The principles of God's law were known from the time of Adam and Eve. Remember that God justly expected Cain to know that murder was wrong. Yet God's law did not bring death to Cain. Sin brought death to Cain.

God seeks to shield us from the evils that result from transgression of his Law of life, love, and liberty. These evils are a natural, inevitable consequence of rebellion against love. Love brings life, joy, and meaning. Sin and selfishness bring sadness, suffering, and death, "Great peace have those who love thy law; nothing can make them stumble" (Psalm 119:165, RSV).

Our loving heavenly Father has given us everything, all of Heaven, through his Son Jesus, in order to draw us back into harmony with his perfect law of life and love. Sadly, many unwittingly unite with Satan in charging upon our Creator the woe, sin, suffering, and death that are the sure result of our rebellion and Satan's rule. Amazingly, in this time of great light, many are still entangled in Satan's lies. For them, Jesus's life and death have still not unveiled Satan's false accusations about the character of God. They worship a mixture of God and Satan, of good and evil, of light and darkness. They cannot keep the law of love because they have not let go of the fear that results from the misapprehension of God's character.

The Law and the Gospel
We can be brought into harmony with God's perfect law

only by understanding God's love and allowing it into our hearts. Only by looking to Christ can we understand, and by faith receive, the perfect character of God's love. The law and the gospel are both describing the same thing, God's love, which is his character, the foundation of Heaven's government. Jesus demonstrated God's love, mercy, forgiveness, and justice.

Christ's sacrifice is not a divine legal maneuver designed to satisfy the broken law and still allow the Father to forgive sinners. Christ's sacrifice reveals that God had already forgiven sinners. The law does not condemn sinners. Neither does Christ condemn sinners. Jesus, through his life, does present the lofty standard (Ten Commandments) of unselfish, unconditional, self-sacrificing love. By contrasting our hearts with Christ's we see that we are sinful, selfish, and destructive. That is not really condemnation at all! Rather, when we look at Christ we see both his goodness and our dire need. "If I am lifted up I will draw all men to myself." The law and the gospel are the same eternal truth:

> And hereby we do know that we know him, if we keep his commandments. He that saith, I know him, and keepeth not his commandments, is a liar, and the truth is not in him. But whoso keepeth his word, in him verily is the love of God perfected: hereby know we that we are in him. He that saith he abideth in him ought himself also so to walk, even as he walked. (1John 2:3-6, KJV)

What an incredible God we serve! What a high standard of love! Christ experienced the second death in order to reveal to us the height, the depth, and breadth of God's law of love! "I have seen the consummation of all perfection, but your commandment is exceedingly broad" (Psalm 119:96, NKJ). Jesus does not condemn us, but shows us his incredible love in order to attract us, to draw us into a saving relationship with him.

Have you ever tried to win someone's friendship by condemning him, remarking on how awful and sinful he is? It wouldn't work, would it? On the other hand, if you got to know him, his hopes and desires, his strengths and weaknesses, his flaws and foibles, and still made him feel comfortable, accepted, and loved you would almost certainly succeed in winning his friendship. If he knew that you loved him, he might even listen to your gentle suggestions in matters of a relationship with Jesus.

God is wise and practical. He accepts us and loves us. By this powerful, loving acceptance, God begins to change our hearts. Love generates love. God's heart is love. The reason that God's law of love could not save us is because we could not understand it without a Person demonstrating it. We needed to see Jesus living out its principles and expressing its depths of meaning through death. The life and self-sacrificing death of Jesus Christ unfold the principles of God's Ten Commandments. In this sense God's moral law, the Ten Commandments does save us, as its principles are unfolded, glorified, exalted, made visible in the person of Jesus. By beholding we become changed. By beholding Jesus our faith is strengthened.

The Sabbath Rest in Christ

Each of God's Ten Commandments instructs and blesses us. God designed the Ten Commandments to prevent us from falling into the black hole of sin. Gerald Schroeder teaches at Hebrew University in Jerusalem. In *The Hidden Face of God*, he asserts:

Time is the continuing reality of life. The relativity of time, discovered by Einstein, was the first of the steps that moved physics into the realm of metaphysics. I find it intriguing that time is also the first item that the Bible makes holy, holy, in the biblical sense of being separate from the remainder of existence. Not a place, not a person, but totally abstract, intangible time - the seventh day, the Sabbath. The Sabbath predates Moses, Abraham, Noah. Only Adam and Eve, the biblical parents of all humanity, predate the Sabbath. Long before the ritual of religion made its way into theology, the Sabbath was established.

156

The Sabbath is the Bible's gift to all humanity; the crown of the six days of creation. It is the undersold superproduct of the Bible. It ritualizes contemplation, fits it into a timely rhythm, superimposing its cycle onto the other cycles that nature has imprinted through light and dark, satiation and hunger, phases of the moon.

The word Sabbath comes from the Hebrew shabat, meaning to rest, to cease from work. The essence of the Sabbath is rest. Erich Fromm, in *The Forgotten Language*, described it perfectly: "Rest is a state of peace between man and nature. Rest is an expression of dignity, peace and freedom."

The Bible understands the human psyche. It realizes that harmony between the two lives we live, the temporal wants of the body and the transcendent needs of the soul, is rarely a spontaneous happening. Without a ritualized, established routine there is always a reason for the tangible immediate demands of life to take precedence over our more abstract spiritual desires.[2]

God does not demand that we go to a specific location, such as the North Pole, or Mount Everest, in order to worship him. Although meeting together for church is a blessing. In the beginning, God made a special date with all mankind. He continues to be there for us each Sabbath, waiting to bless us with a double portion. All that we have to do is meet God at the specified time. Through the Sabbath, God comes to each person once a week. The Holy Spirit and the Sabbath both are a sign or seal of God's people:

In Him you also trusted, after you heard the word of truth, the gospel of your salvation; in whom also, having believed, you were sealed with the Holy Spirit of promise, who is the guarantee of our inheritance until the redemption of the purchased possession, to the praise of His glory. (Ephesians 1:13, 14, NKJ)

Speak also to the sons of Israel, saying, Truly you shall keep My sabbaths. For it is a sign between Me and you throughout your generations, to know that I am the LORD who sanctifies you. (Exodus 31:13, MKJ)

Remember the Sabbath day, to keep it holy. Six days you shall labor and do all your work. But the seventh day is the Sabbath of the LORD your God. You shall not do any work, you nor your son, nor your daughter, your man-servant, nor your maidservant, nor your cattle, nor your stranger within your gates. For in six days the LORD made the heavens and the earth, the sea, and all that is in them, and rested the seventh day. Therefore the LORD blessed the Sabbath day, and sanctified it. (Exodus 20:8-11, MKJ)

The seventh-day Sabbath is the seal of God's law of un-conditional, benevolent love. We can only keep the Sabbath holy if we are filled with the Holy Spirit and have God's noble law of love written in our hearts. Only as we are willing to sac-rifice our time, possessions, money, pride, lives, and even our immortal inheritance for others, even for our enemies, can we enter into true Sabbath rest. When we have Jesus in our hearts we will be able to delight in the law of God's love. Then we will bring forth fruit and prosper:

Blessed is the man who walks not in the counsel of the wicked, nor stands in the way of sinners, nor sits in the seat of scoffers; but his delight is in the law of the LORD, and on his law he meditates day and night. He is like a tree planted by streams of water, that yields its fruit in its season, and its leaf does not wither. In all that he does, he prospers. (Psalm 1:1-3, RSV)

So says Jehovah, "Stand by the ways and see, and ask for the old paths, where the good way is, and walk in it; and you shall find rest for your souls." (Jeremiah 6:16, GLT)

If you fulfill the royal law according to the Scripture, "You shall love your neighbor as yourself," you do well. So speak and do as those who shall be judged by the law of liberty. (James 2:8, 12, MKJ)

So shall I keep thy law continually for ever and ever. And I will walk at liberty: for I seek thy precepts. (Psalm 119:44, 45, KJV)

[The Sabbath] is a sign between Me and you throughout your generations, that you may know that I am the Lord who sanctifies you. (Exodus 31:13, NKJ)

Only as we understand the incredible depths of God's love for us can we fully open our hearts to him so that he can write his law in our hearts. For this to happen, we need to spend the Sabbath day each week, communing with Jesus, fellowshipping with believers and reaching out to the lost. We need our daily worship time as well. Then we will receive the seal of God's law of love through faith and the mighty power of the Holy Spirit. Then we will be ready to stand in the judgment.

When we love others as Christ has loved us, we will be ready to face persecution. With Christ filling our hearts with his benevolent love, we will love our persecutors more than our own lives. Then our interest in the salvation of men will exceed our interest in food, water, security, safety, or any worldly comfort. Then our faces will shine with the glory of God's law as Moses' face shined from the glory of God's law. It is God's law, his character of love that motivated him to sacrifice all to save us. What an awesome God we serve!

1 Hawking, Stephen (1996). A Brief History of Time. New York: Bantam Books

2 Schroeder , Gerald (2001). The Hidden Face of God. New York: The Free Press.

Many waters cannot quench love;

neither can rivers drown it.

If a man tried to buy love

with everything he owned,

his offer would be utterly despised.

(Song of Songs 8:7, NLT)

And when

I passed by and saw you again,

you were old enough to be married.

So I wrapped my cloak around you

to cover your nakedness

and declared my marriage vows.

I made a covenant with you,

says the Sovereign Lord,

and you became mine.

(Ezekiel 16:8, NLT)

8

The Bride and
The Groom

Royal Invitation

Living between the imaginary kingdoms of Elelath and
Eleutheria, Arielle turned heads, even with the conservative
clothing she chose to wear. She had an aura of calm kindness
and compassion that won her the admiration and loyal friendship of all those who had the pleasure of making her acquaintance. Her father, Aaron, and her mother, Rebekah took pride in
their daughter.

Arielle's reputation for great beauty reached to the royal
court of Elelath. The handsome and eligible Prince Damien
sent one of his trusted servants to deliver an invitation to
Arielle for the upcoming royal banquet. With great excitement
Arielle accepted the royal invitation.

Prince Damien arranged to have one of the court seam-
stresses fit Arielle with a gorgeous gown from the finest silks
and silver and gold threads fit for a princess! Finally the day
came and Arielle looked radiant as Prince Damien assisted
Arielle into the royal carriage.

She and the prince made pleasant small talk on the long
journey to the palace. Then Damien escorted her to the im-

mense banquet hall. Arielle commented on the dazzling beauty of the light that shone through and reflected off the elaborate crystal chandeliers, lamp covers, the stained glass windows, and the polished gold and silver. "Yes," Damien replied, "this banquet hall is beautiful, but its beauty is nothing in comparison to your exquisite beauty!" Arielle hoped that the rainbow of colors would help to hide the blush she felt warming her cheeks. She politely thanked the prince for his kind compliment as he seated her next to him at the immense table. The conversation was pleasant. The main course was as colorful and artistic as it was delicious. The pastries were marvelous as well. Then came the fruit; Arielle had never seen such a variety of tropical fruits. Arielle spent the night in the royal castle dreaming of being a princess.

The next day, Prince Damien took Arielle on a tour of the palace. Prince Damien collected statues. Some were gold-plated, others silver, still others seemed to be cast from bronze. As she gazed at one of the finer marble statues, the lady portrayed was so lifelike that Arielle almost felt embarrassed to stare at it, half expecting her to finish the motion of releasing a dove to flight. Noticing Arielle's delight, Prince Damien explained that a sculptor of rare talent from a distant land had the gift of putting the sense of motion and life into stone. He continued, "The price for that statue was ten times higher than any other in my collection, but when I see something I like I buy it." He also had many fine paintings and a large collection of imaginative and lovely jewelry. Everything sparkled with diamonds, rubies, and other precious gems. Gold and silver were in abundance. Prince Damien showed her the royal treasury. Then Prince Damien turned to her and said, "Arielle, you are the most beautiful woman in the kingdom. I want you. I love you. Now, I will give you and your family one thousand pounds of gold, ten thousand pounds of silver, and more diamonds, emeralds, and rubies than you can carry, as the price for your love. Will you marry me?"

Arielle's stomach started to churn, her mouth tasted sour, and she broke out into a cold sweat. She looked away from

Prince Damien as the question formed in her mind, "He claims that he loves me. Yet, does he think that he can buy my love? Does he know what love is?" Mistaking the cause of Arielle's hesitation, Prince Damien quickly added, "if that is not enough I'm prepared to double the offer." Sensing her continued discomfort, Damien smoothly added, "Don't answer now, take your time; talk it over with your father." Maintaining her poise and grace, Arielle politely listened as the prince showed her the gorgeous gardens, including a large zoo.

At last the evening ended, and they bid each other good night. In an upper room in the large castle as she lay in the soft down bed, Arielle's thoughts troubled her. Prince Damien was so handsome and charming. His declaration of love and his offer of riches echoed in her mind. Prince Damien's expression of love intrigued her. To become part of the royal family would be exciting. But, her father had taught her that status and money could not buy love or happiness. He had taught her that she could only find success in marriage with a man that had won her respect, friendship, and love. "I hope he doesn't mean it to sound that way, but his offer makes me feel like he thinks that I am just an expensive addition to his collection of beautiful statues," she mused. "Why do some men think that they can buy a woman's love?" she fumed as she fell asleep. Arielle had a disturbing dream. She had on a beautiful gown, and was riding on a horse in a parade. People were throwing things at her. They were throwing large gold coins and sharp-edged gemstones at her. The heavy gold coins left bruises and the precious stones left little cuts. At the head of the parade rode a strong man with a great bloody sword held high in the air. Though he turned to look from side to side, Arielle wasn't able to see who he was.

A Picnic

The next day, to Arielle's surprise and delight she received another royal invitation, yet the occasion was kept a mystery. She received a clue to the mysterious event when the royal seamstress arrived, this time providing her with riding clothes.

"A picnic," Arielle was excited. She loved horses and delighted in the living greens of the forest and vibrant rainbow of colors of the flowers in the meadows.

After she had changed, Prince Damien escorted Arielle out to the stables. Arielle nearly stumbled when she saw the largest, strongest, and fastest-looking white stallion that she had ever seen. This was going to be fun, she thought, as she mounted the noble-looking steed. She was relieved that Prince Damien did not mention his previous offer. He was even more charming than before.

They rode through the forest of giant trees, crossed babbling brooks and quiet streams at times slowly and at times at an exhilarating pace. The panoramic view from the mountaintop brought tears to Arielle's eyes. Then they rode down into a pretty meadow, filled with lovely flowers. The picnic was delightful. Perhaps because of the fresh air, the simpler food of the picnic tasted even better than the extravagant dinner at the banquet hall. The attendants were prompt, well mannered, and attentive. Arielle noticed, though, that occasionally one of the servants would cast a fearful glance at Prince Damien. While they were eating, some of the servants set up the royal tents, while others made a large stack of wood. After the picnic lunch, Prince Damien played music like she had never heard before. It was exciting, exhilarating, and a bit hypnotic.

That evening as they sat around a large bonfire, Prince Damien told exciting tales of adventure and daring. Arielle listened, enraptured by his charismatic charm.

An Offer You Can't Refuse

The next day they headed back to the palace in his carriage. On the way, Damien took Arielle on a tour of some of his factories. One factory extracted large quantities of pitch from logs. Another factory extracted tar from the oil that was pumped from the ground. Arielle asked what these materials were used for. Prince Damien's eyes hardened as he responded enigmatically, "You will see."

As they watched the sunset from the highest tower in his

castle, Prince Damien turned and looked Arielle straight in the eyes and said, "I love you, with all my heart." Arielle's heart began to beat faster. "I want you to love me and to marry me. If you do, my enchanters will keep you forever young." Arielle became slightly light-headed with the thought of living forever-young. "If you agree to love and marry me, you will have immense riches and live happily ever after." She was beginning to fall under his charm when, with a cruel smile on his handsome face and a hint of coldness in his eyes that Arielle had noticed before, Prince Damien said in a soft, yet intense voice, "If you do not agree, I must follow my great law. No one is allowed to refuse my sovereign commands. I will send my servants to your home. They will tie you up and take you down to the lower caves. They will put tar and pitch on you and torture you with fire. My enchanters will keep you alive forever! For your sake, please say yes! I love you and I do not want you to suffer this fate!" Her dreams of love, royal privileges, castles, rubies, and eternal youth came crashing to the ground. "How can you expect me to love you?" Arielle thought, as tears formed in her eyes. Her silent thoughts continued, "Now that you have made me afraid of you, how can I ever love you? You are wealthy and have great power; you may have the title of a prince, but in your heart you are a tyrant." Prince Damien, seeing her distress graciously added "I will give you time to consider my words. Do not take too long, though. Even though it grieves me, I will have to carry out the punishment, or risk losing control of my subjects. Fear is an important part of the foundation of my kingdom." With that Arielle quickly turned away and left the confused and saddened Prince Damien standing alone. Arielle spent a restless night dreaming of evil enchanters and eternal fire. Arielle felt relieved when morning came. She hoped to never enter his courts again.

On the long journey home, Arielle couldn't hear the joy in the songs of the birds nor relish the bright warmth of the sun. Everything looked gray and dark. When she arrived home, Arielle told her father the whole story, between sobs. She told her father of Damien's enchanters that would keep her forever

young, if she married him. Or, they would keep her alive forever in the caves of torture if she didn't marry him! "Should I
try to love him? How can I love him when he threatens me with
such an awful fate? If I don't, I'm doomed! But it is impossible
to love or even respect such a man! How could I ever trust such
a man? To live forever with someone that works by such cruel
principles would be misery."

"After such a long ride and the stress you are under, a
walk will be just the thing," her father wisely suggested. With
a concerned, yet proud smile he told her, "Daughter, you have
learned well. You are right; love cannot be bought or sold, not
even by a prince. By its very nature love must be free." Her
father Aaron was right, a walk in the warm summer evening
soothed Arielle's troubled spirit.

Michael

As they neared home, Arielle asked, "What are those piles
of dirt around the house?" "Oh," Aaron replied, "while you
were gone, I hired Michael, the carpenter, to fix the crack in the
ceiling and to see if he couldn't get the dining room window to
open properly." "Yes, but what about those piles of dirt?" "Michael pointed out that the crack in the ceiling and the stubborn
window were symptoms of a sagging foundation. He seems to
know what he's doing; he is efficient and strong. You will meet
him at supper tonight. He's from the kingdom of Eleutheria.
Since your brother is gone to school, Michael will be sleeping
in his room."

As Arielle was taking her place at the table, Michael
entered the room. She nearly fell out of her chair. He was so
handsome, tall, and well muscled. But it was his eyes that
almost caused her to land on the floor instead of the chair. His
eyes were powerful, expressive of a sparkling joy and a compassion that hinted at an unlimited capacity for sympathy and
sorrow. Michael carried himself with regal dignity, yet his face
and voice bespoke a gentle humility that invited confidence.

Introductions were made and everyone sat down to a simple meal of fresh baked bread and vegetable stew. Not wanting

to talk about her trip to Elelath over supper, Arielle asked a lot of questions about Michael and the kingdom of Eleutheria. The king was well liked by his subjects. He had a strong army. The majestic castle was thought to be impregnable. The kingdom of Eleutheria had a form of government that combined the principles of a republic, based on the rule of law, combined with a monarchy. No one could change the law. The law was simple, plain, and made good sense. Basically, it could be summed up as the golden rule. Crime was rare. When someone did break the law, the punishment was always aimed at restoration, rehabilitation, and reconciliation rather than revenge. After supper they moved into the living room and Michael asked if he might read from a book of poetry and prophecy. Everyone was delighted to hear Michael's rich musical voice bring life and rhythm to the lovely poems. Arielle shared a short version of her trip to Elelath and what Prince Damien had offered her. Then she told how he had threatened her. Michael listened silently, but his eyes betrayed a burning indignation and sorrow. When Arielle had finished, Michael smiled and assured everyone that Prince Damien could only rule over those that accepted his dominion. If Arielle and her family desired, the king of Eleutheria would put them under his protection.

Breakfast conversation was pleasant, but short as everyone had things to attend to. Lunch found everyone busy and at different places. Arielle waited impatiently for the evening hours. She looked forward to getting better acquainted with Michael. She felt that Michael also was interested in her.

Supper time finally arrived and again the conversation was lively and moved from lighter things to the deeper things of life. Michael seemed to know a lot about the wide range of topics that came up. Still, he kept his comments short and seemed rather more interested in hearing about the issues the family faced than talking about himself.

Day blended into day and suddenly a week had gone by. Michael asked if anyone knew of a pretty place to go for a walk and maybe a picnic. Plans were made and everyone agreed that a day off would be just the thing. There was a small lake nearby with a lovely meadow that was a family favorite. Michael and Arielle took a walk around the lake.

The friendship was developing into a little more than casual acquaintance. Another week slipped by and romance had blossomed. Another picnic day spent at the lake and Arielle knew that Michael was the man for her.

Michael was just about done with the foundation. Arielle wished he would slow down a little so they could have more time together. He was just too efficient. All too soon the last day arrived. Aaron paid Michael. Michael sadly took his leave of the family, but said that he would write to Arielle during the time that he had to spend back at Eleutheria.

True to his word, Michael wrote Arielle every day. The prose, and the poetry! Arielle began to wonder if Michael was the author of the book of poetry that he had occasionally read from, while he had been staying with them. There was something familiar in the style and content.

A month went by, and then it was six months. The letters still came daily. Arielle faithfully responded. Then the last letter came. But what a letter! Michael wrote that he was coming to see Arielle. He also indicated that he had some things to talk over with her that he would prefer to do in person. Arielle felt sure that she knew the subject! Her heart and mind agreed that marriage would be the item for discussion.

The Wedding

It was. He asked for her hand in marriage. Arielle, even though expecting it, still nearly fainted from the powerful emotion that swept through her. She still managed to say an exuberant "yes." Aaron and Rebekah gladly gave their permission. Michael insisted that the wedding take place back at Eleutheria. He said that he would make all the arrangements. He would even supply their wedding garments.

Finally the day came for Arielle and her family to make the long trip to Eleutheria. They started out very early in the morning, while the stars were still visible. They wanted to arrive in time to see something of the city. The wedding would be the next day. As they drew closer to the city, they could see the castle high above the city. It became evident that preparations were underway for some grand festival. Banners were flying and people were busy making festive, bright-colored decorations everywhere.

Arielle was at once excited and a little bit apprehensive. Festivals were exciting and fun, but she hoped that this one wouldn't distract Michael's family and friends, or perhaps keep them from coming to the wedding. Ah well, he said that the wedding would be an occasion to remember. He had made arrangements for them to stay in the castle. He had even arranged to have one of the royal suites for the honeymoon. Arielle had worried that Michael might be spending too much money on the wedding. However, he said not to worry. He would have no problem covering the expenses.

The city and castle were situated in a wide, lovely valley with high mountains for a backdrop. There were lush fields and gardens surrounding the city. Finally they arrived at the castle and asked directions to the inn that Michael had reserved for them. A friend of Michael's was waiting for them. His face brightened as they introduced themselves. He introduced himself and showed them their rooms. After they had freshened up and rested a bit, he took them out to supper. After supper he explained some of the protocol for the wedding, when they should stand, what they should do at what time, etc. He said that Michael was busy overseeing some last minute details for the wedding and would come see them early the next day.

Arielle could hardly sleep that night. Tomorrow was the big day. Finally she would be with Michael. She had looked forward to this for so long! Promptly arriving just as they were finishing a light breakfast, Michael caught Arielle's eye as he came into the inn's dining room. "I cannot stay for long just now," he said. "I have a few things to do, but here's my sister, Teresa, she'll take care of you and show you where to change. He smiled and said, "I hope that you'll like the wedding gown."

She did. It almost seemed to glow with gold and silver

threads woven into the fabric of the finest, whitest linen. Arielle looked and felt radiant. Teresa showed Arielle the jewelry that would be used for the occasion. Arielle wondered out loud, "What must all this have cost? Just look at this tiara, it is gorgeous!" Teresa just smiled. As Arielle finished her preparations she asked, "By the way, Teresa, what is this festival? "Oh look at the time!" Teresa exclaimed, "We must hurry to the hall. I think we'll be just in time." Teresa took Arielle to a small side room. She could hear the sound of music. It sounded like a large choir, orchestra, and band. She hoped that Michael hadn't gone into debt for all this. "How could a carpenter afford all this fine jewelry, and the large hall and this exquisite gown?" Arielle wondered out loud. "Michael loves you so much, he wanted you to have a wedding fit for a..." Just then the music changed, signaling the time for Arielle to walk up the aisle to the altar. Arielle was glad that her father escorted her up to the altar. When she saw the large hall filled with a multitude of people her knees felt a bit weak. When she finally arrived at the altar she whispered to Michael "You're not just a carpenter are you?" He replied. "I am a carpenter, but I am also a king. I wanted to be sure that you loved me for who I am. Now we both know that we love each other for who we are." Michael and Arielle lived happily ever after.

Jesus and his Bride

The Bible refers to our Savior, Jesus, as the bridegroom and his followers as his bride. Paul brings this out quite clearly, "As the Scriptures say, 'A man leaves his father and mother to get married, and he becomes like one person with his wife.' This is a great mystery, but I understand it to mean Christ and his church" (Ephesians 5:31, 32, CEV). The Holy Spirit inspired Paul to write this in order to show us the kind of relationship that Jesus wants with us. Through the prophet Hosea God speaks to Israel as his prospective bride:

> Therefore, I will now allure her, and bring her into the wilderness, and speak tenderly to her...There she shall re-

spond as in the days of her youth, as at the time when she came out of the land of Egypt. On that day, says the Lord, you will call me, "My husband." (Hosea 2:14-16, NRSV)

Jesus died on the cross to reveal God's infinite love for the whole world and to thereby allure his wayward bride back into an intimate, healing, and saving, love relationship. Eternal life is not a bribe designed to buy our love. No. Eternal life is a wedding gift that Christ gives to his bride. Eternal life is more about quality than quantity. He does not offer us Heaven in order to buy our love. Our heavenly Father sent his son, Jesus to this world to reveal what he is like. He wants us to love him for who he is, not for what he can offer us. Stephen, Moses, Paul, and many others have had the opportunity to demonstrate that they loved God and would serve him, whether or not eternal life was part of the package. If Heaven is our motivation for being good, if eternal life is our main goal, we have missed the message of the cross. We may be the last generation to live on the Earth before Jesus comes. Jesus is coming soon! We will have the same opportunity that Moses, Paul, and Stephen had to show the genuineness of our love for God.

You Cannot Buy Love

Solomon (the wisest man to ever live) understood that love could not be bought or sold. The Holy Spirit inspired him to reveal to us this foundation principle of human and heavenly relationships, "Many waters cannot quench love; neither can rivers drown it. If a man tried to buy love with everything he owned, his offer would be utterly despised" (Song of Songs 8:7, NLT).

Everyone would condemn the imaginary Prince Damien. Clearly, Damien is a mixture of good and evil. Our heavenly Father is no such mixture of good and evil, "Can a mortal be more righteous than God? Can a man be more pure than his Maker?" (Job 4:17, NKJ). He is righteous, loving, wise, and just. God is love. Paul explains some of the characteristics of God's love:

171

Love is patient and kind; it is not jealous or conceited or proud; love is not ill-mannered or selfish or irritable; love does not keep a record of wrongs; love is not happy with evil, but is happy with the truth. (1Corinthians 13:4-6, TEV)

Paul again mentions the same principle, "Our message is that God was making the whole human race his friends through Christ. God did not keep an account of their sins, and he has given us the message which tells how he makes them his friends" (2Corinthians 5:19, TEV).

In the story, Prince Damien represents the distorted view some people have of Jesus. Satan has foisted his destructive lies about God where it would hurt God the worst, in the heart and mind of his bride, his church. In the Bible, Jesus does ask us to love and obey him. The Bible also indicates that unrepentant sinners will be cast into a lake of burning fire. A superficial reading of the Bible would seem to support a Prince Damien view of God. The principles developed in the life and death of Jesus Christ argue strongly against a Prince Damien view of God. Our God-given sense of right and wrong properly rejects such a view of God as well. We are not more righteous, more loving than God!

No Christ-like man would try to buy the love of a woman, even if he owned the whole world, or even if he could offer her Heaven itself. Neither would any Christ-like man use coercion or threats of violence to win a woman's love. Any man that would try to bribe or coerce a woman to love him would rightfully be held in contempt by Christian society. The reason no Christ-like man would try to coerce a woman to love him is because it would be against the principles of Heaven, God's law of love, the perfect law of liberty. Jesus does not say, "Do as I say and not as I do! Neither will Jesus woo his bride, the church, using such evil, dark methods:

So men ought to love their wives as their own bodies. He who loves his wife loves himself. For no man ever yet hated his own flesh, but nourishes and cherishes it, even as the Lord loves the church. For we are members of His body, of His flesh, and of His bones. "For this cause a man shall leave his father and mother and shall be joined to his wife, and the two of them shall be one flesh." This is a great mystery, but I speak concerning Christ and the church. (Ephesians 5:28-32, MKJ)

Neither Hope of Reward Nor Fear of Punishment

Jesus is not a cruel tyrant and neither is our heavenly Father a cruel tyrant. God is not like Prince Damien! Our Father does not threaten to punish us with eternal torment if we choose not to fall in love with him and his Son Jesus, "There is no fear in love, but perfect love casts out fear; for fear has to do with punishment, and whoever fears has not reached perfection in love. We love because he first loved us" (1John 4:18, 19, NRSV).

Still, our Father is just and righteous. Sin does have consequences. The wages of sin is death. At the end of the age there will be a lake of fire and sin and sinners will be consumed, but hell is not an arbitrary punishment for those that God hates. No. God never stops loving even his most wayward children. Hell is a natural consequence of sin. Sin is far more destructive than any of us can imagine. Isaiah pins the blame right where it belongs, "For wickedness burns as the fire; It shall devour the briers and thorns, And kindle in the thickets of the forest; They shall mount up like rising smoke" (Isaiah 9:18, NKJ). Briers and thorns represent sin and sinners. Forests and trees represent people. Also consider:

Let grace be shown to the wicked, yet he will not learn righteousness; In the land of uprightness he will deal unjustly, And will not behold the majesty of the Lord. Lord, when Your hand is lifted up, they will not see. But they will see and be ashamed For their envy of people; Yes, the fire of Your enemies shall devour them. (Isaiah 26:10, 11, NKJ)

Please do not blame God for granting us freedom. It is wickedness, rather than our Father that destroys sinners. Without freedom we would be robots or mindless slaves. Freedom brings risks. Sin is a high price to pay for freedom. Nevertheless, God, in his love and wisdom, counted the cost, and paid it. True love always grants freedom and pays the price for it.

Love does not threaten. Love does not use bribes. A lover seeks to win the heart of his beloved by expressing loving words, by kind actions—by revealing his own heart of love.

God's kingdom of love grows one heart at a time. Jesus fully expressed his Father's love during his life and his death. God has chosen to woo us by opening his heart of love to us.

We love God because he first loved us. God's love saves us by alluring us away from our self-destructive, self-centered rebellion. Hope of reward (eternal life in Heaven) and fear of punishment (eternal torment in hell fire) are motivations that would only reinforce our self-centered, carnal nature. People who stubbornly hang onto a shallow, tyrannical view of God block the healing streams of God's love that the Holy Spirit longs to pour out into their hearts. They cannot have the faith needed for this time.

Nothing we can do will make God love us more, or less. We cannot earn salvation, for it is a free gift based on his love for us. Jesus did not die in order to be able to forgive us, but to demonstrate that he is the personification of forgiveness. Jesus came to reveal his Father's heart, his character, which is the foundation principle of the kingdom of Heaven. God is love. His very character is one of self-sacrificing love. He wants us to see the beauty of his holiness, his pure character of love. Our Father wants us to love him for who he is.

Jesus's display of God's incredible love for us is the mechanism, the means, the wooing of our hearts that saves us by drawing us into a relationship with him. Now we must ask ourselves, Does God use the same principles that Prince Damien uses? Does God try to bribe our obedience by offering us Heaven? No. Does God try to coerce our behavior by threatening us with the fires of hell? No. We must not believe in a God that behaves as our imaginary Prince Damien. Otherwise, just as Arielle, we will find ourselves unable to respect, love, trust, obey, or worship him. Prince Damien represents a mixture of truth and error, good and evil.

It is possible to have the entire Bible memorized and still not understand the deeper things of God. Just look at the Pharisees at the time of Christ's first advent. They found scriptural support for their misguided, selfish desires and beliefs. A shallow, superficial reading of the Bible has led to the proliferation of hundreds of different Christian denominations. We must search the Bible for the foundation principles of God's government, character, and plan of salvation. We must dig for the treasure that is buried there:

> Listen to what is wise and try to understand it. Yes, beg for knowledge; plead for insight. Look for it as hard as you would for silver or some hidden treasure. (Proverbs 2:2-4, TEV)

> This is what the LORD says: "Let not the wise man gloat in his wisdom, or the mighty man in his might, or the rich man in his riches. Let them boast in this alone: that they truly know me and understand that I am the LORD who is just and righteous, whose love is unfailing, and that I delight in these things. I, the LORD, have spoken! (Jeremiah 9:23, 24, NLT)

God's way's are much higher than our ways. His justice and mercy spring from the same fountain of love. One does not cancel or dominate the other. God does not change. Only we do. God allows us freedom to choose. We bear full responsibility for the consequences of our choices, for we are made in his image.

Then my anger shall be kindled
against them in that day,
and I will forsake them,
and I will hide my face from them,
and they shall be devoured, and
many evils and troubles shall befall them;
so that they will say in that day,
Are not these evils come upon us,
because our God is not among us?
(Deuteronomy 31:17, KJV)

And the LORD said to Satan,
Behold, all that he has is in your power.
Only do not lay your hand upon him.
And Satan went forth
from the presence of the LORD.
(Job 1:12, MKJ)

9

Job and Fire,
Pigs and Lies

Killing Warps the Soul

At dawn, two guards led the prisoner out into the courtyard. They secured his hands behind his back, tying them to the post in front of the stone wall. One guard softly asked him, "Do you have any last words to say?" The prisoner mournfully replied, "I am sorry for the crime that I have committed. I know that I deserve to die. May God forgive me." The ten guards then put a black hood over his head. The appointed marksmen, carrying their rifles, filed out in a row and lined up a short distance from the man tied to the post. The warden said, "As you know, all but one of you have been given blanks. None of you will know for certain whether or not you have fired the fatal round. Ready. Aim. Fire."

It is interesting that even when executing a convicted criminal, traditions have been established to shield the executioners from the effects of taking another man's life. We instinctively know that it is damaging to shed blood, even when carrying out the requirements of the law.

Instinct means the instructions that God has written into our bodies, the genetic code that he has provided for all living things. Of course sin has damaged our genes. We are prone to sickness, disease, and death. The lion now kills. Skunks stink. But in the New Earth the lion will eat straw as God originally designed. Skunks won't stink. There will be no sickness or death.

The horror of killing others during war always changes those who are involved. No one comes back unaffected. Some never readjust to "normal" society. Even killing someone in legitimate self-defense can haunt a sensitive person for the rest of her life. God knows how damaging it is to be involved in taking the lives of people. God is more sensitive to the negative effects of sin than any other being in the universe.

Why Does God Allow Suffering?

Many people ask the question, "Why does God allow the suffering of innocent people?" The book of Job provides one answer. Satan accuses people of worshiping God for the blessings that they get. Satan demands access to test God-fearing people. In the book of Job, Satan presents himself before God claiming to represent the Earth and all mankind. In order to understand God and Satan's conversation, we need to keep in mind that Adam was called the "son of God." It is true that all people are the children of God (see Acts 17:28, TEV). God is our Creator, our Father. However, Adam is the son of God in a special sense, for he has no other father than God. Also, God gave Adam authority and dominion over the Earth. Adam was God's representative on Earth:

> Then God said, "Let Us make man [Hebrew *Adam*] in Our image, according to Our likeness; let them have dominion over the fish of the sea, over the birds of the air, and over the cattle, over all the earth and over every creeping thing that creeps on the earth." So God created man in his *own* image; in the image of God He created him; male and female He created them. Then God blessed them, and God said to them, "Be fruitful and multiply; fill the earth and subdue it; have dominion over the fish of the sea, over the

birds of the air, and over every living thing that moves on the earth." (Genesis 1:26-28, NKJ)

When Adam sinned, Satan claimed to have the right to Adam's lost dominion. But, God is the source for all authority and dominion. God had a plan to restore Adam's dominion. God did not use brute force or kingly authority to deny Satan's claim to the Earth, but rather used reason, and evidence to demonstrate and establish the truth:

And a day came when the sons of God came to present themselves before Jehovah. And Satan also came among them. And Jehovah said to Satan, From where have you come? And Satan answered Jehovah and said, From going to and fro in the earth, and from walking up and down in it. And Jehovah said to Satan, Have you set your heart on My servant Job because there is none like him in the earth, a perfect and upright man, fearing God and turning away from evil? (Job 1:6-8, GLT)

"The sons of God came." The meeting place would have been Heaven, God's throne, of course. The word, *came,* suggests that the sons of God had been elsewhere. The gathering of the "sons of God," then, would be the gathering of the representatives from the worlds of the universe. Each has authority and dominion over the world that God has given them. God recognized each of the "sons of God" as legitimate representatives of their worlds.

There is a deeper meaning to the question that God asked Satan, "Where do you come from?" Of course God knew where Satan had come from. God's question informs Satan and the sinless universe that he disputes and challenges Satan's usurped dominion over our fallen world. Satan's answer "From going to and fro in the earth..." is his claim to the Earth. What Satan means is, that he can go anywhere on the Earth that he wants; all the people of the Earth are sinners and are therefore his rightful subjects. God then counters Satan with another question that disputes Satan's claim and offers evidence that Satan is not the legitimate representative of the Earth. "Have you considered my servant Job?" Then God reasons, "Job is perfect, he fears [worships] God and turns away from evil." In other words, Job is my servant, not yours, Satan. He worships me, not you. Satan then disputes God's point with a question:

> And Satan answered Jehovah and said, Does Job fear God for nothing? Have You not made a hedge for him, and for his house, and for all that is his all around? You have blessed the work of his hands, and his livestock have increased in the land. But put out Your hand now, and touch against all that is his, and see if he will not then curse You to Your face. And Jehovah said to Satan, Behold, all that is his is in your hand! Only, do not lay your hand on him. And Satan went out from the face of Jehovah. (Job 1:9-12, GLT)

Notice that it is God who protects and Satan who seeks to destroy. In order to prove that Satan's claims were false, God gives him permission to destroy Job's family and possessions. This brings us to the point in the story where Job's breathless servants relate to him the awful news of sudden disaster. Notice that Satan waited until the day that Job would be the most vulnerable, when he would be the most concerned for the spiritual well-being of his children, the day his sons and daughters were feasting, and drinking wine:

> Now there was a day when his sons and daughters were eating and drinking wine in their oldest brother's house; and a messenger came to Job and said, "The oxen were plowing and the donkeys feeding beside them, when the Sabeans raided them and took them away—indeed they have killed the servants with the edge of the sword; and I alone have escaped to tell you!" While he was still speaking, another also came and said, "The fire of God fell from heaven and burned up the sheep and the servants, and con-

sumed them; and I alone have escaped to tell you!" While he was still speaking, another also came and said, "The Chaldeans formed three bands, raided the camels and took them away, yes, and killed the servants with the edge of the sword; and I alone have escaped to tell you!" While he was still speaking, another also came and said, "Your sons and daughters were eating and drinking wine in their oldest brother's house, and suddenly a great wind came from across the wilderness and struck the four corners of the house, and it fell on the young people, and they are dead; and I alone have escaped to tell you!" (Job 1:13-19, NKJ)

The Fire of God?

Pay special attention to the statement, "The fire of God fell from heaven and burned up the sheep and the servants, and consumed them." Job's servant contended that the fire came from God. Job, his servants, and friends believed that the destroying fire came from God. Yet the first chapter of Job, verse twelve puts the blame right where it belongs: "And the Lord said to Satan, 'Behold, all that he has is in your power; only do not lay a hand on his person.' So Satan went out from the presence of the Lord" (NKJ).

God allowed Satan to destroy Job's possessions and family. Satan destroys whenever God allows it. In order to be able to refute Satan's accusations, in order to clear his name before the "sons of God," to be fair, and to give Satan the room to fail, God has to allow him to destroy. God never uses the same methods of warfare that Satan does. It is Satan that brought the fire down from Heaven to destroy Job's flocks and caused all the other disasters that befell Job and his family. Notice, though, that God never explained to Job the reason for his suffering.

Job was a prince, a leader both financially and spiritually. Job's friends would have been of the same social level. Job had a relationship with God. He knew that God loved him. Job proclaimed his innocence to his friends. Job's friends ridiculed his claim to innocence. They maintained that Job's afflictions

181

were the judgments of God against some secret sin. At first, the calamities that befell Job mystified him. However, using these trials, God brought Job to a far better understanding of his character than the other "church" leaders of his time had.

Who is Right about God?

Listen carefully to the theological discussion between Zophar and Job. Zophar calls things as he sees them. He does not pull any punches:

> Zophar from Naamah said: So much foolish talk cannot go unanswered. Your words have silenced others and made them ashamed; now it is only right for you to be put to shame. You claim to be innocent and argue that your beliefs are acceptable to God. But I wish he would speak and let you know that wisdom has many different sides. You would then discover that God has punished you less than you deserve. Can you understand the mysteries surrounding God All-Powerful? They are higher than the heavens and deeper than the grave. So what can you do when you know so little, and these mysteries outreach the earth and the ocean? (Job 11:1-9, CEV)

Zophar trumpets a mighty mixture of truth and error, "wisdom has many different sides." "Can you understand the mysteries surrounding God...?" Zophar's main point is that man, especially a sinful man like Job, cannot understand much of anything about God because God is infinite and man is limited. Zophar is making the case that we can't know God. Many people feel the same way today. Zophar informs Job that he is a sinner and that is why God has punished him. The sarcastic implication is that Job ought to be ashamed to disagree with his obviously more righteous and knowledgeable brethren who are not being punished by God. Zophar continues his good-sounding, but erroneous assessment of Job's situation:

> Surrender your heart to God, turn to him in prayer, and

give up your sins—even those you do in secret. Then you won't be ashamed; you will be confident and fearless. Your troubles will go away like water beneath a bridge, and your darkest night will be brighter than noon. You will rest safe and secure, filled with hope and emptied of worry. You will sleep without fear and be greatly respected. But those who are evil will go blind and lose their way. Their only escape is death! (Job 11:13-20, CEV)

Zophar declares that it is obvious that God is punishing Job on account of some secret sin. Yet none of Job's friends could convict him of any particular sin. The only evidence that Job's friends could offer was the string of disasters that had befallen him. Zophar eloquently expresses his mainstream theology. They all thought that God was in the business of punishing sinners and giving wealth and good health to the righteous. Many preach the same thing today.

The Tabernacles of Robbers Prosper

However, Job does not buy that mainstream view. Nor should we. Job knows that God works differently. So should we. Job had three good reasons to conclude that God was not punishing him for his sins.

Reason 1. God had given Job a clear conscience. Amid the calamities and the condemnation of his friends, Job walked the path toward the knowledge of God. Job knew that God was not punishing him for his sins:

But I have understanding as well as you; I am not inferior to you: yea, who knoweth not such things as these? I am as one mocked of his neighbour, who calleth upon God, and he answereth him: the just upright man is laughed to scorn. He that is ready to slip with his feet is as a lamp despised in the thought of him that is at ease. The tabernacles of robbers prosper, and they that provoke God are secure; into whose hand God bringeth abundantly. But ask now the beasts, and they shall teach thee; and the fowls of the air, and they shall tell thee: (Job 12:3-7, KJV)

Job rebuts Zophar's mistaken view of God, "My feet are ready to slip but I am as God's lamp, even though those who are at ease [Job's friends] despise the light." Job cautions his miserable comforters that they shouldn't allow the calamities that have befallen him to cause them to reject the light on the character of God that he is seeking to share with them.

Job's story foreshadows the experience of God's elect at the end of time. The entire world will believe that the elect have been rejected by God. People won't listen to the elect because they will be poor, the outcasts of society. The preachers of the prosperity gospel will ridicule God's elect. But only for a while.

Reason 2. "The tabernacles of robbers prosper." Job is pointing out that bad things can happen to good people and that God blesses even robbers and those who provoke him.

Reason 3. Job makes an additional point, "ask now the beasts." God feeds all the beasts of the Earth. God blesses all his created beings, both good and bad.

In the last chapter, God rebukes Jobs friends. God vindicates Job, "After the Lord had finished speaking to Job, he said to Eliphaz, "I am angry with you and your two friends, because you did not speak the truth about me, as my servant Job did" (Job 42:7, TEV). God is not in the business of punishing sin; He is in the business of rescuing his lost children who are caught in sin. Imagine if God gave you an electric shock every time you cherished a sinful thought!

Imagine what would happen if God brought disaster on every person the moment he or she sinned! The consequences would be horrendous. The fear of God would take on a perverted and destructive meaning. Everyone would learn to view God as a tyrant and hate him. Or, people would try to obey God from fear of the consequences. Fear-based obedience is not obedience at all. Jesus told us, "If you love me, you will obey my commandments" (John 14:15, TEV). Love is the only way to obedience. Also, punishment of sin would destroy freedom of choice. We would be nothing more than robots. God has made it clear that we are free to choose:

> Now if you are unwilling to serve the LORD, choose this day whom you will serve, whether the gods your ancestors served in the region beyond the River or the gods of the Amorites in whose land you are living; but as for me and my household, we will serve the LORD." (Joshua 24:15, NRSV)

In order to provide freedom of choice, God must bless the good and bad alike. Otherwise, everyone would become a Christian to get the material benefits. Christ restated the principle that God blesses the good and the bad alike:

> You have heard that it was said, "Love your friends, hate your enemies." But now I tell you: love your enemies and pray for those who persecute you, so that you may become the children of your Father in heaven. For he makes his sun to shine on bad and good people alike, and gives rain to those who do good and to those who do evil. Why should God reward you if you love only the people who love you? Even the tax collectors do that! And if you speak only to your friends, have you done anything out of the ordinary? Even the pagans do that! You must be perfect— just as your Father in heaven is perfect! (Matthew 5:43-48, TEV)

Fortunately for us, God loves his enemies; He blesses those that curse him. Christ here clearly states that his Father does not punish sinners, but blesses them. He wants us to be just like him. But make no mistake about it; sin does bring negative, destructive, eternal, and fatal consequences. However, these bad results do not come from God! Also, obedience does bring blessings that are unavailable to the wicked, such as a clear conscience.

185

Love Versus Demons

Everything that Christ did tended to reveal the character of God, and unmask the true source of sin and suffering. Let's watch as Christ and Satan meet in hand to hand combat on the shores of the sea of Galilee. As the demoniac came running toward Christ, his disciples would likely have trembled in terror, or even ran away. But Christ does not tremble, or run:

When they arrived at the other side of the lake, a demon-possessed man ran out from a graveyard, just as Jesus was climbing from the boat.

This man lived among the gravestones and had such strength that whenever he was put into handcuffs and shackles—as he often was—he snapped the handcuffs from his wrists and smashed the shackles and walked away. No one was strong enough to control him.

All day long and through the night he would wander among the tombs and in the wild hills, screaming and cutting himself with sharp pieces of stone.

When Jesus was still far out on the water, the man had seen him and had run to meet him, and fell down before him.

Then Jesus spoke to the demon within the man and said, "Come out, you evil spirit." It gave a terrible scream, shrieking, "What are you going to do to me, Jesus, Son of the Most High God? For God's sake, don't torture me!"

"What is your name?" Jesus asked, and the demon replied, "Legion, for there are many of us here within this man."

Then the demons begged him again and again not to send them to some distant land.

Now as it happened there was a huge herd of hogs rooting around on the hill above the lake. "Send us into those hogs," the demons begged.

And Jesus gave them permission. Then the evil spirits came out of the man and entered the hogs, and the entire herd plunged down the steep hillside into the lake and drowned. The herdsmen fled to the nearby towns and

186

countryside, spreading the news as they ran. Everyone rushed out to see for themselves. And a large crowd soon gathered where Jesus was; but as they saw the man sitting there, fully clothed and perfectly sane, they were frightened. Those who saw what happened were telling everyone about it, and the crowd began pleading with Jesus to go away and leave them alone! So he got back into the boat...(Mark 5:1-18, Living Bible)

How did Christ cast out the demons? What power did he use? The mightiest power in the universe! Jesus was ever connected to his omnipotent heavenly Father. What are God's weapons? Did God force the demons out of the demoniac against the man's will, using some mysterious force, or power? No. The very presence of Christ awakened hope in the afflicted man, and kindled a small spark of faith, "When Jesus was still far out on the water, the man had seen him and had run to meet him, and fell down before him." The mighty power of God's love was present and expressed in the face of our Saviour.

As the demoniac rushed toward Jesus, the light, the infinite power and glory of God's love, in mighty streams began to pour forth into the heart and mind of the demon-possessed man. The demons could no more stay in control of this man than darkness can abide in the presence of light. Jesus demonstrated that God's powerful love is more than a match for sin, Satan, and even the degrading bonds of demon possession. Satan did not give up without a fight, though. That is why he had his demons ask permission to enter the pigs. Satan knew that if he destroyed the pigs that he could get the people to blame it on Jesus.

God and Satan were battling for the hearts and minds of the people on the shores of the Sea of Galilee (also called Lake Gennesaret). The principles are the same as in the book of Job. When Satan is allowed to destroy, he does it in such a way as to cast the blame on God. However, God, in his infinite love and wisdom, patiently waits for the opportunity of vindication.

Many people from the local villages, most certainly including the owners of the pigs, quickly gathered to see what had happened. The herdsmen told everyone about the pigs drowning in the lake. Together with the destruction of the pigs, the restoring of the demon-possessed man was too much for the local people.

Just as Satan wanted, the people rejected Jesus and asked him to leave. Even so, Jesus did not reject those who asked him to leave. Always patient, kind, and loving, Jesus required the restored man to stay. He knew that his story would have a powerful influence. It did. The next time Jesus came to the area the people eagerly received him with joy. Jesus also knew that the man's faith would be strengthened as he shared what Jesus had done for him.

This story of how Christ rescued the man from the evil grasp of demons presents a powerful contrast between God's principles of healing and freedom, and Satan's principles of degradation, slavery, and destruction. The demon-possessed man represents the condition, the end result of a life of sin. He shows what happens to a person that lives by Satan's principles. He had no self-control. He lived alone among the tombs. Sin separates. It destroys relationships. Sin causes guilt and self-hatred. Notice how the demon-possessed man cut himself with rocks. This man had followed his heart rather than reason. He had set reason aside so many times that he had none left. Satan would have us all follow our hearts. If it feels good, do it. But the end result of this path is ugly. Our intellect and heart must be guided by the loving power of the Holy Spirit.

Jesus represents the condition, the result of following Heaven's principles. Jesus had full control of himself. The multitudes followed him wherever he went. Jesus had close relationships with the disciples and many others. Jesus's face expressed innocence and love. He never engaged in mindless, self-destructive behavior. Jesus had strong emotions. He was more sensitive and had deeper feelings than any other person that has ever lived. But he always set reason above feelings. Jesus controlled his emotions. They never controlled him. He had appetites and passions. But he always controlled them.

To unreasoningly follow the dictates of emotions, appetite, or passion is to enter into Satan's dominion. Let's look at a story where Christ rescues two men from Satan's evil grasp:

Fire from Heaven?

Now it came to pass, when the time had come for Him to be received up, that He steadfastly set His face to go to Jerusalem, and sent messengers before His face. And as they went, they entered a village of the Samaritans, to prepare for Him. But they did not receive Him, because His face was set for the journey to Jerusalem. And when His disciples James and John saw this, they said, "Lord, do You want us to command fire to come down from heaven and consume them, just as Elijah did?"

But He turned and rebuked them, and said, "You do not know what manner of spirit you are of. "For the Son of Man did not come to destroy men's lives but to save them." (Luke 9:51-56, NKJ)

Those who seek to destroy are of Satan's spirit and kingdom. God's methods and Satan's methods are completely separate. God is holy. God's Ten Commandments are holy; they are his law of love. God does not use any of Lucifer's principles. None. Never. God never degrades himself by using the dark methods and principles of Satan's government!

I Will Hide My Face

God's principles never change. The same foundation principles that God explained to Moses, regarding the children of Israel, he will use to deal with the unrepentant, unbelieving sinners at the end of time. God hides, or veils his face. Just as fast as God hides his face, destruction comes:

And the LORD said unto Moses, Behold, thou shalt sleep with thy fathers; and this people will rise up, and go a whoring after the gods of the strangers of the land, whither they go to be among them, and will forsake me, and break my covenant which I have made with them.

Then my anger shall be kindled against them in that day, and I will forsake them, and I will hide my face from them, and they shall be devoured, and many evils and troubles shall befall them; so that they will say in that day, Are not these evils come upon us, because our God is not among us?

And I will surely hide my face in that day for all the evils which they shall have wrought, in that they are turned unto other gods.

Now therefore write ye this song for you, and teach it the children of Israel: put it in their mouths, that this song may be a witness for me against the children of Israel.

For when I shall have brought them into the land which I sware unto their fathers, that floweth with milk and honey; and they shall have eaten and filled themselves, and waxen fat; then will they turn unto other gods, and serve them, and provoke me, and break my covenant. (Deuteronomy 31:16-20, KJV)

God gave Moses, his prophet, an accurate, behind the scenes preview of the history of the children of Israel. When Israel sinned by choosing another master, God would hide his face from them. Reluctantly, God would hand Israel over to their chosen master—Satan. Even so, God put limits on what Satan could do to Israel. God's love grants freedom of choice. Even when God had to hide his face from Israel, he was longing to teach them his ways:

Give ear, O heavens, to my voice; let the earth take note of the words of my mouth:

My teaching is dropping like rain, coming down like dew on the fields; like rain on the young grass and showers on the garden plants:

For I will give honour to the name of the Lord: let our God be named great.

He is the Rock, complete is his work; for all his ways are

righteousness: a God without evil who keeps faith, true and upright is he.

And the Lord saw with disgust the evil-doing of his sons and daughters.

And he said, My face will be veiled from them, I will see what their end will be: for they are an uncontrolled generation, children in whom is no faith. (Deuteronomy 32:1-4, 19, 20, GLT)

When the children of Israel chose other gods, they were placing themselves under Satan's banner, "Yea, they turned back and tempted God, and limited the Holy One of Israel" (Psalm 78:41, KJV). "Neither murmur ye, as some of them also murmured, and were destroyed of the destroyer" (1Corinthians 10:10, KJV). Yes, our heavenly Father's heart churned within him and he longed to protect his beloved nation, Israel. However, backsliding Israel limited the Holy One of Israel.

God, in his perfect righteousness, desired good things for Israel. As Israel departed from God, their self-centered fears came upon them, "The desire of the righteous is only good, But the expectation of the wicked is wrath" (Proverbs 11:23, NKJ).

Satan worked through nature, foreign armies, internal strife, plagues, and as a destroying angel. He even brought fire down from Heaven in the sight of men. Satan made it look like all of these calamities came from our Father in Heaven.

Satan uses the same pattern over and over again. Our Father patiently endures the false accusations, biding his time, until people are ready to receive more light. God was constrained by the limitations of Israel's capacity to understand. The full light of God's glory is too much to receive all at once. It takes time. God's wrath is not opposite, or even separate from his glory.

Wheat and Grapes, Wrath and Fire

The seven last plagues of Revelation describe the wrath of God. We have noted that the Bible defines the wrath of God to be the hiding of his face, or to give up a person or nation to the

191

consequences of the decisions that have been made. In other words, our Father turns hardened sinners over to their chosen master—Satan.

Last night as I lay in my bed, I meditated on Revelation 14. John, in the last part of Revelation 14 delineates the wheat harvest, which represents the gathering, of the saved. Jesus, in the parable of the wheat and the tares (Matthew 13:24-43), identifies the wheat: "The good seed are the children of the kingdom." The grape harvest, in symbolic language denotes the fate of the wicked. The treading of the grapes denotes the wrath of God, the seven last plagues falling on the lost:

> And I looked, and behold, a white cloud. And on the cloud sat one like the Son of man, having a golden crown on His head, and a sharp sickle in His hand.
> And another angel came out of the temple, crying in a great voice to Him sitting on the cloud, Thrust in Your sickle and reap, for the time has come for You to reap, for the harvest of the earth was dried.
> And He sitting on the cloud thrust in His sickle on the earth, and the earth was reaped.
> And another angel came out of the temple in Heaven, also having a sharp sickle.
> And another angel came out from the altar, who had authority over fire. And he spoke with a great cry to him who had the sharp sickle, saying, Thrust in your sharp sickle, and gather the clusters of the vine of the earth, for her grapes are fully ripe.
> And the angel thrust in his sickle into the earth and gathered the vine of the earth, and cast it into the great winepress of the anger of God.
> And the winepress was trodden outside the city, and blood came out of the winepress, even to the bridles of the horses, for the space of a thousand, six hundred stadia. (Revelation 14:14-20, MKJ)

In verse 18, John describes an angel who, "came out from

the altar, who had authority over fire." That phrase had puzzled me. Why would God make known to us that the angel directing the initiation of the grape harvest had "authority over fire?" That information seemed completely incidental, useless. What could literal fire have to do with a symbolic grape harvest? Last night, the Holy Spirit impressed me with the importance of this concept. It can best be understood in the light of God's love.

Revelation is a highly symbolic book. The angel coming from the altar has authority over fire—symbolic fire. This fire symbolizes the results of the whole world following the desires of their heart, passions, and appetites rather than God's principle of unselfish love.

Revelation 16 describes the seven last plagues. The first plague brings a sore, which comes upon people taking the mark of the beast. Taking the mark is a spiritual/intellectual decision. The sore could come from a negative reaction to an injected biochip, or some other method of enforcing the mark of the beast. Or it could come form bad health habits, adulteration of the food supply, a virus, a vaccination, or perhaps a reaction to a pharmaceutical drug.

The Greek word for sorcery is Pharmakeia. Strong's Concordance defines Pharmakeia as:

1. the use or the administering of drugs.
2. poisoning.
3. sorcery, magical arts, often found in connection with idolatry and fostered by it.
4. metaphysics: the deceptions and seductions of idolatry.[2]

During the second and third plagues the seas and the rivers are turned to blood. Rodney Barker, in his book *And the Waters Turned to Blood*, outlines how pollution has started to unleash a bacterial scourge on the east coast that could at any time explode into a worldwide scourge. It would then fit the description of the plagues turning the waters to blood.[1] The same mind-set that leads the world, including apostate Christians, to destroy God's creation by polluting it will lead them to seek to destroy God's elect. The angel declares that shedding the blood of saints results in receiving blood to drink:

> And the second angel poured out his vial upon the sea; and it became as the blood of a dead man: and every living soul died in the sea.
> And the third angel poured out his vial upon the rivers and fountains of waters; and they became blood.
> And I heard the angel of the waters say, Thou art righteous, O Lord, which art, and wast, and shalt be, because thou hast judged thus.
> For they have shed the blood of saints and prophets, and thou hast given them blood to drink; for they are worthy.
> And I heard another out of the altar say, Even so, Lord God Almighty, true and righteous are thy judgments. (Revelation 16:3-7, KJV)

God has been shielding the world from the full consequences of sin. But when the world chooses Satan, God must hide his face. He must allow the world to suffer their fate at the hands of their chosen master. Satan has no mercy in his heart. None. The fourth plague, the sun scorching the Earth, might be the result of global warming or perhaps the destruction of the ozone layer. Or it could combine these two with a massive solar flare.

However the sun scorches the Earth, it is a case of the punishment fitting the crime. Nearly the entire Christian world honors the sun by worshipping on Sunday, or the day of the Sun. Remember, Lucifer means *Daystar*, or in other words, *Sun*. Lucifer has always claimed Sunday as his day. Sun worship all throughout history has used Sunday for worship.

The seventh-day Sabbath is the Creator's (Jesus) day.

The fifth plague brings darkness and pain. This is a fitting result of rejecting God's light and truth as it is in Jesus. Hot volcanic ash filling the air? Perhaps. The world will soon experience the horrific results of turning from God and embracing Satan.

The sixth plague is the great battle of Armageddon. Satan will gather the nations to battle God's people. Satan wants them to annihilate God's special people. This vast throng of people will turn on themselves, though. They have set reason and love aside. They are so degraded and impassioned that they can no longer cooperate with one another.

Preview to Armageddon

God has given us several previews of Armageddon in the Old Testament. We will choose the story in 2Chronicles 20. It tells the story of the nations of Moab, Ammon, and Mount Seir gathering together to destroy Israel. Satan was always trying to move the nations to destroy Israel:

> "This battle is not for you to fight; take your position, stand still, and see the victory of the LORD on your behalf, O Judah and Jerusalem. Do not fear or be dismayed; tomorrow go out against them, and the LORD will be with you." Then Jehoshaphat bowed down with his face to the ground, and all Judah and the inhabitants of Jerusalem fell down before the LORD, worshiping the LORD. And the Levites, of the Kohathites and the Korahites, stood up to praise the LORD, the God of Israel, with a very loud voice.
> They rose early in the morning and went out into the wilderness of Tekoa; and as they went out, Jehoshaphat stood and said, "Listen to me, O Judah and inhabitants of Jerusalem! Believe in the LORD your God and you will be established; believe his prophets." When he had taken counsel with the people, he appointed those who were to sing to the LORD and praise him in holy splendor, as they went before the army, saying, "Give thanks to the LORD, for his steadfast love endures forever."
> As they began to sing and praise, the LORD set an ambush against the Ammonites, Moab, and Mount Seir, who had come against Judah, so that they were routed. For the Ammonites and Moab attacked the inhabitants of Mount Seir, destroying them utterly; and when they had made an end

of the inhabitants of Seir, they all helped to destroy one another.

When Judah came to the watchtower of the wilderness, they looked toward the multitude; they were corpses lying on the ground; no one had escaped. (2Chronicles 20:17-24, NRSV)

Don't miss *how* God ambushed Satan's horde. God allowed Ammon and Moab to destroy the people of Mount Seir! Then they turned on one another. No one survived! This story foreshadows the battle of Armageddon. God's people will praise him with songs and shouts of joy. Satan's hordes, Gog and Magog, which are all the nations of the Earth, will finally understand that they have been deceived and that they are lost. The multitudes will first focus their hatred on the false teachers, ministers, and leaders who have deceived them. Enraged and in despair, they will turn on one another with desperate fury and destroy one another totally.

This is the treading of the winepress of Revelation 14. First the wheat harvest and then the plagues of the grape harvest. Our God is sovereign. God has chosen to allow the wicked to destroy themselves. Who are we, finite mortals, to tell God that he must violate his infinite love to directly punish, kill, and destroy?

Notice, that the "Son of man," (Jesus) harvests the wheat, or in other words, saves the righteous. Notice also, that the angel throws grapes into the winepress, but blood is what comes out! God uses symbolic language to reveal to us what will happen shortly. The blood coming out of the winepress is the blood of the lost. When the Holy Spirit is finally grieved away from the multitudes of the lost, violence, murder, and war will cause the blood to flow.

The angel who "had authority over fire" signals the beginning of the fiery passions, the winds of strife, the rage, grief, terror, and anguish of the lost. John also here describes this as the treading of the winepress.

This occurs when everyone on Earth has decided to accept

or reject Jesus, "He that is unjust, let him be unjust still: and he which is filthy, let him be filthy still: and he that is righteous, let him be righteous still: and he that is holy, let him be holy still" (Revelation 22:11, KJV). Our Father will hand the lost over to Satan, the master they have chosen. Our Father will hide his face and Satan will torment and destroy those that God has reluctantly relinquished into his power. John refers to this time, this event:

God Will Grieve Alone
Then I looked and saw that the Temple in heaven, God's Tabernacle, was thrown wide open! The seven angels who were holding the bowls of the seven plagues came from the Temple, clothed in spotless white linen with gold belts across their chests. And one of the four living beings handed each of the seven angels a gold bowl filled with the terrible wrath of God, who lives forever and forever. The Temple was filled with smoke from God's glory and power. No one could enter the Temple until the seven angels had completed pouring out the seven plagues. (Revelation 15:5-8, NLT)

The reason no one can enter the temple in Heaven at the time of the pouring out of the seven last plagues is because no one could understand, or even survive the passionate display of our Father's infinite anguish, and wrath at seeing his precious lost children fall into the horrific hands of Satan, the Destroyer.

Jesus separated from his disciples when he knew that he faced extreme soul anguish. Our Father also surrounded the cross with darkness during Jesus's extreme suffering. The Father will also separate himself from all created beings when he begins to endure the unspeakable sorrow and soul anguish when he is constrained to hand his lost children over to Satan's control. God never stops loving sinners, even those that finally reject him. The greater one's love, the greater one's risk of pain. God's love is infinite. The plagues cause God immeasurable pain.

197

Satan leads the lost to blame the plagues on God. The lost "blasphemed the name of God, which hath power over these plagues: and they repented not to give him glory" (Revelation 16:9, KJV).

The seventh plague ends Earth's history of sinner's persecution of the saved. God thunders from his throne in the temple saying, "It is done!" (Revelation 16:17, NRSV). The worst earthquake of all time and hundred pound hailstones will devastate the people of the Earth. The mountains and cities will be leveled, and the islands will disappear. The wicked of the Earth will curse God, blaming him for the plagues, which is blasphemy.

History Repeats

In Heaven, Lucifer sowed the seeds of discontent. Then he blamed the results on God. Lucifer assumed the part of peacemaker, reconciler. But he was the one that had caused the trouble. So it continues on today. Satan causes catastrophes on the left hand and on the right, all the while teaching men to blame God. As a result of Satan's lies, men shake their fist toward Heaven and blame God, when it is Satan who brings these destructive natural disasters.

Satan uses men's guilt against God. Men sin, and so feel guilty. Then men blame God for the guilt. Satan leads men to look upon our Father as a stern and harsh Judge. This error leads to another. Satan's destructive actions and man's own warring, crime and destructive actions, are presumed to be the "judgments of God." Satan is the one that advocates stern justice, and harsh punishment against man. Satan is the Accuser of the brethren (Revelation 12:10). The Destroyer and all who choose his side of the war will come to an awful end.

However, God does not arbitrarily destroy the wicked. God in his infinite wisdom and mercy has been shielding Satan from the full effects of sin and rebellion. However, Satan will suffer for the sins he has caused. In the sanctuary, this was symbolized during the Day of Atonement when the high priest transferred Israel's sin and guilt to the scapegoat, Azazel. Then the scapegoat was led out into the wilderness, by the hand of a fit man (symbol of Jesus), and left there to die.

The wilderness is a fit symbol for the abyss (the empty place) that Satan and his angels will be confined to during the Sabbath millennium of rest. The abyss is empty because all the wicked people are dead and all the saved have been taken to Heaven with Jesus. No hand was laid upon the scapegoat. Nor will God actively destroy Satan. Satan will bear the weight of his own sins, which include leading people into sin. Satan does not save us from our sins. But, he does carry the heavy responsibility for initiating sin.

God used the sanctuary service to shed the light of his love upon Israel. Despite this, through the long centuries, selfishness and sin blinded Israel and they remained in deep spiritual darkness. That same darkness covers much of the world today.

God's Battle Plan

Jesus came into our dark world to bring the light of the truth of the beautiful knowledge of God's character of love to his precious children, "The people who sat in darkness saw a great Light; and Light has sprung up to those who sat in the region and shadow of death" (Matthew 4:16, MKJ).

A lack of knowledge, or a misunderstanding of God's character can cause people to perish, "My people are destroyed for lack of knowledge" (Hosea 4:6, KJV).

There will be no pain and suffering, no death and destruction in Heaven. Our heavenly Father explains why this will be, "They shall not hurt nor destroy in all my holy mountain: for the earth shall be full of the knowledge of the LORD, as the waters cover the sea" (Isaiah 11:9, KJV). The "knowledge of the Lord" means knowledge about our Father's heart, character, personality and law. God hates to see our pain and death.

It might seem a difficult task for God to wage war without using force and destruction. It is! That is why it is taking six thousand years for God to bring sin to an end. If God had been willing to use threats, coercion, or destructive force, the rebellion would have been brought to a swift end. Adam and Eve would never have even been tempted by the devil. However, God's subjects would have lived in fear. Rebellion would have simmered beneath the surface, in the hearts of God's children. God could not truly bring security to Heaven with force. God found it prudent to give sin time to burn itself out.

God chose to do battle by revealing his love through his Son, "that through death he might destroy him that had the power of death, that is, the devil" (Hebrews 2:14, KJV).

God saved us, and the whole universe, through his Son. By looking to Jesus and meditating on his life and death, we can come to know what our heavenly Father is like. Through his powerful love, God can destroy Satan's hold on us. To know God is to love him. To know God is to enter into eternal life, "And this is life eternal, that they may know You, the only true God, and Jesus Christ whom You have sent" (John 17:3, NRSV).

Remember that God loves sinners with a deep, infinite love that led him to lay down his life for us. God's infinite love never changes. Our good deeds won't make him love us more. Our bad deeds won't make him love us less. Jesus showed us that God's anger, his wrath is more akin to our human grief than to fury, "And when he had looked round about on them with anger, being grieved for the hardness of their hearts, he saith unto the man, Stretch forth thine hand" (Mark 3:5, KJV).

God's wrath is also shown to mean: to hide his face, (withdraw his protection), to honor the decision of those sinners that have persistently rejected him and chosen Satan and his kingdom. God allows evil angels to destroy those that fully reject his love. "He cast upon them the fierceness of his anger, wrath, and indignation, and trouble, by sending evil angels among them" (Psalm 78:49, KJV). That is his strange work, his strange act.

Admah and Zeboiim

Isaiah and Moses gave us insights into the heart of our heavenly Father. Paul restates these same truths. Paul defines God's wrath for us as handing over the sinner to his own desires and the dire consequences that brings. God's anger, his wrath is to withdraw his protection, to hide his face from those who have persistently rejected his love and care:

> For the wrath of God is revealed from heaven against all ungodliness and unrighteousness of men, who suppress the truth in unrighteousness, Therefore God also gave them up to uncleanness, in the lusts of their hearts, to dishonor their bodies among themselves, For this reason God gave them up to vile passions. For even their women exchanged the natural use for what is against nature. And even as they did not like to retain God in their knowledge, God gave them over to a debased mind, to do those things which are not fitting; (Romans 1:18, 24, 26, 28, NKJ)

Listen to the heart of God as he weeps over his apostate children:

> My people are bent on backsliding from Me. Though they call to the Most High, None at all exalt Him. How can I give you up, Ephraim? How can I hand you over, Israel? How can I make you like Admah? How can I set you like Zeboiim? My heart churns within Me; My sympathy is stirred. (Hosea 11:7, 8, NKJ)

Don't miss, "How can I hand you over Israel? How can I make you like Admah." Admah and Zeboiim were among the cities that were destroyed with Sodom and Gomorrah. In other words, God is saying, "How can I hand Israel over, as I handed Sodom and Gomorrah over, for Satan to destroy. Our Father in Heaven lives and rules by eternal principles. "For I am the LORD, I do not change; Therefore you are not consumed, O sons of Jacob" (Malachi 3:6, NKJ). Sin has not caused our Father to alter the principles of his government at all. The foundation principle of the government of Heaven is the principle, or law, of self-sacrificing love.

God's Ways and Ideas

If the appearance of sin on Heaven's scene had made it necessary to change any of God's eternal principles, then Lucifer would have been proven right, for Lucifer claimed that God's law of love could not deal with open rebellion. Therefore it needed to be improved upon. It was Satan's idea that sin and rebellion should be punished. But this was not God's idea. God expressed his idea through the life and death of Jesus Christ. Punishment and death are not part of God's eternal principles. Rather, suffering and death result naturally from living out of harmony with God's law of unselfish love. The cross has proven God right.

Sin brings guilt, self-condemnation, suffering, and death. We judge and condemn other sinners based on the measure of our own self-condemnation and guilt. This error leads to another error—that sinners need to be punished. It also results in people taking revenge into their own hands, for example, the Palestinian-Israeli conflict.

Innocent people die on both sides of the conflict. Each side wants to avenge itself. The Palestinians send a suicide bomber into Israel and innocent people die. Israel responds with tanks or helicopter gunships and more innocent people die. Hatred breeds hatred. The only good solution to this conflict is for both Palestinians and Israelis to learn of God's love and to accept it. They must learn to respect and love one another, or they will keep destroying one another, despite temporary, futile efforts at peace.

A self-righteous religion always leads to the condemnation of others. The condemnation of others, in reality is self-condemnation. Both of these problems come from a mistaken understanding of the character of God and an underestimation of the destructive power of sin. A self-righteous religion always ends up resorting to force. False religion will yet persuade our government to enforce her decrees. And God's people will suffer.

When God's people suffer, God suffers. "In all their affliction he was afflicted." Remember how Jesus interrupted the

202

triumphal entry to weep over Jerusalem! What an awful, sad, strange act for God!

Remember that Christ could only do what he saw his Father doing. Our heavenly Father also wept when he was "limited" by his people Israel, when he had to give them over to their chosen ruler, Satan. This is God's strange act! This is the wrath of God.

Beholding God's holy character of love, experiencing his love for us is the truth that sets us free to love and obey him, which is eternal life. It is the only way that we can learn to truly love one another.

The death of Christ fully revealed the character of God's love and also the dark destructive power of sin. No one except Christ has ever experienced the full results of sin. God has always spared his creatures from the fullness of the natural destructive consequences of sin, "Because sentence against an evil work is not executed speedily, therefore the heart of the sons of men is fully set in them to do evil" (Ecclesiastes 8:11, KJV). This same principle applies with equal force to fallen angels.

Sin Burns Itself Out

As we discussed in chapter one, if Lucifer had believed that God would punish his rebellion with death, Lucifer out of fear would have tried to stay loyal to God, even if not out of love. What Lucifer did not immediately understand, was that the inevitable, natural, unassisted, outcome of rebellion (sin) is self-destruction (eternal death). The wages of sin is death. Lucifer knew that the Creator-God had infinite power, and could easily destroy him for his rebellion. God does not desire a fear-based worship. Lucifer understood that God's character was pure love. Lucifer knew that God would not destroy any of his created beings, for that would be inconsistent with the foundation law of all Heaven—unconditional, unselfish, holy, love.

However, rebellious Lucifer and sinful, deceived mankind alike underestimate the self-destructive power of selfishness, which is sin, the transgression of God's law of love. Lucifer has led men to accuse our holy, loving God of sending those sinners who, in human weakness and foolishness, failed to reach his high standard of holiness to an eternal fiery torment (hell).

Unbelieving, rebellious men and angels who reject God's merciful offer to carry their sin, to be their Sin-Bearer do come to an end. God's strange act is to grant them the desire of their hearts, which is to hang onto their sins. Sin destroys totally. They have rejected Christ's mercy, their only hope. Sin killed Jesus on the cross. Let's not blame it on God the Father.

Satan's rebellion played out here on our planet shows the entire universe once, and for all time, the shameful, degrading, and destructive results of sin. Satan's principle of self-seeking has degraded men and angels. Look at the demon-possessed people in the Bible; No one wants to be like one of them! Even so, that is the end result of anyone who chooses to hang on to sin and thereby come under the full control of Satan.

The Cross Guarantees Peace

God's law of love is the only path to harmony, peace, happiness, and security for all his children. Satan's method of harsh punishment and rigid justice have failed here on Earth. The death penalty has not succeeded in deterring serious crime. The torture of terror suspects only breeds more terrorists. Nor does torture provide reliable information, as a person will make up lies to escape the pain. Notice the corruption that fills the political and corporate world today. Our elected government officials lie to us regularly. Crime continues unabated. Our earthly system of reward and punishment is not working. Satan's system has failed. Perhaps it is time to give God's principles a try!

After the close of this Earth's painful history no one will ever again think to set aside God's law of love. None will ever again doubt the goodness and love of God. The cross of Calvary, Jesus the Son of God, and his infinite sacrifice will have fully won every heart that has responded to and accepted Jesus's love.

Nowhere in all the universe, in all of time, have we ever,

or will we ever see a more intense revelation of God's wrath and his love than in the suffering and death of Jesus Christ on the cross of Calvary. Humanity's history of sin will be a protection for the ages of eternity. The cross will keep us safe.

Jesus, on the cross of Calvary fully revealed God's love, his mercy and justice, and his wrath. I stand in awe of the pure, practical wisdom of our heavenly Father.

Those who are open to the Holy Spirit can look at Jesus on the cross and begin to see a revelation of infinite love. They can also begin to see the infinite depths of the Father's wrath against sin. God's wrath against sin is to hide his face. Please do not make the terrible mistake of thinking that "God hiding his face" is a trivial thing! Remember the Son of God's reaction as the world's sin and guilt began to block his view of the Father's face!

> At noon the sky turned dark and stayed that way until three o'clock. Then about that time Jesus shouted, "Eli, Eli, lema sabachthani?" which means, "My God, my God, why have you deserted me?" (Matthew 27:45, 46, CEV)

Christ suffered our fate, the results of sin, "For the wages of sin is death, but the gift of God is eternal life in Christ Jesus our Lord" (Romans 6:23, NKJ). Sin brings death. God brings life. God hates sin, because it brings suffering and death to those whom he loves. Remember that God loves the world:

> For God so loved the world that He gave His only begotten Son, that whoever believes in Him should not perish but have everlasting life. For God did not send His Son into the world to condemn the world, but that the world through Him might be saved. (John 3:16, 17, NKJ)

> But God demonstrates His own love toward us, in that while we were still sinners, Christ died for us. (Romans 5:8, NKJ)

The Deep Things of God

But we speak the wisdom of God in a mystery, the hidden wisdom which God ordained before the ages for our glory, which none of the rulers of this age knew; for had they known, they would not have crucified the Lord of glory. But as it is written: "Eye has not seen, nor ear heard, nor have entered into the heart of man The things which God has prepared for those who love Him." But God has revealed them to us through His Spirit. For the Spirit searches all things, yes, the deep things of God. (1 Corinthians 2:7-10, NKJ)

God's glory is his character of love. If the rulers of Christ's age had understood the glory of God's unconditional love, they would have recognized the holiness of Christ's love, glory, and power. They would not have crucified the Lord of glory. Today, we too must pay attention to what Paul taught. We must avoid the errors the Jewish leaders fell into. They believed that God used force to overcome his enemies. He does not. God risked everything to turn his enemies into his friends!

The Holy Spirit has revealed the deep things of God to us. There's nothing deeper, higher, broader, or more powerful than God's infinite, unconditional love. God showed us his love by creating us. When we fell, God showed us his love by redeeming us. Soon God will show us his love again and come to take us home! God's love gives each human being infinite value. We can see that in the sacrifice of Jesus.

God has shown the value he places on each human being by allowing his Son to die the second death, to save us from sin. The life and death of Christ rebukes sin and points out its dangers and its inevitable end result—eternal death. But Christ never once punished sin. Nor did he kill anyone. Jesus is the embodiment of the law, which is a transcript of the character of the Father. Since Christ is the law lived out, we can safely conclude that the law does not punish or kill either. Christ is the express image of the Father.

God Loved the Egyptians

When we see calamities fall on other sinners, our guilt, our self-condemnation causes us to misunderstand the true issues involved. Pharaoh was a sinner. Did God harden Pharaoh's heart? Did God send the plagues upon the Egyptians? Did God slay the firstborn sons of the Egyptians? Our heavenly Father had blessed Egypt. He is the One that had given them sunshine and rain (Matthew 5:45). He had caused their crops to grow. His power had kept the frogs in the river. He had protected them from the swarms of locusts. He had kept the flies and the lice in check. He had kept the hail from destroying animals and crops. Why did God pour out all these blessings upon the Egyptians? Because he loved them! Remember that God didn't love Israel instead of the other nations. God is no respecter of persons. God wanted to love the other nations through Israel. Israel limited the Holy One.

Every soul was precious in his sight. But the Egyptians worshiped other "gods." Satan claimed the right to destroy them, as they had chosen him. Remember Job chapters one and two, and Deuteronomy 31:16-30. God allowed Satan to test a perfect, godly man like Job. Satan destroyed all Job's possessions and family. Then Satan plagued Job with boils. If Satan is allowed to bring all this destruction on a man loyal to God, imagine what he could do to those who finally reject God!

God sent Moses to the Egyptians as a mediator, a type of Christ. God sent Moses to save Egypt, not to destroy it. Pharaoh repeatedly rejected his only mediator:

> And afterward Moses and Aaron went in, and told Pharaoh, Thus saith the LORD God of Israel, Let my people go, that they may hold a feast unto me in the wilderness. And Pharaoh said, Who is the LORD, that I should obey his voice to let Israel go? I know not the LORD, neither will I let Israel go. (Exodus 5:1, 2, KJV)

Even though the Creator-God had poured out his blessings upon Egypt, Pharaoh in his ignorance and pride chose not

207

to recognize the Source of these blessings. His sorcerers and enchanters convinced Pharaoh that Egypt's prosperity was a result of natural causes. Every time that he hardened his heart, God was forced to honor Pharaoh's decision and step-by-step give the land of Egypt over to the destroying angel—Satan.

Jesus hardened Pharaoh's heart in the same way he hardened Judas' heart—by loving him. But every warning, every blessing rejected, we turn into a curse upon ourselves. It is the same warm sun that melts butter, but hardens clay:

> They remembered not his hand, nor the day when he delivered them from the enemy. How he had wrought his signs in Egypt, and his wonders in the field of Zoan: And had turned their rivers into blood; and their floods, that they could not drink. He sent divers sorts of flies among them, which devoured them; and frogs, which destroyed them. He gave also their increase unto the caterpiller, and their labour unto the locust. He destroyed their vines with hail, and their sycomore trees with frost. He gave up their cattle also to the hail, and their flocks to hot thunderbolts. He cast upon them the fierceness of his anger, wrath, and indignation, and trouble, by sending evil angels among them. He made a way to his anger; he spared not their soul from death, but gave their life over to the pestilence; And smote all the firstborn in Egypt; the chief of their strength in the tabernacles of Ham. (Psalm 78:42-51, KJV)

God had been protecting the land of Egypt. As God allowed Satan to afflict the Egyptians with each new plague, God longed for them to recognize his love and care for them. If the Egyptians had turned to God, he would have had the right to spare them. Remember that God and Satan are at war. There are rules of engagement.

But Pharaoh insisted on believing that all God's blessings and all Satan's plagues were the result of natural causes. God's wrath against the Egyptians was to hand them over to the consequences of sin. Notice the phrases: "by sending evil angels among them;" "he gave them up;" and "he gave them over."

In the light of the cross we need to understand this to mean that God allowed Satan and his evil angels to bring the plagues on the Egyptians because they had chosen Satan. Satan glories in destroying God's children. Through Moses, God warned his beloved Egyptian children:

> Give an order now to bring your livestock and everything you have in the field to a place of shelter, because the hail will fall on every man and animal that has not been brought in and is still out in the field, and they will die. Those officials of pharaoh who feared the word of the Lord hurried to bring their slaves and their livestock inside. (Exodus 9:19, 20, NIV)

God loved the Egyptians as well as the people of Israel. He warned both peoples about the plague of hail. Note that some of the Egyptians "feared the word of the Lord" and were saved from the plague.

God's wrath is an expression of his love. Even when God reluctantly has to hand over some of his children to taste the bitter consequences of sin, he hopes to draw them to feel their need for him.

God's Wrath and Abortion

The Old Testament often mentions God's anger and wrath. The Hebrew word *aph* is commonly translated as anger or wrath. According to Strong's Concordance, the Hebrew word *aph* can mean forbearing, long-suffering, face, nostrils, nose, angry, before, countenance, forehead, and snout. *Aph* is derived from the primitive root *anaph*: to be angry, to be displeased, or to breathe hard[2]. A deep breath could be a sigh. God has led me to view his anger and wrath toward humans as long-suffering, anguish, and forbearing rather than mere human anger:

> And when he had looked round about on them with anger, being grieved for the hardness of their hearts, he saith unto

the man, Stretch forth thine hand. And he stretched it out: and his hand was restored whole as the other. (Mark 3:5, KJV)

Our loving, long-suffering, heavenly Father must surely sigh and cry in sadness and in pain when he sees his children choose the path of self-destruction. Jesus reveals to us the Father's heart. When Jesus saw rebellious and unrepentant Jerusalem, during the triumphal entry, he wept in uncontrollable anguish. He did not want to let his children go. That is a demonstration of the wrath of God. In English *anger* and *anguish* come from the same root word. God creates and saves life. Satan destroys life.

Life begins at conception. Life is a gift from God. Taking life at any stage is unethical, immoral, contrary to God's character of love, and against God's law; in short, abortion is murder, a violation of the sixth commandment. Abortion approved by our nation's laws brings negative results upon our great country. This should cause Christians to be concerned and to take action. We should speak out against such things, contact our representatives, educate, etc. However, using violence to oppose abortion would not be in harmony with God's principles.

God does not promote sin in order to fight sin. Absolutely not! God does allow sinners to fight each other to stop some of sin's excesses. Even so, people that shoot doctors and bomb clinics that practice abortion are also guilty of murder. I do not judge their motives, just the actions. God tells us how to battle against evil, "Do not be overcome by evil, but overcome evil with good" (Romans 12:21, RSV). Fighting fire with fire just creates a bigger fire. Fighting sin with sin just adds to the misery, suffering, and guilt in our world. God is not honored with such practices.

If God had wanted to punish sin by using the perverted principles Lucifer advocated, he would have destroyed Lucifer as soon as he had rebelled. Lucifer is alive and well, actually sustained by God's power. The fact that sinners sometimes live long, prosperous lives strongly argues that God doesn't use force in the way that Lucifer had promoted.

Were God to withdraw his power from any of his creatures, life would cease, "When you turn away, they are afraid; when you take away your breath, they die and go back to the dust from which they came" (Psalm 104:29, TEV). That applies even to Satan, "All the prosperous of the earth shall eat and worship; All those who go down to the dust shall bow before Him, even he who cannot keep himself alive" (Psalm 22:29, NKJ). The phrase "even he who cannot keep himself alive includes angels as well as humans. God is the Source and Sustainer of all life; Satan lives only because God upholds him. God sustains Lucifer in order that we may freely choose between good and evil. Evil must be given the full opportunity to burn itself out.

God is just, fair, merciful, kind, wise, and loving. God is wise to allow Satan to continue so that we can choose between the two proposed governments. Also, God wants us to see how he deals with rebellion, which is with great patience, care, and gentleness. Christ struck the deathblow to Satan's claims at the cross. Time, sin, and the rebellion continue, however, until we as humans can fully see the difference between Jesus and Satan. And until everyone has made their final decision. Let's help bring this world of suffering to an end by accepting Jesus for who he really is!

> The Lord isn't really being slow about his promise to return, as some people think. No, he is being patient for your sake. He does not want anyone to perish, so he is giving more time for everyone to repent (2Peter 3:9, NLT).

1. Barker, Rodney (1997). And the Waters Turned to Blood. New York: Simon and Schuster

2. Strong, James (1990). New Strong's Exhaustive Concordance of the Bible. Nashville, TN: Thomas Nelson Publishers.

*What matters is faith
that works through love.
(Galatians 5:6, TEV)*

*Meanwhile these three remain:
faith, hope, and love;
and the greatest of these is love.
(1 Corinthians 13:13, TEV)*

*Do we destroy the Law
by our faith? Not at all!
We make it even more powerful.
(Romans 3:31, CEV)*

*So then faith cometh by hearing,
and hearing by the word of God.
(Romans 10:17, KJV)*

10

Faith

A Son's Faith

In the movie "The Day After Tomorrow," maverick, but brilliant climatologist Jack Hall warns government leaders of extreme weather to be followed by catastrophically cold weather systems that will lead to a new ice age. The leaders downplay Jack Hall's warnings until it is too late to do much about it.

As a result of the rapid climate change a severe storm system hits the east coast and New York gets flooded. Jack's son, Sam is on a trip to New York for a high school science decathlon. Sam and a few friends get stranded in New York City. From a nearly submerged pay phone, Sam calls his father, who is in Philadelphia. Jack persuades him to wait for him, explaining that the storm will be too dangerous to travel in. Jack emphasizes that he will come for Sam.

Jack loves his son; Sam knows that. He also knows that his father is smart, determined, and strong. During the killingly cold storm, Sam and his friends follow his father's advice and stay in the city library.

Many others brave the unimaginable cold and perish. Sam and his friends keep warm by burning books in the library fireplace. Some of Sam's friends contend that his father won't be able to come for him. They maintain that the storm is too severe. Sam calmly responds that his father will come. He knows his father; they do not. Facing great risk and hardship, Jack and two close friends set out to rescue Sam. They drive as far as they can. When they can drive no further, they continue on skis. One of Jack's friends dies on the way. Using all his strength, ingenuity, and sheer will power, Jack beats the ravages of the storm. He comes for his son. Sam was happy to see his father, but not surprised.

Sam is a good example of faith in action. Sam does not just affirm that he believes his father—he makes life and death decisions based on his father's word. Jesus also made life and death decisions based on his Father's word, "I can do nothing of My own self. As I hear, I judge, and My judgment is just, because I do not seek My own will, but the will of the Father who has sent Me" (John 5:30, MKJ). Jesus depended on his Father for everything he did throughout his ministry. Jesus was our example in all things. Jesus's faith in his Father sustained him in the challenges of day-to-day life.

Sin Separates, Faith Unites

Faith is what sustained Jesus through the darkest hours of his life, for Jesus knew and trusted his heavenly Father. When they were nailing him to the cross, Jesus had prayed, "Father forgive them for they know not what they do." He used the endearing term *Father*. This indicates that his faith was strong and that he felt close to his Father at that point. Yet, as Jesus hung dying on the cross, Satan tempted him to think that God had rejected him. Notice the shift to the more formal and distant term, "My God."

Now from the sixth hour there was darkness over all the land unto the ninth hour. And about the ninth hour Jesus cried with a loud voice, saying, Eli, Eli, lama sabachthani? that is to say, My God, my God, why hast thou forsaken me? (Matthew 27:45, 46, KJV)

This expresses the feeling of rejection that Christ experienced. Christ was sliding into the depths of the pit, the abyss of hell. He felt separated from God.

All his life, Jesus knew the height and depth of the Father's love. Jesus knew that nothing could stop the infinite stream of love flowing from the Heavenly Father's heart. Not even sin could separate Jesus from his Father. When we sin, our sense of justice accuses us. We feel guilty. We naturally *feel* that God condemns us. He does not:

> Behold, the LORD'S hand is not shortened, that it cannot save; neither his ear heavy, that it cannot hear: But your iniquities have separated between you and your God, and your sins have hid *his* face from you, that he will not hear. (Isaiah 59:1, 2, KJV)

Have you ever felt that your prayers went no higher than the ceiling? I have. No one ever felt the insidious strength of the temptation to doubt to the degree that Jesus did. Two things can cause that feeling.

1. Hanging on to sin causes us to feel separated from God, when we are not.

2. Having a wrong concept of God's character. Remember what Jesus told Nicodemus, "For God sent not his Son into the world to condemn the world; but that the world through him might be saved." (John 3:17, KJV).

Neither Jesus nor the Father judge or condemn sinners. God does not arbitrarily decree that sinners must die. Yet sin causes the sinner to feel that God condemns him. Witness Adam and Eve hiding from God in the Garden of Eden. Jesus carried the sin and guilt of the entire human race. He felt condemned. He was tempted to believe the feelings of condemnation. But he knew his Father better than that. Jesus knew that his sense of condemnation did not come from his Father.

Jesus had explained the plan of salvation to Nicodemus, "The man who has faith in him does not come up to be judged; but he who has no faith in him has been judged even now, because he has no faith in the name of the only Son of

God" (John 3:18, BBE). Name means reputation, or character. God's character is unconditional love. God loves sinners. Jesus knew that God loved sinners unconditionally. That is what allowed Jesus to see past the infinite load of sin and guilt. The substance, the essence, the vision of faith is the knowledge, based on theory and experience, that God loves sinners unconditionally. Jesus survived the cross by faith alone, faith in his Father's character of unconditional, unselfish love.

One major problem with sin is that it causes us to fear and flee from God, "And this is the test by which men are judged: the light has come into the world and men have more love for the dark than for the light, because their acts are evil" (John 3:19, BBE). But sin, even the whole world's sin couldn't make Jesus try to hide from his Father. A knowledge of God's goodness, his unconditional love, draws us to him. His love overcomes sin and doubt the way a powerful searchlight overcomes darkness. Faith, through the mighty power of love wins the victory over sin, doubt, and hell.

The Faith of Jesus

While on the cross, Jesus had been suffering the agonies of the second death, or hell. Our intrepid Savior wrestled with all the lies, temptations, doubts, and infernal devices of hell. Even though Satan and all his evil angels bombarded Jesus with their fierce temptations, they could not stop Jesus from relying on his Father's love. The blind and self-centered church leaders could not stop Jesus from relying on his Father. The full weight of all our sin and guilt could not stop God's love. Men's rejection of Jesus could not stop his faith from resting in the knowledge of his Father's love.

Jesus relied on the evidence, the experience of his Father's love. He had seen God's love in action. Jesus knew that he had been the vessel for God's love that had rescued Mary Magdalene from sin and destruction. She had anointed his body for burial. She was one of the few to accept Christ's testimony that he was going to die.

When the thief on the cross accepted Jesus as Lord, that

also brightened the darkness that pressed down on Jesus's heart and mind. At the end, the faith of Jesus broke through Satan's lies about God, "And when Jesus had cried with a loud voice, he said, Father, into thy hands I commend my spirit: and having said thus, he gave up the ghost" (Luke 23:46, KJV). At the end, Jesus again used the intimate word "Father." This reveals that Jesus had regained his sense of closeness to his Father. His feelings followed his reason.

Faith, Feelings, and Reason

Feelings are beautiful, a gift from God. But they are not a substitute or even a foundation for faith. Feelings must follow faith and reason.

From time to time, we too may feel that God has abandoned us. However, as Jesus did, we may trust that our loving God is always with us. The better we come to know the character of our Father, the more fully we will be able to trust him. The cross of Jesus proves that sin and guilt cannot separate us from the love of God, unless we allow it to. No matter how dark our world may appear to be, it can never be as dark as it was for Jesus!

Sin does not cause God to stop loving us, or to turn away from us. It is the guilt and attraction of sin that cause us to turn away from our loving God. We too, through the power of the Holy Spirit, must break through Satan's lies about God, his law, and the nature of faith. The key to stronger faith in God is to know him better:

Thus says the Lord: "Let not the wise man glory in his wisdom, Let not the mighty man glory in his might, Nor let the rich man glory in his riches; But let him who glories glory in this, That he understands and knows Me, That I am the Lord, exercising lovingkindness, judgment, and righteousness in the earth. For in these I delight," says the Lord. (Jeremiah 9:23, 24, NKJ)

"And this is life eternal, that they might know You, the

217

only true God, and Jesus Christ whom You have sent" (John 17:3, MKJ). To know God is to love him. To love God is to have faith in him. Faith in God brings eternal life. We can enter into eternal life now, by turning to Jesus.

When we turn to Jesus, we are choosing to live by God's eternal principles, his Ten Words of love. We have then entered into the heavenly realms of eternal life. Faith in, and love for God will cause us to hate sin. God's character is summed up in his law, the Ten Commandments. Therefore, to love God is to love his law. One cannot love God and love sin at the same time, "No man can serve two masters: for either he will hate the one, and love the other; or else he will hold to the one, and despise the other" (Matthew 6:24, KJV).

"Here is the patience of the saints: here are they that keep the commandments of God, and the faith of Jesus" (Revelation 14:12, KJV). In this Scripture, the apostle John affirms that the last generation of Christians will, like Christ, keep God's Ten Commandments. They will also have the faith of Jesus. The faith of Jesus was so strong that, even though carrying the sin and guilt of the world, he still knew that his Father loved him!

As Jesus was rejected by the world and by the nominal church leaders of his day, so God's elect will be rejected by the world, and by nominal Christian leaders of our day. History will be repeated. God's elect will even be tempted to feel rejected by God as Christ was. But their previous experience with Jesus will sustain their faith. That kind of love and faith is only possible by the grace of God. When we understand the right relationship between God's law and his grace, our faith will be strengthened to endure the difficult times ahead.

Faith (trust) is based on the deep knowledge of, and love for God. Faith cannot be blind, or it would only be a mirage, a poor substitute that would be better identified as presumption. Both God's law and his grace are expressions of his character of love. Faith, trust, and belief in Jesus are words the Bible uses to describe our relationship with God, "And this is his law, that we have faith in the name of his Son Jesus Christ, and love for one another, even as he said to us" (1John 3:23, BBE).

What Is Faith?

Faith is simple to experience, yet it can be controversial to define. In order to have faith in God, we must know about God. But, faith means much more than knowing things about God. For example, the prosecutor in the sensational murder trial of Jeffrey Dahmer certainly came to know a lot about Mr. Dahmer (He ate his victims). Most certainly this did not lead the prosecutor to trust Jeffrey Dahmer. Nor did Jeffrey Dahmer come to trust the prosecutor. In order to develop a relationship of trust with God we must spend time getting to know him. Moreover, we must come to experience that he is good, that he is worthy of our trust, and that he loves us. Also, as a result we will come to see that we cannot trust ourselves. When we claim that we have faith in God we are affirming that:

1. We have come to see that God loves us unconditionally.
2. God's love led him to sacrifice himself in order to rescue us from sin and death.
3. We recognize that we are sinful (selfish) by nature.
4. We desire to let go of our selfishness because we admire, worship, and prefer the generous love of God as displayed by Jesus on the Cross of Calvary.

Our heavenly Father is eager to have us get to know and experience his love. Experiencing God's love is true faith. As we understand and appreciate the incredible, pure, holy, and noble beauty of Jesus's love, we see the hideous, destructive darkness of our self-centered hearts.

The clearer we see Jesus's loving character the more we realize how sinful we are. When God shows us through his Word that he loves us so unselfishly that he is willing to lay down his life to rescue us sinners, our hearts begin to soften. The softening of our hearts is faith. We begin to see that Jesus wants us to love others as he loves us, "And this is His commandment, that we should believe on the name of His Son Jesus Christ, and love one another, as He gave us commandment" (1John 3:23, MKJ). The New Testament speaks often of faith and love:

Faith and Love

I have loved you even as the Father has loved me. Remain in my love. When you obey me, you remain in my love, just as I obey my Father and remain in his love. I have told you this so that you will be filled with my joy. Yes, your joy will overflow! I command you to love each other in the same way that I love you. And here is how to measure it—the greatest love is shown when people lay down their lives for their friends. (John 15:9-13, NLT)

For this cause I bow my knees unto the Father of our Lord Jesus Christ, Of whom the whole family in heaven and earth is named, That he would grant you, according to the riches of his glory, to be strengthened with might by his Spirit in the inner man; That Christ may dwell in your hearts by faith; that ye, being rooted and grounded in love, May be able to comprehend with all saints what is the breadth, and length, and depth, and height; And to know the love of Christ, which passeth knowledge, that ye might be filled with all the fulness of God. (Ephesians 3:14-19, KJV)

Peace be to the brethren, and love with faith, from God the Father and the Lord Jesus Christ. Grace be with all them that love our Lord Jesus Christ in sincerity. Amen. (Ephesians 6:23, 24, KJV)

Though I speak with the tongues of men and of angels, but have not love, I have become sounding brass or a clanging cymbal. And though I have the gift of prophecy, and understand all mysteries and all knowledge, and though I have all faith, so that I could remove mountains, but have not love, I am nothing. And now abide faith, hope, love, these three; but the greatest of these is love. (1 Corinthians 13:1, 2, 13, NKJ)

Faith without love is useless, dead. Righteousness is thinking, feeling, speaking, and acting, motivated and guided by love for Jesus. Faith is love for and dependence upon Jesus. Love and faith walk so closely together that they leave only one set of footprints across the pathways of our heart.

Righteousness by faith means that God counts us as perfect. God is just to count us perfect because Jesus is our Substitute. It is fair because by beholding His love, we are becoming loving as he is. Our sinful hearts have no innate righteousness, or agape (unselfish) love.

Apart from Jesus Christ we are selfish and unloving. Righteousness by faith means much more than an intellectual belief that our sins are forgiven. Righteousness by faith is not an illegal declaration that the law (the standard of righteousness) does not apply to us any more.

It is a legal declaration. In fact it is a pardon. A pardon does not set aside the law. For example the president and state governors have the right to pardon convicted criminals. They are not breaking the law when they pardon someone. In fact those that are pardoned are expected to keep the law after they have been pardoned. God fulfills His law of love when he pardons us. Jesus died in order to express God's pardoning love. And through the Holy Spirit, he empowers us to keep his eternal law of love.

Faith Versus Presumption

Faith is much more than merely admitting a fact to be true. If we mentally accept the fact that Jesus paid the penalty for our sins without understanding and accepting His love in our hearts, we will still be lost. We must be born-again, or in other words, we must let go of our selfishness and receive God's love into our hearts.

There is great danger in looking at the cross of Jesus Christ in a legal, or court of law (forensic) setting. We may know that Jesus died for our sins. Good. But if our hearts remain unchanged and we have not chosen to serve Jesus, we still have not experienced saving faith in Jesus.

To live with Jesus in Heaven we must die with him here

on Earth by dying to selfishness. In fact, when we die to self we enter into eternal life right now. Eternal life means living by God's law of love. When God declares the sinner to be righteous by faith, he is not lying. He counts, he considers, the future as though it were the present. When we behold the infinite sacrifice of Jesus on the Cross of Calvary, the Holy Spirit begins to fill our heart with love. We begin to see selfishness, or sin, for the hateful, and destructive thing that it is. We long to be like Jesus.

The Holy Spirit begins the most difficult task in the universe—changing our sinful heart into a Christ-like heart. When the accuser of the brethren comes before God and points out our flaws and sins, God points to Jesus and asserts, "They have entered the paths of righteousness. They are becoming more and more like Jesus. You may not judge them as they are now. You must look at Jesus, for given enough time they would become like him."

That is how Christ is our substitute. By faith, the sinner is immediately counted as righteous (Justification). And over time he is becoming righteous (Sanctification). To say, "becoming more like Christ," means to come into harmony with the Ten Commandments, because Jesus kept the Ten Commandments every moment of his life.

As a person comes to have faith, she understands, and knows God and naturally makes a decision to walk with God and to turn away from sin. Anything short of this would be presumption. In order to surrender our hearts to God, we must see that he is someone worthy of falling in love with. We can only do this by getting to know Jesus, for he is the path to the Father.

He is the express image of God the Father. Jesus is the truth. To the degree that we reject the truth we reject Jesus. And to the degree that we reject Jesus we reject the truth. Heavenly Father, grant us the gift of your Holy Spirit that we may accept the fullness of the truth about you as it has been revealed in your Son, Jesus Christ, amen.

Jesus Versus Baal

If we ascribe incorrect attributes to God, we may, in the end, find that we have been worshiping a false god. Faith is useless if its focus is on a false picture of God. A rose by any other name would smell as sweet. In other words, Jesus is more than a set of letters in the English language. He has a character.

If Satan comes claiming to be Jesus, does his use of the name *Jesus* make it so? Of course not. If a person mixes satanic principles with divine principles and calls the result *Jesus*, does that make it so? I think not. Our faith must be based on correct knowledge of the attributes, the character of Jesus.

The mixing of false principles with the true has an Old Testament precedent, Baal worship. Originally Baal just meant lord or master. It could refer to a king or a nobleman as well as to the Lord. Pagan principles based on a pagan deity became mixed up with the worship of YHWH (God).

At different times in Israel's history the large majority of Israel worshiped Baal. That was the issue when Elijah confronted Israel on Mount Carmel, "And Elijah came unto all the people, and said, How long halt ye between two opinions? if the LORD be God, follow him: but if Baal, then follow him. And the people answered him not a word" (1Kings 18:21, KJV).

Hosea wrote about the same issue, "And it shall be at that day, saith the LORD, that thou shalt call me Ishi [My Husband]; and shalt call me no more Baali [My Master]. For I will take away the names of Baalim out of her mouth, and they shall no more be remembered by their name" (Hosea 2:16, 17, KJV, brackets mine). "And shalt call me no more Baali." Clearly, some in Israel had, up to that time, been calling God *Baal*.

The more of God's infinite, self-sacrificing, gentle, and powerful love that we see, the easier it is to trust him and enter into a saving relationship with him. God designed the relationship between a husband and a wife to develop into the most vulnerable, intimate, loving, and trusting [faith] relationship possible between human beings.

This is the kind of relationship that our Father wants with

each of us. Our Father wants us to know him deeply and intimately. Only then can we develop the faith relationship necessary to endure the difficulties of our day-to-day lives and the time of trouble that will come upon the last generation.

Many have grown up as I did, relating to God as Baal, which is to say, "My Master." Even now, most Christians tend to worship God because he is the Almighty, the powerful Creator-God, because He's the one that made the rules. Many look at God as a divine travel agent that will do little more than give them a ticket to Heaven, or to hell; they had better worship him; They had better be afraid of God.

The desire for self-preservation, the desire for Heaven, the fear of hell, are poor substitutes for the adoring love, the close-knit relationship that Our Father longs for. He understands our weakness and tendency to be afraid of him. He longs to relieve our fears. These selfish, fear-based motives are the inevitable result of a false gospel, a mistaken view of God.

Our heavenly Father loves us. The life and sacrifice of Jesus demonstrate this love. The more that we understand the law of God (His Character of love) and the gospel (His Character of love), and the relationship between these, the easier it is to trust God. The relationship between the Law and the Gospel is that they are two different descriptions of the same thing— God's character of love, "And this is life eternal, that they might know thee the only true God, and Jesus Christ, whom thou hast sent" (John 17:3, KJV). To understand the relationship between the law and the gospel is to enter into a deeper level of faith.

Faith and Works

When a husband and wife come together, a child is produced. We are the bride of Christ. If Christ's seed enters us we will produce the "fruit of the womb." Just as pregnancy is difficult to hide, so our relationship with Jesus is hard to hide. If Jesus's love is in us we will bear fruit. God's character is love. Remember that the law of God is a transcript of his character. Love begets love, "We love him, because he first loved us" (1John 4:19, KJV). Love and faith are as closely tied together as a husband and wife. The natural result, the child of love and faith is works. Faith without love is presumption. Love without faith is mere sentimentalism. Faith and love that don't produce works are barren. When faith and love come together, the natural result, the child of love and faith is works. The Scriptures often link faith, love, and works one with another:

> For through the Spirit we wait for the hope of righteousness by faith. For in Jesus Christ neither circumcision avails any thing, nor uncircumcision; but faith which works by love. (Galatians 5:5, 6, NKJ)

> Peace be to the brethren, and love with faith, from God the Father and the Lord Jesus Christ. Grace be with all them that love our Lord Jesus Christ in sincerity. Amen. (Ephesians 6:23, 24, KJV)

> What good is it, my brothers and sisters, if you say you have faith but do not have works? Can faith save you? If a brother or sister is naked and lacks daily food, and one of you says to them, "Go in peace; keep warm and eat your fill," and yet you do not supply their bodily needs, what is the good of that? So faith by itself, if it has no works, is dead. But someone will say, "You have faith and I have works." Show me your faith apart from your works, and I by my works will show you my faith. You believe that God is one; you do well. Even the demons believe—and shudder. Do you want to be shown, you senseless person, that faith apart from works is barren? Was not our ancestor Abraham justified by works when he offered his son Isaac on the altar? You see that faith was active along with his works, and faith was brought to completion by the works. Thus the scripture was fulfilled that says, "Abraham believed God, and it was reckoned to him as righteousness," and he was called the friend of God. You see that a person is justified by works and not by faith alone. Likewise, was not Rahab the prostitute also justified by works when she

welcomed the messengers and sent them out by another road? For just as the body without the spirit is dead, so faith without works is also dead. (James 2:14-26, NRSV)

But the fruit of the Spirit is love, joy, peace, longsuffering, gentleness, goodness, faith, Meekness, temperance: against such there is no law. (Galatians 5:22, 23, KJV)

I know your works—your love, faith, service, and patient endurance. I know that your last works are greater than the first. (Revelation 2:19, NRSV)

And the grace of our Lord was exceeding abundant with faith and love which is in Christ Jesus. (1Timothy 1:14, KJV)

But let us, who are of the day, be sober, putting on the breastplate of faith and love; and for an helmet, the hope of salvation. For God hath not appointed us to wrath, but to obtain salvation by our Lord Jesus Christ, Who died for us, that, whether we wake or sleep, we should live together with him. (1Thessalonians 5:8-10, KJV)

But thou, O man of God, flee these things; and follow after righteousness, godliness, faith, love, patience, meekness. (1Timothy 6:11, KJV)

Hold fast the form of sound words, which thou hast heard of me, in faith and love which is in Christ Jesus. (2Timothy 1:13, KJV)

Then you will ask in my name. I'm not saying I will ask the Father on your behalf, for the Father himself loves you dearly because you love me and believe that I came from God. (John 16:26, 27, NLT)

I am praying not only for these disciples but also for all

226

who will ever believe in me because of their testimony. My prayer for all of them is that they will be one, just as you and I are one, Father—that just as you are in me and I am in you, so they will be in us, and the world will believe you sent me. I have given them the glory you gave me, so that they may be one, as we are—I in them and you in me, all being perfected into one. Then the world will know that you sent me and will understand that you love them as much as you love me. Father, I want these whom you've given me to be with me, so they can see my glory. You gave me the glory because you loved me even before the world began! O righteous Father, the world doesn't know you, but I do; and these disciples know you sent me. And I have revealed you to them and will keep on revealing you. I will do this so that your love for me may be in them and I in them. (John 17:20-26, NLT)

I beseech you therefore, brethren, by the mercies of God, that ye present your bodies a living sacrifice, holy, acceptable unto God, which is your reasonable service. And be not conformed to this world: but be ye transformed by the renewing of your mind, that ye may prove what is that good, and acceptable, and perfect, will of God. For I say, through the grace given unto me, to every man that is among you, not to think of himself more highly than he ought to think; but to think soberly, according as God hath dealt to every man the measure of faith. (Romans 12:1-3, KJV)

If I have all faith, so as to remove mountains, but do have not love, I am nothing. (1Corinthians 13:2, RSV)

When we see the beauty of Jesus, and as his love fills us, he will change our tastes so that anything that would dull, or distract the mind will become unattractive to us. The more completely we give our hearts to Jesus, the more we live in harmony with his love, the more fully he can reveal himself to us. Only the grace of God as revealed through Jesus can accomplish these things in us.

Then we will see every person as infinitely valuable in the light of our Savior's sacrifice. We will not think of our opinions and ourselves more highly than we ought to. Faith must lead to the overcoming of sin and selfishness in the heart, in the thoughts, feelings, and actions, or else it is only the imposter—presumption, "Do you not know that if you present yourselves to anyone as obedient slaves, you are slaves of the one whom you obey, either of sin, which leads to death, or of obedience, which leads to righteousness?" (Romans 6:16, NRSV). What we don't overcome will overcome us.

To the degree that we have Christ's love in our hearts, we will be willing to sacrifice anything that damages or distracts from our relationship with God, or our fellow human beings. Jesus's love led him to sacrifice his life, his soul for us. If we are born-again, the Holy Spirit will begin to re-create us into Jesus's image. We will live to please and serve him. No sacrifice will be too great. No sacrifice will be too small. No job will be too hard. No sin will be too attractive.

It is only in this life that we have the opportunity to suffer for Jesus and our fellow human beings. In Heaven there will be no suffering, no sacrifice, no pain, and no tears. Now is the time that we can truly show our love for God and man. Now, by faith we can offer the sacrifice of obedience. No pain, no gain. Faith and love bring pain, healing pain. Sin brings pain too, destructive pain.

A Measure of Faith

"But I say to every one of you, through the grace given to me, not to have an over-high opinion of himself, but to have wise thoughts, as God has given to every one a measure of faith" (Romans 12:3, BBE). God has put in every man's heart a yearning desire to believe that God must be good. If you ask an atheist what God would be like if he existed, often he will give you a quite beautiful description of a kind and loving God. God has placed that desire, that instinctive knowledge within his heart. That is "the measure of faith." God has given even atheists a measure of faith.

Tragically, misunderstood doctrines, especially in regard to hell, have caused many to totally reject God and become atheists. If our view of God is warped and tainted, our characters can rise no higher than our warped view. When we as Christians believe, live, present, and reflect a more deeply beautiful view of God's character, many atheists and other non-Christians will fall in love with Jesus.

It is by beholding Christ that we become changed into his image. Behold Christ in the garden of Gethsemane as he weighs the cost of our salvation.

Faith is not something that we produce. Rather, faith and repentance are a response to the goodness of God, "The goodness of God leads you to repentance" (Romans 2:4, NKJ).

As we more fully see, accept, and experience his goodness, it is inevitable that faith and love will grow and fill our hearts, for that is how God designed us. Look to Jesus:

> Wherefore seeing we also are compassed about with so great a cloud of witnesses, let us lay aside every weight, and the sin which doth so easily beset us, and let us run with patience the race that is set before us, Looking unto Jesus the author and finisher of our faith; who for the joy that was set before him endured the cross, despising the shame, and is set down at the right hand of the throne of God. (Hebrews 12:1, 2, KJV)

Truly, sin (unbelief), which comes from a false view of God's character and our own selfish desires, are weights that will slow us down and cause us to stumble in our race to become like Jesus. Let us lay them aside. Let us spend time looking unto Jesus, the author and finisher of our faith!

His own iniquities entrap the wicked man,
And he is caught in the cords of his sin.
He shall die for lack of instruction,
And in the greatness of his folly
he shall go astray.
(Proverbs 5:22, 23, NKJ)

11

Sin

By Beholding We Become Changed

September 11, 2001. The whole world knows what happened on that day. That day changed our lives forever. Nineteen terrorists damaged the pentagon, destroyed the twin towers, killed thousands of innocent people, violated our trust, our privacy, and, to an ever-increasing degree, are causing us to give up our freedom.

Why did they do it? Some contend that they were jealous of our wealth and ease. Some maintain that they did it because of our hard-nosed favoritism of the Israelis over the Palestinians. Some suggest they were angered by our corrupting influence on world morality. Others say because of American arrogance and disregard of other nation's rights. Yet others say mostly just because of the hatred that filled the terrorists hearts. Each of these rationales probably has some truth to it. Yet none of these rationales speaks to the fundamental reason, though the last one heads in the right direction.

These terrorists came from an extremist Islamic sect that paints Allah as vengeful and violent, who will shower his wrath on infidels. By beholding we become changed. Our view of God determines what our character becomes. By beholding a wrathful image of God, these men became changed into the image of God that their leaders had painted.

Certainly, one cannot doubt their sincerity, seeing that they were willing to sacrifice their lives to carry out what they considered to be God's will. They felt that it was their duty to attack the United States, which in their minds was *evil*, or the *great Satan*.

Each person's view of God has a powerful impact on her personal philosophy and her character. An evil picture of God leads to evil feelings, then evil words, followed by evil actions. A beautiful picture of God, on the other hand leads to loving feelings, then to loving words, followed by loving actions. Much of the sin in our world comes from a warped view of God:

> A disciple is not greater than his master, or a servant than his lord. It is enough for the disciple that he may be as his master, and the servant as his lord. If they have given the name Beelzebub to the master of the house, how much more to those of his house! (Matthew 10:24, 25, BBE)

Every Christian battles sin in his life. We all desire to overcome sin. It is helpful to identify the characteristics of the enemy that we fight. The Bible writers use various words for sin. Essentially, there are four basic concepts.

1. Breaking the Law.

This basic Bible concept of sin is found in 1John 3:4, "Whoever commits sin transgresses also the law: for sin is the transgression of the law" (NKJ). The law that John refers to is the Ten Commandments, God's law of love. Our words and actions flow from our heart. The prophet Jeremiah proclaims that the human heart "is deceitful above all things, And desperately wicked; Who can know it?" (Jeremiah 17:9, KJV). Only as we allow God to write his law of love in our hearts can we keep the Ten Commandments.

Jesus is the only one that, with perfect confidence, could ask the question "Which of you convicts Me of sin?" (John 8:46, KJV). Jesus kept the Ten Commandments, revealed the self-sacrificing love (glory) of God, lived an unselfish life, and under the worst possible circumstances trusted (had faith in) God. The life and death of Christ as told in the Bible present to us the standard of behavior. Anything less is sin. Jesus never sinned:

> Seeing then that we have a great High Priest who has passed through the heavens, Jesus the Son of God, let us hold fast our confession. For we do not have a High Priest who cannot sympathize with our weaknesses, but was in all points tempted as we are, yet without sin. (Hebrews 4:14, 15, NKJ)

He kept the law, The Ten Commandments. He is our example. We must walk in his footsteps:

> If you keep My commandments, you shall abide in My love, even as I have kept My Father's commandments and abide in His love. (John 15:10, MKJ)

> Think not that I am come to destroy the law, or the prophets: I am not come to destroy, but to fulfil. For verily I say unto you, Till heaven and earth pass, one jot or one tittle shall in no wise pass from the law, till all be fulfilled. (Matthew 5:17, KJV)

Jesus always pleased God by living according to the law of God's love, "And he who sent me is with me; he has not left me alone, because I always do what pleases him" (John 8:29, TEV).

2. Falling Short of God's Glory.

The apostle Paul gives us this Bible definition of sin, "For all have sinned, and come short of the glory of God" (Romans 3:23, KJV). Paul asserts that to fall short of the glory of God is sin. That's a high standard. The glory of God is his law of love, his character as revealed by the life and death of Jesus Christ, (see also Exodus 33:18-20 and 1Corinthians 13). Jesus glorified his Father by suffering for our sin and guilt. Through his life, death, and teachings, Jesus showed us the glory, or character, of his Father:

> And this is eternal life, that they may know You, the only true God, and Jesus Christ whom You have sent. I have glorified You on the earth. I have finished the work which You have given Me to do. And now, O Father, glorify Me together with Yourself, with the glory which I had with You before the world was. (John 17:3-5, NKJ)

Jesus never fell short of the glory of God. He always died to self and lived for others. Everything he did, from his birth to his last breath, displayed the holy beauty of God's love. To glorify God, then, is to be willing to suffer and die for those that hate and misunderstand you. It also means that we should willingly live to serve others, making our desires subservient to those around us. Living for others takes more effort than to physically die for others. Jesus did all this and more.

3. Iniquity.

The Hebrew word iniquity means bent, or warped. In the beginning, God created man to be a channel for his love. Love would flow outward from the heart of man to all those around him. When Adam and Eve fell, sin warped their hearts; God's perfect, unselfish love did a U-turn. Now, each human naturally loves only himself unconditionally. We all instinctively look out for number one. In other words, iniquity is selfishness. Our hearts are naturally selfish.

Jesus had absolutely no iniquity (selfishness) in him. Consider the contrast between Jesus and Lucifer (Satan). Earlier we saw that iniquity (selfishness) started in the heart of Lucifer, the covering cherub. The covering cherub stood in the presence of God among the stones of fire, the highest position any angel can have.

Because of his vanity, Lucifer started to desire the very

throne of God. He desired the worship of the other angels. Lucifer wanted to exalt himself. He imagined climbing higher and higher, surpassing God. He would stop at nothing to grasp the position and honor he wanted. Lucifer would destroy anything and anyone to get what he wanted.

Even if Lucifer had attained the throne of God, he would not have been satisfied. Warped, selfish ambition can never be satisfied. Iniquity causes an emptiness of soul that cannot be filled by any material object or social status. Owning the entire universe (Heaven) wouldn't have been enough. Having all power and authority over the entire universe would not make Satan happy.

Jesus, on the other hand, willingly gave up his status as King in Heaven to become a servant here on Earth. Jesus had no selfishness, that is to say, no iniquity, in him, "I will no longer talk much with you, for the ruler of this world is coming, and he has nothing in Me" (John 14:30, NKJ).

The Holy Spirit inspired my favorite poet, David, to share some insights on sin with us. After David had Uriah the Hittite killed to take his wife Bathsheba, he repented of his sin and wrote these powerful words:

> Have mercy upon me, O God, according to thy lovingkindness: according unto the multitude of thy tender mercies blot out my transgressions. Wash me throughly from mine iniquity, and cleanse me from my sin. For I acknowledge my transgressions: and my sin is ever before me. Hide thy face from my sins, and blot out all mine iniquities. Create in me a clean heart, O God; and renew a right spirit within me. For thou desirest not sacrifice; else would I give it: thou delightest not in burnt offering. The sacrifices of God are a broken spirit: a broken and a contrite heart, O God, thou wilt not despise. (Psalms 51:1-3, 9, 10, 16, 17, KJV)

4. Unbelief.

A fourth Biblical concept of sin is to not believe in Jesus:

235

Nevertheless I tell you the truth; It is expedient for you that I go away: for if I go not away, the Comforter will not come unto you; but if I depart, I will send him unto you. And when he is come, he will reprove the world of sin, and of righteousness, and of judgment: Of sin, because they believe not on me. (John 16:7-9, KJV)

Here Jesus defines sin as not believing in him. "Believe" and "faith" come from the same Greek root word. Sin is lack of faith in Jesus. In Hebrews 11:6, we read that without faith it is impossible to please him. Faith means knowing God well enough to trust him with your life. Faith is not blind, but rather based on experience and knowledge. Faith is a matter of the heart and mind. Paul applies the principle that unbelief equals sin in regard to Israel as they wandered forty years in the wilderness:

Wherefore I was grieved with that generation, and said, They do alway err in their heart; and they have not known my ways. So I sware in my wrath, They shall not enter into my rest.) Take heed, brethren, lest there be in any of you an evil heart of unbelief, in departing from the living God. (Hebrews 3:10-12, KJV)

But with whom was he grieved forty years? was it not with them that had sinned, whose carcases fell in the wilderness? And to whom sware he that they should not enter into his rest, but to them that believed not? So we see that they could not enter in because of unbelief. (Hebrews 3:17-19, KJV)

Unbelief kept one generation of Israelites out of the Promised Land. Unbelief is what keeps the wicked out of Heaven. Jesus's temptation in the wilderness provides another perspective on sin. After Jesus had fasted for 40, days, Satan tried four basic temptations against him. We face these same four basic temptations today.

236

1. Doubt.

Satan used the phrase, "If You are the Son of God" to tempt Jesus to doubt:

> Then Jesus was led by the Spirit up into the wilderness, to be tempted by the Devil. And when He had fasted forty days and forty nights, He was afterwards hungry. And when the tempter came to Him, he said, "If You are the Son of God, command that these stones be made bread." But He answered and said, "It is written, 'Man shall not live by bread alone, but by every word that proceeds out of the mouth of God.'" (Matthew 4:1-4, MKJ)

Satan wanted Jesus to doubt that he was the Son of God. Notice that Satan had insinuated doubt about the goodness and truthfulness of God to tempt Eve:

> Now the serpent was the shrewdest of all the creatures the Lord God had made. "Really?" he asked the woman. "Did God really say you must not eat any of the fruit in the garden?"
> "Of course we may eat it," the woman told him. "It's only the fruit from the tree at the center of the garden that we are not allowed to eat. God says we must not eat it or even touch it, or we will die."
> "You won't die!" the serpent hissed. "God knows that your eyes will be opened when you eat it. You will become just like God, knowing everything, both good and evil." (Genesis 3:1-5, NLT)

Doubt, or unbelief, then, is one of the four basic temptations we face as well. When we hang on to sin we support Satan's claims against God. We also strengthen our doubts. Love for sin crowds out love for God. Faith rests on our love for God. Every time we sin we make it easier to doubt.

We have never had to face as strong a temptation to doubt God's goodness as Jesus did. Moreover, Jesus faced that temptation while carrying the whole worlds sins. Today, doubt seems to be a badge of honor, or a symbol of free thought. It seems to me that false tolerance has led to the acceptance of the concept that all ideas are equal. Relativity of morals has over-shadowed God's law in our society. The results are not good.

2. Appetite.

Satan combined the temptation to doubt with that of appetite. Appetite, combined with doubts about the goodness of God, took Adam and Eve down. Sticking with a previous pattern of success, Satan hit Jesus at his weakest moment, after he had fasted forty days. I rarely fast more than one day at a time. I can't imagine forty days. After forty days of fasting, food would be attractive. Certainly even plain bread would have tasted good to Jesus after forty days of fasting.

Even so, Jesus did not give in to appetite, but answered Satan by quoting Scripture. Jesus didn't go by his feelings. He made his decisions based on principles. Biblical principles. Jesus was more sensitive and had stronger feelings than any other man. Yet he made his feelings subservient to reason and principle.

Today appetite seems to rule the world. Janet Raloff reports in *Science News*, April 2, 2005:

Since the mid-1960s, the rate of obesity in the United States has nearly tripled to one in three adults. Over the same period, U.S. citizens have deducted, on average, about 2 hours from their nightly slumber. Is there a connection? Endocrinologist Eve Van Cauter strongly suspects that there is. She points to seven studies that have linked body weight to how long people sleep.

Again Ben Harder confirms this concept in *Science News* April 1, 2006:

Widespread sleep deprivation could partly explain the current epidemics of both obesity and diabetes, emerging data suggest.

Too little sleep may contribute to long-term health problems by changing the concentrations of hormones that control appetite, increasing food intake, and disrupting the biological clock, according to Eve Van Cauter of the University of Chicago.

God has designed us with the need for love. We try to fill that empty spot in our hearts with food, television, sports, sex, drugs, and rock and roll, as well as the outward forms of religion. Of course it doesn't work. That empty spot can only be filled by Jesus's love, through the word of God.

I think that it is useful to know that we need the proper amount of sleep in order to resist the temptation to eat more than we need. I wonder if there might be a relationship between lack of sleep and a reduced ability to resist other temptations as well. Satan knows about the relation of rest to spiritual strength. God spoke to Pharaoh through Moses and Aaron, requesting that he allow the Israelites to go out into the wilderness to worship him. Listen to how Pharaoh, Satan's spokesman, reacts:

"Who do you think you are," Pharaoh shouted, "distracting the people from their tasks? Get back to work! Look, there are many people here in Egypt, and you are stopping them from doing their work." That same day Pharaoh sent this order to the slave drivers and foremen he had set over the people of Israel: "Do not supply the people with any more straw for making bricks. Let them get it themselves! But don't reduce their production quotas by a single brick. They obviously don't have enough to do. If they did, they wouldn't be talking about going into the wilderness to offer sacrifices to their God. Load them down with more work. Make them sweat!" (Exodus 5:6-9, NLT)

Satan knows that if he can keep us overly busy that we won't have time for God. We need our daily physical rest in order to battle temptation. We also need our daily spiritual rest in order to keep our friendship with our heavenly Father. Jesus took time for communion with his Father, "And in the morning, rising up a great while before day, he went out, and departed into a solitary place, and there prayed" (Mark 1:35, KJV). We also need a weekly time of spiritual rest to keep our relationship with Jesus alive.

Another aspect of appetite is the desire to accumulate material goods. Sexual appetite is yet another area that Satan tempts fallen humanity with great success. Jesus passed the test on every aspect of appetite.

3. Presumption.

Satan had more temptations up his sleeve, though. He encouraged Jesus to doubt and presume on God's protection:

> Then the Devil took Him up into the holy city and set Him upon a pinnacle of the Temple. And he said to Him, "If you are the Son of God, cast yourself down. For it is written, 'He shall give His angels charge concerning You, and in their hands they shall bear You up, lest at any time You dash Your foot against a stone.'" Jesus said to him, "It is written again, 'You shall not tempt the Lord your God.'" (Matthew 4:5-7, MKJ)

Again, Satan tried to cause Jesus to doubt that he was the Son of God. Again Satan combined two temptations, presumption and doubt. Faith and presumption outwardly resemble one another. Presumption carries within it a mixture of doubt and disregard for the principles of love. Satan tempted Jesus to use God's promises to force his Father to prove his love for Jesus. Faith and love need not resort to force.

In this modern age we can easily slide into presumption. We can be tempted to feel that we will be saved no matter what we do. However, faith and love show regard for other's feelings and desires. God wants us to show our love for him by allowing his principles into our hearts. Faith allows God to create a new heart in us. Faith realizes that God only wants what is good for us. And he only asks us to give up that which would destroy us. A new heart speaks good, kind words. Kind words lead to kind actions. Jesus spells it out for us:

> Your words show what is in your hearts. Good people bring good things out of their hearts, but evil people bring evil things out of their hearts. I promise you that on the day of judgment, everyone will have to account for every careless word they have spoken. On that day they will be told that they are either innocent or guilty because of the things they have said. (Matthew 12:34-37, CEV)

Presumption contends "God will save me in my sins. I don't need a new heart." Faith says, "Please change it or I will die."

4. Greed and Idols.

Closely related to presumption are greed, vanity, pride of possession, the desire for power, and idol worship:

> Again, the Devil took Him up into a very high mountain and showed Him all the kingdoms of the world and their glory. And he said to Him, "All these things I will give You if You will fall down and worship me." Then Jesus said to him, "Go, Satan! For it is written, 'You shall worship the Lord your God, and Him only you shall serve.'" Then the Devil left him. And behold, angels came and ministered to Him. (Matthew 4:8-11, MKJ)

Satan tempted Jesus to enter into a business deal. "You worship me and I will give up my claim to the Earth and its inhabitants." Of course Satan was lying. Satan tempted Jesus to follow the easy path. Reading beneath the surface words, Satan insinuated to Jesus that he didn't have to go to the cross in order to gain control of the world. Satan offered Jesus control of the world, but at a cost. Satan tempted Jesus to enter into the principles of force. However, if God had wanted to use force to gain control of the world, he wouldn't have needed Satan's help to do it.

We too, face the temptation to use power, or force. Look at the political races. People will do or say most anything to gain political power. Some people will even break the law to obtain the political or corporate position they want. Other people try to gain power through amassing money, persuasive speaking, fraud, or other means of climbing the corporate ladder. That is why we see so many accounting scandals and other types of fraud in the large corporations. People are trying to move up the ladder, at any cost to others or even themselves.

Even those who have large amounts of money and power seek more. Greed is never satisfied. Power, prestige, and pride of possession hypnotize many, causing them to sell their soul for fleeting pleasures. This same principle occurs on a smaller scale as well.

I have found myself in that mode of thought. In the past, I have convinced myself that a new car would make me happy. Then it was a new computer. After that it was getting a new, more powerful stereo system that I thought would make me happy. Solomon warns us, "If you love money, you will never be satisfied; if you long to be rich, you will never get all you want. It is useless. The rich, however, have so much that they stay awake worrying" (Ecclesiastes 5:10, 12, TEV).

Church board meetings can bring out the satanic principle of force. People want control, power over others, and over the material structures of the church. If you have ever sat on a church board, or know someone who has, you likely have heard of the battles that occur over such weighty matters as the color of the carpet, curtains, or the paint on the walls. One church board I know of even voted not to have an evangelistic series because they had just installed new carpet! They didn't want to get it dirty, or wear it out too quickly. Often, Patience slips out of the boardroom just after Christian Kindness and the Spirit of Listening have left.

The Way Up Is Down

Lucifer thought he would be happy if he could have the throne of God. He thought he could have the status and worship without the character of self-sacrificing love. He was wrong. The end of the path of self-exaltation is dishonor, death, and destruction, "And whosoever shall exalt himself shall be abased; and he that shall humble himself shall be exalted" (Matthew 23:12, KJV). This is not an arbitrary law that God enforces, but rather a natural principle that God himself has chosen to live by. God has humbled himself more than any other being ever could. Jesus, though God, became a human being, took the from of a servant, took all our sins upon himself, and died in our place!

We need to stay focused on Jesus and his love for us. We have never faced the level of temptation that Jesus did. He overcame, even while carrying the weight of the world's sin and guilt!

Jesus is the Antidote to sin. How did Jesus overcome temptation? And how can we?

Jesus was the King of Kings. Though he was the Creator-God, Jesus left the honor, security, and pleasures of Heaven that were rightfully his. Jesus laid aside his royal robes and his divine prerogatives to combine his divinity with our humanity. God became a human baby! He grew up in a city renowned for its sinfulness. He lived to serve others. He worked as a carpenter until he was thirty years old. And Jesus had to deal with temptation on a daily basis.

When tempted by Satan, Jesus quoted the Old Testament. During his ministry, Jesus often prayed. Prayer strengthened Jesus. Jesus felt the need for prayer, even though he was perfect. Or, perhaps it was because Jesus was perfect that he felt the need to pray. The closer we come to God, the more we will feel our need to pray, "And in the morning, rising up a great while before day, he went out, and departed into a solitary place, and there prayed" (Mark 1:35, KJV). "And it came to pass in those days, that he went out into a mountain to pray, and continued all night in prayer to God" (Luke 6:12, KJV).

243

We too, must pray for strength to overcome sin in our lives. Jesus instructed his followers, "Keep watch and pray that you will not fall into temptation" (Matthew 26:41, TEV). Paul advised Christians to, "Pray without ceasing" (1Thessalonians 5:17, KJV). Prayer is vital to overcoming temptation and sin.

Jesus healed others. Jesus fed others. By serving others, we enter into the Spirit of Jesus and become more resistant to sin.

Jesus forgave others' sins. Jesus didn't judge others. When we forgive others of their sins against us, God strengthens us. When we refrain from judging others, we partake of the Spirit of God's mercy and thereby avoid one of the most grievous of sins.

Would you like to know one of the most powerful weapons against sin? Jesus used it. Moses used it. Paul used it. Now you can use it. "Most important of all, continue to show deep love for each other, for love covers a multitude of sins" (1Peter 4:8, NLT). Imagine that, love covers a multitude of sins. Love cuts a wide swath through the sin problem. Love is the answer to sin. God's love through Jesus destroyed the power of sin. The cross shows that.

OK. How do you get love for God and others? By meditating on Jesus, you will become more like him. Spend time in the word every day. First thing in the morning is best. It is also good to end the day with Jesus. Prayer and meditation on God's great love will change your heart. Also, putting his love into practice will speed the whole process. Find ways to serve others. Jesus served us.

Jesus took the path that went down, down, down. Jesus would stop at nothing to rescue others. He sacrificed everything. He would rather take destruction upon himself than to allow it to fall on us. The end of the path of humility, self-sacrifice, and service is honor, happiness, and life. Jesus revealed that his Father is the greatest Servant. Jesus wants us to be like him.

Often, like Lucifer, we are more concerned with ourselves than with others. However, God loves others more than he loves himself! That is the source of his power. That kind of love can change hearts. That kind of power can overcome sin. Sin shows itself in the little things of life.

Road Rage and the Cross

How do we feel when someone tries to cut us off on the freeway? Do we automatically and graciously slow down to make room for the aggressive or careless driver? Or are we instead tempted to speed up, and try to stay ahead of the other guy and thereby save two or three seconds? Remember, love covers a multitude of sins.

The contrast between our selfishness and the glory of God's love becomes very clear in the light of the cross of Jesus. In the cross we see that God was willing to die to save everyone, even those that hated him, and whipped, punched, and spit on him, and finally nailed him to the cross.

Would we be willing to die for a man that had just spit on us? No, I don't think so. Our natural reaction would be at least to respond with some harsh words, or depending on his size, slap him, or perhaps spit back.

How few of even professed Christians would react with a humble kindness and forgiveness and a desire to love him as Christ did. Humility versus pride. Pride is one of the most dangerous sins. It suggests that we don't need God's power in our lives. Pride of opinion can keep us from growing in knowledge and experience in Jesus.

How do we feel when someone disagrees with us in Bible study? How do we react when someone criticizes us? Do we thank them for the new information and their concern for our happiness? Or do we perceive them as critical, judgmental, and legalistic? Did Jesus become defensive? Would you give your life for someone that you perceive as being critical and legalistic? Jesus did. Meditate on Jesus.

Human love whines, "if you are good to me, I'll be good to you. God loves others because he is love, not because others deserve it.

Love is the opposite of sin. The standard of love that Jesus reveals on the cross goes way beyond reluctantly letting someone cut in front of you on the freeway. It goes beyond stopping a bullet for a friend or enemy. Paul, in Hebrews 2:9, tells us that Jesus tasted death for every man. Sin is destructive. It brings guilt.

Every time we do something wrong we feel guilt. If we lie to someone, steal some money from a friend, or gossip about a best friend, we feel guilt, especially if we get caught. The shame, the guilt that we feel is very uncomfortable. Remember that Jesus carried the shame and guilt of the whole world. Sin, and the sense of separation from his Father, broke the heart of Jesus, "Reproach hath broken my heart; and I am full of heaviness: and I looked for some to take pity, but there was none; and for comforters, but I found none" (Psalm 69:20, KJV).

What is the problem with sin? If sin is such fun, why does the Bible use such negative terms in describing sin? Why does God hate sin so much? God wants us to enjoy life. God's law is the law of liberty. We know that sin is transgression of God's law of life and love. God's law is wisdom. Wisdom calls out to us, "But those who miss me have injured themselves. All who hate me love death" (Proverbs 8:36, NLT).

Sin leads to death. That doesn't sound like much fun. Selfishness may appear fun, but it causes loneliness, stress, and death. God wants us to enjoy life. Talking with friends, rejoicing in the beauty of nature, helping others, these are activities that God has designed for us to enjoy. These bring true, lasting joy. Satan's counterfeits look exciting, glitzy, fun, and sweet, but they are hollow, trite, and leave a bitter aftertaste.

God's law is not arbitrary. God's law brings true freedom. James calls the Ten Commandments, "the perfect law of liberty" (James 1:25, KJV). God hates sin because it brings slavery. Take appetite, for example. If you let children eat just what they want, many would find themselves enslaved to a perverted appetite. They would eat chips, chocolate cake, and ice cream all day. But that would lead to illness and death. Slavery to sin causes misery and at last, leads to death. Tobacco. I don't need to spell it out, do I. The advertisers make smoking look fun, but just try to quit!

246

Have you, or someone you know struggled with a really bad temper? Have you ever told anyone "You made me angry"? That is an admission that someone else is in control of your temper! A bad temper controls many. That's slavery. God can give you freedom. Anger only lasts three seconds, unless you feed it. I've tried it, it's true. Hang on for three seconds without adding fuel to the fire, without justifying your anger, and it goes away. That feels good! Why should we let anger enslave us? Anger destroys.

Freedom to Sin Versus Freedom from Sin

Give control of your thoughts to Jesus. Make a habit of guarding your thoughts. When negative thoughts and feelings come, pray and give the thought or feeling to Jesus. And let it go. Each time you do this it will get easier. Don't let sinful, negative thoughts dwell in your mind. Pray without ceasing. Jesus can free us from slavery to our negative emotions and passions. Jesus will fill us with positive emotions, such as joy, satisfaction, peace, and many others. Freedom brings these emotions. Why let either Satan or your own desires make you into a slave?

> God will bless you, if you don't give up when your faith is being tested. He will reward you with a glorious life, just as he rewards everyone who loves him. Don't blame God when you are tempted! God cannot be tempted by evil, and he doesn't use evil to tempt others. We are tempted by our own desires that drag us off and trap us. Our desires make us sin, and when sin is finished with us, it leaves us dead. (James 1:12-15, CEV)

Jesus died to rescue us from sin, not to enable us to live in our sins. When, through the cross of Jesus, we see the high cost of sin and God's great love for us, sin will become disgusting to us. The goodness of God leads us to repentance. Our hearts will be filled with unselfish love rather than selfishness and negative desires. We will choose faith, love, and life over sin, doubt, and death. By taking the sins of the entire world on himself, Jesus showed us the natural consequences of sin. Truly, the wages of sin is death. Remember that God does not *consider, reckon* or *impute* (Greek *Logizomai*) our sins (2Corinthians 5:19 and 1Corinthians 13:5). God is love:

> Love is patient and kind; it is not jealous or conceited or proud; love is not ill-mannered or selfish or irritable; love does not keep a record of wrongs; love is not happy with evil, but is happy with the truth. Love never gives up; and its faith, hope, and patience never fail. Love is eternal. (1Corinthians 13:4-8, TEV)

God is not the source of death, but life. God is the Creator, not the Destroyer. There is one who accuses, keeps track of sins, and loves to destroy; it is Satan. Judging, keeping track of wrongs in order to punish or take revenge is sin. God doesn't reckon or impute other's sins. Neither should we.

Another powerful tool in the fight against sin is nature. God has placed healing power within his creation. We were designed to live in a garden, the Garden of Eden. Cities contain many temptations that we could avoid by living in the country. Spending time in nature can help us to overcome sin. In God's handiwork, as we observe the beautiful, living things we see more of God's love. The songs of the birds, the fluffy white clouds against the blue sky, the colorful flowers, and many other lovely, vibrant things testify to God's love.

We can walk with God and receive deep impressions of his love for us by spending time in nature, his beautiful creation. By beholding God in nature we will be changed into his image. To be sure, sin has tainted God's perfect creation, as we can see in the thorns and decay, as well as in poisonous and destructive things. Rather than dwelling on the negative, we can look for God's love. The principle that we find what we look for holds true. We also know that our Father will shortly re-create our world. We too, need to be re-created.

Mankind was the pinnacle of God's creation, so it is here

in our fallen, selfish humanity, in our body, mind, and character that we can see most clearly the principles and results of sin and unbelief. It stains our nature, "While we were living in the flesh, our sinful passions, aroused by the law, were at work in our members to bear fruit for death" (Romans 7:5, RSV).

The Wicked Fall into Their Own Pit

Sin leads to a chain reaction of negative events culminating in death. Don't add to your sin by blaming God for either the temptation or the death of the wicked, "The LORD is known by the judgment He executes; The wicked is snared in the work of his own hands" (Psalm 9:16, NKJ). David tells us that God's idea of judgment is to allow the wicked to be caught in his own trap. The Psalmist reaffirms, "Evil shall slay the wicked, And those who hate the righteous shall be condemned" (Psalm 34:21, NKJ). Notice what slays the wicked —*Evil.*

King David experienced some of sin's destructive power in his own life. David's sin with Bathsheba caused disharmony, disrespect, rebellion, (remember Absalom) and death. In Psalm 51 we read that David fully repented of his sin. God forgave David. But God did not remove all the effects of David's sin. David lost four of his sons just as he had passed judgment on the rich man of Nathan's parable to repay four lambs for the lamb he had stolen.

God knows that we have been deceived. He doesn't hold our sins against us. Yet in his mercy God allows us a small taste of the consequences of sin, hoping that we will turn from sin. All the while he draws us to himself with cords of love.

Because of his great mercy, God shields us from the full consequences of sin, which is the second death. God longs for each of us to clearly see the pain, sorrow, death, and destruction of sin, in full contrast with the peace, joy, and eternal life of his holy law of love.

Our loving and merciful heavenly Father does not want any of us to die for lack of instruction. He has abundantly provided instruction for escaping from the trap of iniquity, and the cords of sin. This instruction is found in the life and death of our Savior, Jesus Christ. The Holy Spirit shared these principles with all mankind, "His own iniquities entrap the wicked man, And he is caught in the cords of his sin. He shall die for lack of instruction, And in the greatness of his folly he shall go astray" (Proverbs 5:22, 23, NKJ). As we noted before, John makes it clear that condemnation doesn't come from God:

> For God so loved the world, that he gave his only begotten Son, that whosoever believeth in him should not perish, but have everlasting life. For God sent not his Son into the world to condemn the world; but that the world through him might be saved. (John 3:16, 17, KJV)

Paul reaffirms it too:

> God's law was given so that all people could see how sinful they were. But as people sinned more and more, God's wonderful kindness became more abundant. So just as sin ruled over all people and brought them to death, now God's wonderful kindness rules instead, giving us right standing with God and resulting in eternal life through Jesus Christ our Lord. (Romans 5:18-21, CEV)

> What shall we say then? Is the law sin? Let it not be! But I did not know sin except through law; for also I did not know lust except the law said, "You shall not lust." But sin taking occasion through the commandment worked every lust in me; for apart from law, sin is dead. And I was alive apart from law once, but the commandment came, and sin came alive, and I died. And the commandment which was to life, this was found to be death to me; for sin taking occasion through the commandment deceived me, and through it killed me. So indeed the law is holy, and the commandment holy and just and good. Then that which is good, has it become death to me? Let it not be! But sin, that it might appear to be sin, having worked out death to me through the good, in order that sin might become

excessively sinful through the commandment. (Romans 7:7-13, GLT)

Here Paul explains that the law (Ten Commandments) arouses, or makes us aware of, our evil, sinful, selfish desires. These evil desires (not the law) produce sinful deeds that result in death. Notice that it is sin itself that brings death. Our God loves sinners enough to lay down his life in order to win our hearts and save us from sin. Our God is not a harsh dictator. And sin is far more dangerous and destructive than any of us realize, or even like to admit.

Jesus, in the garden of Gethsemane, however, understood and experienced the destructive power of sin. In agony, Jesus pleaded with his Father to see if there was any other way to save humanity than carrying the destructive guilt and shame of sin. By his death on the cross of Calvary, Christ demonstrated the incredibly destructive power of sin and guilt. Looking unto Jesus, let us turn from sin:

Then do not let sin rule in your mortal body, to obey it in its lusts. Neither present your members as instruments of unrighteousness to sin, but present yourselves to God as one living from the dead, and your members instruments of righteousness to God. For your sin shall not lord it over you, for you are not under law, but under grace. What then? Shall we sin because we are not under law, but under grace? Let it not be! Do you not know that to whom you present yourselves as slaves for obedience, you are slaves to whom you obey, whether of sin to death, or obedience to righteousness? But thanks be to God that you were slaves of sin, but you obeyed from the heart the form of doctrine to which you were delivered. And having been set free from sin, you were enslaved to righteousness. I speak as a man on account of the weakness of your flesh. For as you presented your members as slaves to uncleanness and to lawless act unto lawless act, so now yield your members as slaves to righteousness unto sanctification. For when

251

you were slaves of sin, you were free as to righteousness. Therefore what fruit did you have then in the things over which you are now ashamed? For the end of those things is death. But now being set free from sin, and being enslaved to God, you have your fruit unto sanctification, and the end everlasting life. For the wages of sin is death, but the free gift of God is everlasting life in Christ Jesus our Lord. (Romans 6:12-23, GLT)

Wages are something that a person earns. Wages are the result of work. Sin is hard work. Satan paints sin as exciting, glamorous, and pleasant, but in reality it is bitter and destructive. Sin is the hard, lonely, stressful work of being selfish. Selfish people may seem to have many friends. And they may seem happily married. But without a new heart, selfish people cannot find true happiness, security, and love. Selfishness is like a wall of separation. The more selfish a person is the thicker and higher the wall of separation. The result (wages) of selfishness (sin) is death. "For the wages of sin is death," means that the natural consequence of selfishness is death. But love breaks down walls and brings life.

As we have seen before, the sacrifice of Jesus clearly revealed the wages of sin in the garden of Gethsemane and on the cross of Calvary. Jesus had unbroken fellowship with his heavenly Father from his birth right up to Gethsemane. In the garden Jesus prayed three times that the "cup" might be taken from him. He knew that if he drank from this cup (the sins of the world) he would feel separated from his heavenly Father. Jesus would feel the shame and guilt of the whole world's sins, even though he himself was perfect. This struggle caused him to sweat blood (see Luke 22:44). The wages of sin horrified the Son of God. Our heavenly Father did not kill Jesus. The physical violence of the cross did not kill Jesus. Sin killed Jesus. My sins and yours killed Jesus. Jesus took the consequences of the sins of the whole world. The burning, crushing weight of the guilt and shame of sin caused Jesus to feel an infinitely deep sense of separation from the Father. That combination caused

Jesus to experience the second death. It is a fatal combination. And if sin and a sense of separation from God killed Christ, the only begotten Son of God, how much more so for sinners at the end of time! Our heavenly Father does not kill sinners at the end of time. Sin, resulting in guilt, and separation from God will destroy sinners at the end of time.

We mustn't hang onto sin, which is unbelief. Unbelief comes from a dark picture of God motivated by our own selfish desires. A dark picture of God prevents us from having saving faith in God. We must see God's goodness so that Jesus can change our hearts, or we will remain slaves to sin. If we remain slaves to sin, we will be lost. Sin carries within it the seeds of death. Through Jesus, God plants within us the seeds of life. The seed of life springs from an understanding of Jesus's love for sinners. If we fertilize and water the seed of life, God will with rejoicing give us eternal life. However, if we fertilize and water the seed of sin and death, the harvest will be death and God will weep. Dear reader, which will you choose? Heavenly Father, I pray that each person who reads this book will not choose the insane path of selfishness, empty pleasures, loneliness, guilt, stress, and eternal death. I pray each precious soul will choose the beautiful path of unselfish love, fellowship, service, fulfillment, joy, innocence, peace, rest from sin, and eternal life, amen.

1 Janet Raloff, Still Hungry?, Science News, (April 2, 2005), Vol. 167, no. 14: page 217

2 B. Harder, XXl from Too Few Zs?, Science News, (April 1, 2006), Vol. 169, no. 13: page 195

You search the Scriptures,
for in them you think you have eternal life.
And they are the ones witnessing of Me.
(John 5:39, NKJ)

But their minds were blinded.
For until this day
the same veil remains unlifted
in the reading of the Old Testament,
because the veil is taken away in Christ.
But even to this day, when Moses is read,
a veil lies on their heart.
Nevertheless when one turns to the Lord,
the veil is taken away.
(2 Corinthians 3:14-16, NKJ)

12

The Old Versus
The New

Interpretation Principle No. 1

Have you ever heard anyone express the feeling that the Old Testament overflows with violence, vengeance, fear, and the wrath of God, but the New Testament abounds in grace, mercy, forgiveness, faith, and love? Perhaps you have felt this way too. I know that I have. There are many Christian churches that are uncomfortable with the Old Testament, and even some that totally reject it. They prefer to focus on Jesus's love rather than God's wrath.

Be that as it may, I believe that the whole Bible is inspired of God. Most Christians do. In this chapter I will suggest several principles of interpretation that I have found useful in studying and reconciling the Old and New Testaments in the light of God's love.

The whole Bible must be interpreted in the light that streams from the life and death of our Savior Jesus Christ. The apostle Paul promotes this one simple, yet powerful principle. Let us prayerfully listen as the Holy Spirit speaks to us through Paul's words:

255

Therefore, since we have such hope, we use great boldness of speech—unlike Moses, who put a veil over his face so that the children of Israel could not look steadily at the end of what was passing away. But their minds were blinded. For until this day the same veil remains unlifted in the reading of the Old Testament, because the veil is taken away in Christ. But even to this day, when Moses is read, a veil lies on their heart. Nevertheless when one turns to the Lord, the veil is taken away. Now the Lord is the Spirit; and where the Spirit of the Lord is, there is liberty. But we all, with unveiled face, beholding as in a mirror the glory of the Lord, are being transformed into the same image from glory to glory, just as by the Spirit of the Lord. (2Corinthians 3:12-18, NKJ)

God has been kind enough to trust us with this work. That's why we never give up. We don't do shameful things that must be kept secret. And we don't try to fool anyone or twist God's message around. God is our witness that we speak only the truth, so others will be sure that we can be trusted. If there is anything hidden about our message, it is hidden only to someone who is lost. The god who rules this world has blinded the minds of unbelievers. They cannot see the light, which is the good news about our glorious Christ, who shows what God is like. (2Corinthians 4:1-4, CEV)

Today we will also have a blurred and distorted view of God unless the veil that obstructs our view of our Father's goodness is removed.

The letter kills, but the Spirit gives life. Reading the surface of the Holy Writings, we can miss the underlying beauty and harmony of God. Nature also reveals this same pattern. Gerald Schroeder in *The Hidden Face of God* highlights the incredible intricacies of the approximately 72 trillion living cells that form our bodies.

He points out the depth of wisdom that precisely tuned the

relationships between atomic particles and the forces of nature that make life possible. He points out that there are deeper truths that the casual observer might well miss. With a contagious sense of awe, he captures this powerful principle from nature:

> Why aren't the subtleties of physics and the phenomenal symphony of which life is composed apparent for all to see, visible, right up front? Why are they sequestered beneath an exterior that looks so simple? The implication is that we can settle for a superficial reading of nature if that's all we want, but the ultimate reality of existence lies below the surface, between the lines.[1]

That same principle applies to the whole Bible. Both the Old and New Testament contain many gems that lie below the surface, between the lines. We can learn the same lesson from the world of art as well. If you stand too close to a large painting, all you can see are smudges, streaks, and chaos. But, if you step back a few feet, the picture will suddenly become coherent, it will become meaningful and beautiful.

When we pile up text after text to prove something that we want to believe, we are standing too close to the painting. We need to step back and get an overview of God's purpose. We need to grasp the foundation principles of God's love.

The veil that lies over our heart when we read the Holy Scriptures will cripple our study and weaken our faith in God, until we learn to harmonize all teachings with the truth about the character of God as portrayed by Jesus. The depths of nature and the Scriptures contain wisdom that at once lies buried far beneath the surface and soars beyond the reach of worldly philosophy:

> God was wise and decided not to let the people of this world use their wisdom to learn about him. Instead, God chose to save only those who believe the foolish message we preach. Jews ask for miracles, and Greeks want

something that sounds wise. But we preach that Christ was nailed to a cross. Most Jews have problems with this, and most Gentiles think it is foolish. (1Corinthians 1:21-23, CEV)

Friends, when I came and told you the mystery that God had shared with us, I didn't use big words or try to sound wise. In fact, while I was with you, I made up my mind to speak only about Jesus Christ, who had been nailed to a cross. (1Corinthians 2:1, 2, CEV)

Interpretation Principle No. 2

All sin, suffering, and death come from Satan. When the Bible appears to give God the blame for the results of sin, which are suffering, and death, we need to reinterpret the passage in the light of the cross of Christ, the history of Job, and other key precepts, or principles.

The story of Job, and other Bible passages clearly reveal that Satan, the Accuser, and the Destroyer, inflicts all suffering and death. While God does not have any part in causing sin, suffering, and death, he, in his great mercy, limits and overrules these for purposes of mercy.

Christ came to reveal the character of God. Christ is the light of the world. Darkness had well nigh covered the Earth. Even the people of God had sunk into great darkness. Lack of knowledge is not as dangerous as wrong knowledge. Many of the heathen, or pagan people eagerly received Jesus. The religious leaders of God's people rejected him. Satan had so blinded the priests and rabbis with wrong information that they did not recognize Jesus, their Creator:

But we impart a secret and hidden wisdom of God, which God decreed before the ages for our glorification. None of the rulers of this age understood this; for if they had, they would not have crucified the Lord of glory. (1Corinthians 2:7, 8, RSV)

258

This should be a warning to us today as well. Satan always goes after the religious leaders. The Bible points out that Satan has rarely failed in this area. In every age the religious leaders think that they have avoided Satan's deceptions, just as he would have them think. They can then speak with sincerity, the better to deceive their followers.

Christ died under the weight of the world's sins. Yet he had done none of them. In him was no sin. Jesus took responsibility for our sins as if they were his, taking our shame, our guilt, and our punishment. The Old Testament follows the same pattern. In the Old Testament, God takes responsibility for the death and destruction of sinners even though he had done none of it.

Interpretation Principle No. 3

The Old Testament contains much that God allowed that was not part of his perfect will. The New Testament, to a far greater degree, reveals the perfect will of God:

> They said to Him, "Why then did Moses command to give a certificate of divorce, and to put her away?" He said to them, "Moses, because of the hardness of your hearts, permitted you to divorce your wives, but from the beginning it was not so. And I say to you, whoever divorces his wife, except for sexual immorality, and marries another, commits adultery; and whoever marries her who is divorced commits adultery." (Matthew 19:7-9, NKJ)

God, in his great mercy, meets people where they are. He does not at once reveal all the truth that he could reveal. In the times of ignorance God allows fallen humanity to believe in and live by customs, guidelines, and principles that are not up to the standard of his perfect will, "And the times of this ignorance God winked at; but now commandeth all men every where to repent" (Acts 17:30, KJV).

Divorce can never be in line with God's perfect will. However, because of the hardness of our hearts, he does permit it. There is a difference between God's permissive will and

259

his perfect will. Our heavenly Father, through the Holy Spirit, inspired Moses to write down these instructions:

> When a man causes a disfigurement in his neighbor, as he has done it shall be done to him, fracture for fracture, eye for eye, tooth for tooth; as he has disfigured a man, he shall be disfigured. (Leviticus 24:19, 20, RSV)

This was a way of limiting the traditional blood feuds and the resulting cycle of violence that were an ingrained part of the culture of that day. Christ makes it clear that was not part of God's perfect will:

> You have heard that it was said, "An eye for an eye and a tooth for a tooth." [Quoting from Leviticus 24:20] But I tell you not to resist an evil person. But whoever slaps you on your right cheek, turn the other to him also. If anyone wants to sue you and take away your tunic, let him have your cloak also. And whoever compels you to go one mile, go with him two. Give to him who asks you, and from him who wants to borrow from you do not turn away. (Matthew 5:38-42, NKJ)

Paul reaffirms Christ's words:

> Instead, as the scripture says: "If your enemies are hungry, feed them; if they are thirsty, give them a drink; for by doing this you will make them burn with shame." Do not let evil defeat you; instead, conquer evil with good. (Romans 12:20, 21, TEV)

Interpretation Principle No. 4

The New Testament writers enlarge, explain, and reinterpret the Old Testament. Christ's words shine new light on the Old Testament. The New Testament writers explain and redefine biblical expressions in the light of God's holy, perfect character of love:

Let no one say when he is tempted, "I am tempted by God"; for God cannot be tempted by evil, nor does He Himself tempt anyone. But each one is tempted when he is drawn away by his own desires and enticed. Then, when desire has conceived, it gives birth to sin; and sin, when it is full-grown, brings forth death. (James 1:13-15, NKJ)

God tempts no one. Every time we read in the Bible that God tempts, tests, or tries someone we need to interpret it in the light of Jesus's sacrifice. We can see the same principle in the cross. God the Father never tempted, tested, or tried Jesus. God never lies or misleads us.

Remember that God takes the blame, the responsibility for our sin. Jesus took our guilt. Jesus also showed us how to interpret the word *fear*. The Old Testament reads: "You shall fear the LORD your God; you shall serve Him" (Deuteronomy 10:20, NKJ). Jesus, quoting from this Old Testament verse, interprets the word *fear* as *worship*: "Then Jesus said to him, 'Away with you, Satan! For it is written,' 'You shall worship the LORD your God, and Him only you shall serve'" (Matthew 4:10, NKJ).

Listen carefully as Jesus seeks to expand our understanding of the Ten Commandments. Watch for the pattern that Jesus uses: "You have heard...[from the Old Testament] But I say to you..." The Son of God lovingly points us away from a superficial reading of the letter of the law and the prophets to a deeper and broader spiritual understanding of the Old Testament Scriptures. The surface letter kills, the deeper spiritual principles bring life. Listen to Jesus and notice this pattern in the next several verses:

You have heard that it was said to those of old, "You shall not murder, and whoever murders will be in danger of the judgment." But I say to you that whoever is angry with his brother without a cause shall be in danger of the judgment. And whoever says to his brother, "Raca!" shall be in danger of the council. But whoever says, "You fool!" shall be in danger of hell fire. (Matthew 5:21, 22, NKJ)

Again you have heard that it was said to those of old,
"You shall not swear falsely, but shall perform your oaths
to the Lord." But I say to you, do not swear at all: neither
by heaven, for it is God's throne; nor by the earth, for it
is His footstool; nor by Jerusalem, for it is the city of the
great King. Nor shall you swear by your head, because you
cannot make one hair white or black. But let your "Yes"
be "Yes," and your "No," "No." For whatever is more than
these is from the evil one. (Matthew 5:33-37, NKJ)

Here again Jesus quotes from the Old Testament Scriptures
(Leviticus 19:12). Moses had, under inspiration, given instructions on the practice of taking oaths. "But I say to you, do not
swear at all." Jesus here teaches us not to get caught up in what
does or does not constitute a binding oath, but he rather tells us
not to make any of these kinds of oaths. Jesus clearly seeks to
lift his listeners above a surface reading of the scriptures.

God, when dealing with the ancient Hebrews, chose to
make allowances for their culture and spiritual ignorance.
However, God's people must continue to grow in their understanding, "The way of the righteous is like the first gleam of
dawn, which shines ever brighter until the full light of day. But
the way of the wicked is like complete darkness. Those who
follow it have no idea what they are stumbling over" (Proverbs
4:18, 19, NLT).

The Old Testament contains much that can cause people
to stumble. All throughout Matthew chapter five, Jesus warns
against a surface reading of the Scriptures, or the use of men's
traditions in understanding them. He points to the deeper principle of unselfish love. Even though a person were to have the
Bible memorized, if he didn't understand the deeper principles
of love and mercy, he would still be lost. Jesus explained this
to the Church leaders of his time, "You study the Scriptures,
because you think that in them you will find eternal life. And
these very Scriptures speak about me! Yet you are not will-

ing to come to me in order to have life" (John 5:39 TEV). Jesus could say these same words today. The vast majority of "Christians" still fail to see and come to Jesus. The veil of letters blinds their eyes. The surface reading of the Scriptures blurs their view of the Lamb of God. Jesus instructs us to look beyond the veil of the surface letters to the golden law of love:

> You have heard that it was said, "You shall love your neighbor and hate your enemy." But I say to you, love your enemies, bless those who curse you, do good to those who hate you, and pray for those who spitefully use you and persecute you, that you may be sons of your Father in heaven; for He makes His sun rise on the evil and on the good, and sends rain on the just and on the unjust. For if you love those who love you, what reward have you? Do not even the tax collectors do the same? And if you greet your brethren only, what do you do more than others? Do not even the tax collectors do so? Therefore you shall be perfect, just as your Father in heaven is perfect. (Matthew 5:43-46, NKJ)

God loves his enemies. We should love his enemies too. That would mean all of humanity. No matter what people do, we should react to them as friends, based on God's love for us rather than our emotions. Remember that Jesus called Judas, *friend.*

Time and Light

God through his Holy Spirit inspired the Old Testament writers, but within the context of their culture and preconceived ideas and beliefs. Sin causes us to be afraid of God. Witness Adam and Eve. After they sinned they hid from God. Many of the Bible writers openly confessed that they were sinners. Many openly confessed that they were afraid of God. Even the twelve disciples were afraid of Jesus at different times.

God does not, even cannot force us to receive knowledge about him, or to fall in love with him faster than our mortal, human limitations allow. God has been giving his children more knowledge about his character of love as quickly as we can bear it. Even Jesus's disciples were not ready to hear everything that he wanted to reveal to them:

> I have yet many things to say to you, but you cannot bear them now. However when He, the Spirit of Truth, is come, He will guide you into all truth; for He shall not speak from Himself, but whatsoever He shall hear, that shall He speak; and He will show you things to come. (John 16:12, 13, MKJ)

Under the mighty power of the Holy Spirit, God's light has been increasing throughout time. According to Solomon (Proverbs 4:18), the last generation of people to live on the Earth will have the greatest light because the light is always increasing "to the perfect day."

One purpose of time is to bring darkness into the light. That's one reason that God said that the evening and the morning were the first day. The Earth, and humanity, start out in darkness. Then God spins the Earth around into the light. Greater light brings greater responsibility.

Gerald Schroeder, in *The Hidden Face of God*, talks about the phrase "the evening and morning." He states that *evening* can be understood as disorder or chaos and *morning* can be understood as order.[1] This concept is true on three levels. First, God brought order out of chaos each literal day of the creation week. Second, God brings order out of the chaos of our lives by bringing us from darkness into spiritual light.

The third way that God will bring order out of chaos takes seven thousand years. God will spin sin-darkened earth around into the harmonious light of his love. The first chapter of Genesis has an interesting prophecy in regard to time and light. While Genesis chapter one is a literal six-day account of creation, it also contains an outline of Earth's six thousand year history, "But, beloved, let not this one thing be hidden from you, that one day is with the Lord as a thousand years, and a

264

thousand years as one day" (2Peter 3:8, MKJ).

1. The first day God made light. God gave Adam and Eve great light to share with their descendants. After his fall, Adam lived just short of one thousand years.

2. The second day God created the waters above and the waters below. This is the only day of the creation week that God does not assert "it was good." That is because it is also referring to the flood. The flood took place in the second millennium. God takes no pleasure in the death of the wicked.

3. The third day describes land rising from the waters. The waters refer to the heathen peoples of the Earth. The land refers to the nation of Israel, which God raised up in the third millennium. As the land was to bring forth herbs yielding fruit, so Israel was to bear spiritual fruit. God raised up Israel to reach out to the other nations by revealing the glory of God's love. Israel failed most of the time. We mustn't fail.

4. The fourth day God made the sun. The sun refers to the Sun of Righteousness, Jesus Christ. Jesus determines the times and seasons, as he is the Creator-God. Historians divide time into two main parts. They denote the years before Christ's life here on Earth as B.C. The abbreviation A.D. stands for anno Domini — the year of our Lord. Truly Jesus divided the night of evil from the day of love, as well as setting the times and years.

5. The fifth day God made the sea creatures and the birds of the air. These creatures refer to the early Christian church leaders. B.G. Wilkinson tells the story of the first millennium's great church leaders such as Lucian, Vigilantius, Patrick, Columba, Papas, Dinooth, Aidan, and many others.[2] These early Christians swam in an ocean of heathen humanity. Some, perhaps like John the Revelator, spiritually soared into the heavens like the birds of the air.

6. The sixth day God made the land animals. This would refer to the great protestant reformers such as Luther, Melanchthon, Knox, Von Amsdorf, Karlstadt, Wycliffe,

Wesley, Huss, Jerome, Calvin, Zwingli, and many others. Toward the end of the sixth day, God made Adam and Eve. God's light has been increasing steadily, "to the perfect day." Adam and Eve were created in God's image. God's image refers to his character.

At the end of time, at the end of Earth's six thousand years, God will have a chosen people, an elect that through the mighty power of the Holy Spirit will be transfigured, transformed into his image, his character of unselfish love. The sixth day is our preparation day for Jesus's seventh-day Sabbath. We use the sixth day to prepare to enter Jesus's day of rest. So at the end of six thousand years we must prepare to enter God's millennium of rest by total dependence on Jesus.

7. God sanctified the seventh day as a memorial of his creative power. God rested in his completed work. The seventh millennium, then, will be a time of rest from sin, suffering, and death. At the end of the seventh millennium God will cause the wicked to judge themselves by presenting to them their own words and deeds. They will perish. After that time God will re-create the Earth. That will be the beginning of the eighth millennium. The number eight symbolizes a new beginning.

Another Old Testament passage confirms this same seven-day/seven-thousand year theme. The weekly cycle of gathering manna also places special emphasis on the sixth day, the day of preparation for the Sabbath:

Then the LORD said to Moses, "Behold, I will rain bread from the heavens for you. And the people shall go out and gather a certain amount every day, that I may test them, whether they will walk in My law or not. And on the sixth day it shall happen, they shall prepare what they bring in. And it shall be twice as much as they gather day by day." (Exodus 16:4, 5, MKJ)

The Children of Israel gathered one portion of manna for

266

the first five days of the week. The sixth day they gathered twice as much manna as they had gathered the first five days. The seventh day, the Sabbath, God provided no manna. The manna refers to Jesus Christ:

> Our fathers ate the manna in the desert, as it is written, "He gave them bread from Heaven to eat." Then Jesus said to them, Truly, truly, I say to you, Moses did not give you that bread from Heaven, but My Father gives you the true bread from Heaven. For the bread of God is He who comes down from Heaven and gives life to the world. then they said to him, Lord, evermore give us this bread. And Jesus said to them, I am the bread of life. He who comes to Me shall never hunger, and he who believes on Me shall never thirst. (John 6:31-35, MKJ)

Jesus is the Manna, the bread of Heaven. All throughout human history, each generation received new and increasing light, the light of God. However, the last generation will receive a double portion of manna, meaning a double portion of Jesus Christ, the Light of the world. The brightness of Jesus's light will burn sin out of our hearts during our walk with him.

God has another principle in relation to time. Time keeps everything from happening all at once. The light and fire of God's love over time, is healing, restorative, saving.

Having stubbornly, persistently refused the measured doses of God's love, his cure for sin, stubborn sinners will have nothing left but fiery hate for themselves and others. Our God is a consuming fire. Sin also consumes. God's fire heals. Sin's fire destroys. At the second resurrection, the unrepentant wicked will be unable, and unwilling to assimilate God's love. They have repeatedly spurned the Holy Spirit. There is nothing more that God can do for them. God's strange act will be to sadly, reluctantly release them to their own heart's desire to be separate from God. Sin will consume itself totally. There are no second probations.

The end of the seventh day is too late for them. On the

seventh-day Sabbath no manna could be gathered. In the same way, the time is soon coming when every heart will either have Jesus or Satan as their lord. There will be no more decisions for Jesus during the millennium of rest. We must gather a double portion of Jesus, now, while it is still the sixth day. We must allow the Master Artist to paint his image in our hearts and minds, now, while there is time. Art takes time.

The Master Artist

A long, long time ago, so long ago that some people now doubt his existence, there was a Master Painter of unparalleled skill. His name was Joshua. Joshua decided to paint something special, something so special that it would reveal the secrets that had been hidden in his heart for a long time. The first day, Joshua stretched out a large canvas. It was so large that if I told you, you wouldn't believe me. And he painted the background with varying shades of light. At the end of the day he stood back and looked at his work. Joshua said to some friends that had watched him work, "It is good." His friends nodded in agreement. In fact, Joshua knew in his heart that it was perfect.

The second day, Joshua painted the blues of the sky, the lakes, rivers, streams, and the seas. It was a lot of work, but Joshua had a reputation to uphold. He made it look easy.

The third day, Joshua painted the land. He covered the land with glorious meadows full of flowers that were so lovely that some of his friends began to cry for joy. He painted lofty trees that reached so high in the sky they could almost make you fall over backward just looking at them. And the fruit trees were so inviting that a few of his friends began to get hungry. At the end of the day Joshua rejoiced, saying, "It is good." You could see in their faces that his friends agreed, it was beautiful.

The fourth day, Joshua painted the brilliant sun and all the shading that went with it. His friends remarked that they didn't see how he could keep improving the painting, it was so glorious already. But he did. At the end of the day Joshua said, "It is good." Joshua's friends danced a happy dance to show their feelings of awe and joy.

The fifth day, Joshua painted birds. He filled the sky with myriads of birds. Big birds, small hummingbirds, medium-sized birds. He painted red birds, blue birds, yellow birds, green birds, and birds of mixed colors that dazzled the eye. It looked like a flying meadow. He painted fish, Beautiful, colorful fish that shimmered in the sunlight with metallic hues that filled the water with so much color that Joshua's friends murmured with a joy too pure for words. It seemed as though Joshua didn't want the fish to feel less important than the birds and the flowers. Then Joshua painted the whales and the dolphins with such grace that his friends had to turn away for a moment and then look again, it was so overwhelming. At the end of the day when he was finished, Joshua said, "It is good." With his keen, artistic eye, Joshua could see that it was perfect.

The sixth day, Joshua painted flying squirrels, chipmunks, koala bears, kangaroos, elephants, lions, and tigers. He painted deer in the meadows, Sheep and goats on the mountains, bears in the woods, and so many other animals that you would fall asleep if I tried to tell you all of them. It was magnificent. The day was winding down, and they thought he might be done. Then Joshua's friends noticed a change in his face. They could see an increase in intensity and tenderness. Then Joshua painted a man and a woman. They weren't ordinary at all. No, they were more beautiful then any other creature that Joshua had painted. What's more, they were getting married! What a wedding it was! Oh the flowers! The animals seemed to jump off the canvas, the birds hovered around and over the happy couple. The fish jumped so high out of the water that the birds thought they were trying to join them. It was so beautiful that Joshua's friends stood looking on with tears streaming down their faces. No one was ashamed of their tears. No one bothered to wipe them away. When Joshua had finished, he said, "It is very good." Joshua's friends were ecstatic beyond words. They gave him a big group hug. Of course, Joshua was smiling.

The seventh day, Joshua came back to look at his finished masterpiece. It was absolutely perfect. There was nothing missing, really. Yet there was. Then Joshua signed his masterpiece.

And it was complete.

The seventh-day Sabbath is Joshua's (Jesus) signature on his masterpiece of creation. Jesus didn't paint, he spoke and it existed. His creation was dynamic, it moved with purpose and was filled with life. The birds flew and sang. The flowers glowed with color and filled the air with perfume. Jesus's creation revealed much more than a surface reading of its beauty could reveal. Creation reveals Jesus's heart of love. Man is the apex of God's creation. Man was designed to share and reveal the glory of our Father's love. Creation is much more than a dry painting.

The Bible is the Word of God. It is more than a set of dry letters. A mere surface reading will head a person toward confusion and division. We need to see Jesus in all that we study in God's word. We must not try to fit Jesus into the mold of our interpretations that come from a shallow set of man's creeds. Nor should we paint Jesus with the surface colors of the Old Testament. We should step back and get an overview of the Master's work of art.

Jesus placed critical importance on digging beneath the surface of the Old Testament; He reinterpreted it in a way that appears contradictory to a shallow reader. We must learn to interpret the Bible in the light of Jesus's life and death. The message of the cross is that our heavenly Father is a life-giving God, the Creator, who in the person of his Son, sacrificed more than eternity itself will ever fully reveal.

God loves each of us more than his own life. Meditate on that. Make it your filter to guide you in your studies and your life decisions. Behold your God and become like him. Today is the day, now is the time. Holy, holy, holy, Lord God Almighty! I choose to worship You in beauty and in truth!

1. Schroeder , Gerald (2001). The Hidden Face of God. New York: The Free Press.

2. Wilkinson, B. G. (1994) Truth Triumphant 254 Donovan Road, Brushton, New York: Teach Services.

End Word

The purpose of The Cross Was Hell is to draw people into a deeper understanding of and relationship with Jesus Christ. I hope and pray that I have been a tool in the hand of God for this purpose. The writing of this book has been a channel that God has used to bless me.

It is clear from the scriptures that Jesus's life and sacrificial death is a full and clear manifestation of our heavenly Father's heart of love. We need to allow God's love to enter and change our hearts. This is called faith. It is also called the new birth. The Holy Spirit brings us into relationship and harmony with Jesus and the Father.

If God is our Father, then all men are our brothers, and all women are our sisters. Christian unity can only occur as we unite our hearts with Jesus. Fear, force, compromise, and negotiations are poor counterfeits and cannot provide true unity.

Let us continue to behold the glory of God in the face of Jesus and allow God to transform our hearts from glory to glory! God's glory is his character of love and mercy. Jesus came to reveal God's glory and to refute Satan's lies about the Father.

If this book has been a blessing to you and you feel that it would be a blessing to others, donations will help me print more books. You may obtain copies by writing to the address below. Or you can go to: www.TheCrossWasHell.com.

Loren James
P.O. Box 448
Elk City, ID
83525

www.TheCrossWasHell.com